WORKBOOK/STUDY GUIDE

for use with

MANAGERIAL
ACCOUNTING

CONCEPTS FOR PLANNING
CONTROL, DECISION MAKING

Seventh Edition

Ray H. Garrison
Eric W. Noreen

Prepared by
Ray H. Garrison
Brigham Young University

IRWIN
Burr Ridge, Illinois
Boston, Massachusetts
Sydney, Australia

©Richard D. Irwin, Inc., 1976, 1979, 1982, 1985, 1988, 1991, and 1994

Printed in the United States of America.

ISBN 0-256-13029-9

2 3 4 5 6 7 8 9 0 WCB 0 9 8 7 6 5 4

Preface

To The Student

This study guide has been prepared for your use as a student in the study of managerial accounting. It is designed to supplement the seventh edition of *Managerial Accounting: Concepts for Planning, Control, Decision Making*, by Ray H. Garrison and Eric W. Noreen. The purposes of the study guide are:

1. To provide suggestions for the study of chapter material.
2. To summarize the essential points in each chapter, thus making it possible to review chapter material quickly, particularly before examinations.
3. To test your knowledge of chapter material by means of a series of *self-test* questions and exercises. Answers to these questions and exercises are provided immediately following the questions and exercises themselves in order to give you immediate feedback and to point out areas that may need additional study.

Each chapter in the study guide begins with a brief section titled *Chapter Study Suggestions*. These study suggestions relate to the corresponding textbook chapter and will help you in your initial reading of the chapter material. Immediately following these study suggestions, a chapter outline is provided which highlights the key points and concepts discussed in the text. The purpose of this outline is to help you review the chapter material before attempting to complete the self-test questions and exercises provided for each chapter in the study guide. The self-test questions and exercises consist of true-false questions, multiple-choice questions, completion statements, and short exercises. This self-test material is designed to both measure and reinforce your understanding.

The way in which this study guide is used may differ from student to student; however, we would recommend the following approach:

1. Before reading the chapter in your textbook, read the *Chapter Study Suggestions* contained at the beginning of the corresponding chapter in the study guide.
2. Study the textbook chapter.
3. Study the outline contained in the *Chapter Highlights* section of the study guide. If you encounter any statements or comments that you do not understand, refer to the textbook for a more detailed discussion of the topic.
4. Work the review questions and exercises contained in the study guide, and then compare your answers to those given in the study guide. If you find something you don't understand, refer to the textbook for help.
5. Work the homework exercises and/or problems assigned by your instructor.

Remember, the study guide is not intended as a substitute for the textbook. Rather, its purpose is to *supplement* the textbook and to serve as an *aid* to learning.

The author welcomes suggestions and comments from users.

Ray H. Garrison

Contents

Chapter 1

Managerial Accounting— A Perspective

Chapter Study Suggestions

As its title indicates, the purpose of this chapter is to provide a perspective of managerial accounting. The chapter describes the work that managers do and the kinds of information they need in order to do this work effectively. Study the section titled "The Work of Management" carefully; it contains a number of key concepts which carry on through the book. Also pay particular note to the similarities between organizations discussed in the chapter.

Many new terms are introduced in the chapter. Study these terms with care, and be sure you understand *how* the terms are used in the chapter discussion.

To ease your transition from financial accounting to managerial accounting, be sure you understand the points made in the "Comparison of Financial and Managerial Accounting" section near the end of the chapter.

CHAPTER HIGHLIGHTS AND STUDY GUIDE

A. An organization is a group of people united together for a common objective or purpose. The objective(s) of an organization are set by its managers, through strategic planning. Strategic planning occurs in two phases: 1) deciding on the product/service to produce/render, and 2) deciding on the best way to market the desired product/service.

B. The work of management centers around the thing to be managed—the organization. Four broad functions are involved in the manager's work:

1. Planning, which involves deciding on the actions to be taken in order to achieve the organization's objectives.

2. Organizing and directing, which involve putting the organization's resources together effectively and overseeing day-to-day activities.

3. Controlling, which involves the obtaining of feedback to ensure that all parts of the organization are following the plans which have been set and approved.

4. Decision making, which involves the making of choices between alternative courses of action. Decision making is an integral part of the *other* functions of management—that is, in order to plan, it is necessary to make decisions; in order to organize, it is necessary to make decisions, etc. As a practical matter, decision making is really the culmination of the work of the manager at key points in the planning and control cycle.

C. The work of management is done most effectively in an organizational structure that is decentralized. Decentralization means the delegation of decision-making authority, by moving the decision-making point to the lowest managerial level possible.

D. The organization chart is designed to show the levels of responsibility and formal channels of communication in an organization. Basically, a manager may occupy either a line position or a staff position as depicted on the organization chart.

1. Line positions are those positions which are directly related to the achievement of the basic objectives of the organization.

2. Staff positions are those positions which provide service, assistance, and specialized support to the line positions. In this sense, accounting is a staff position; however, authority is delegated to the accounting department by top management to prescribe accounting and reporting procedures which line units must follow.

3. The controller is the manager of the accounting department. He or she advises top management and heavily influences the decision-making process through the providing and interpreting of data.

E. Organizations can be divided into three basic groups: 1) profit-oriented business enterprises, 2) service-oriented agencies and associations, such as the Red Cross, and 3) service-oriented agencies, such as the Department of Defense, which are created and controlled by governmental bodies. All these organizations share five basic similarities:

1. Each has an objective toward which it is working.

2. Each has a set of strategies designed to assist it in achieving its basic objective.

3. Each has a manager or managers who plan, organize, direct, and control its activities, and who make numerous decisions.

4. Each has an organizational structure that shows responsibility relationships between managers, and that shows line and staff relationships.

5. Each has an insatiable need for information to assist in the execution of its strategies.

F. Information is the "fuel" that makes management go. Information comes to management from many directions, one of which is from the accounting department. The information provided by accounting is largely quantitative in nature and is provided to help management do three things:

1. To plan effectively
2. To direct operations
3. To solve problems

G. There are at least eight major differences between financial and managerial accounting. Managerial accounting:

1. Focuses on providing data for internal uses.

2. Places more emphasis on the future.

3. Emphasizes the relevance and flexibility of data.

4. Places less emphasis on precision and more emphasis on nonmonetary data.

5. Emphasizes the segments of an organization rather than just looking at the organization as a whole.

6. Draws heavily from other disciplines.

7. Is not governed by generally accepted accounting principles.

8. Is not mandatory, whereas most financial accounting data are required.

As these differences suggest, managerial accounting is less structured and less mechanical than is financial accounting. Thus, in order to master the concepts involved in managerial accounting, you will need to devote the bulk of your time to understanding *logic* rather than *mechanical procedure*.

H. The role of managerial accounting is expanding rapidly, due to the operation of many forces on the organization and on its managers.

1. These forces include increased business competition, a severe cost-price squeeze, and rapidly developing technology.

2. For the most part, these forces have intensified the manager's need for information beyond that which is contained in the traditional balance sheet and income statement.

I. Trade barriers in international markets are slowly being eliminated, making it easier to conduct international trade. Firms can no longer be complacent in their "home" markets, since competition may suddenly come from a competitor half way around the world.

1. The implication for managerial accounting is that firms' accounting systems must be "world class" in order to compete.

2. Throughout this book we highlight the differences between obsolete accounting systems and well-designed accounting systems.

J. Ethics can be defined as "The study of standards of conduct and moral judgment." In recent years, many concerns have been raised regarding ethical behavior in business.

1. Ethical problems occur at several organizational levels. These include the corporate level, the intercorporate level, the intracorporate level, the professional level, and the personal level.

2. Many companies have developed codes of ethical conduct. These codes are broad-based statements of a company's responsibilities to its employees, customers, suppliers, and others.

3. A code titled *Standards of Ethical Conduct for Management Accountants* has been developed as a guide to management accountants in their duties. Codes of ethical conduct also exist on the international level that control cross border activities.

REVIEW AND SELF TEST
Questions and Exercises

True or False

For each of the following statements, enter a T or and F in the blank to indicate whether the statement is true or false.

____ 1. Managerial accounting is equally as concerned with providing information to stockholders as it is with providing information to managers.

____ 2. An organization consists of buildings, equipment, and other physical assets dedicated to a common purpose.

____ 3. The steps to be followed in implementing an organization's objectives are set down through strategic planning.

____ 4. Strategic planning is sometimes referred to as setting policy.

____ 5. "Controlling" refers primarily to setting maximum limits on spending in an organization.

____   6. The plans of management are expressed in quantitative form as budgets.

____   7. In practice, the planning, organizing, and controlling functions of management are kept separate from the decision-making function.

____   8. A performance report is a device for obtaining feedback for the manager.

____   9. Staff departments in an organization generally have direct authority over line departments.

____   10. Profit-oriented organizations and service-oriented organizations share many basic similarities.

____   11. The information needs of management are all supplied through the accounting system.

____   12. Managerial accounting focuses more on the segments of an organization than on the organization as a whole.

____   13. International competition is decreasing as firms become more content to focus on "home" markets.

____   14. Ethical problems are generally confined to the professional level such as with lawyers, politicians and other professionals.

____   15. Codes of ethical conduct exist for professional groups and also exist on the international level.

Multiple Choice

Choose the best answer or response by placing the identifying letter in the space provided.

____   1. The work of management: a) consists only of strategic planning; b) is clearly explained by the organization chart; c) follows a well-defined cycle; d) responses a, b, and c are all correct; e) none of these.

____   2. Staff positions: a) are not shown on the organization chart; b) are superior in authority to line positions; c) are equal in authority to line positions; d) none of these.

____   3. Organizations: a) share only one basic similarity—the need for information; b) share similarities only with other organizations that have like objectives; c) are divided into three basic groups; d) responses b and c are both correct; e) none of these.

____   4. The controller: a) has delegated authority over line departments; b) occupies a line position; c) has little influence in the decision-making process; d) none of these.

____   5. Managerial accounting: a) is governed by generally accepted accounting principles; b) places more emphasis on precision of data than does financial accounting; c) draws heavily from other disciplines; d) is geared primarily to the past rather than to the future; e) none of these.

____   6. Financial and managerial accounting are similar in that: a) both are mandatory; b) both rely on the same accounting information system; c) both focus on providing data for internal uses; d) none of these.

____   7. In a decentralized organization, decisions are made: a) only by top management; b) only by managers occupying staff positions; c) at the lowest managerial level possible in the organization; d) none of these.

____   8. In large part, "control" in an organization is achieved through: a) decentralization of decision-making authority; b) obtaining feedback on how well the organization is moving toward its objectives; c) preparing an organization chart which shows both line and staff functions; d) none of these.

Complete the Statements

Fill in the necessary words to complete the following statements.

1. An _____ can be defined as a group of people working together for some common purpose.

2. The implementation of an organization's objectives is known as _____ _____ .

3. Essentially, the manager carries out four broad functions in an organization: 1 _____, 2 _____ and _____, 3 _____, and 4 _____ .

4. In _____, the manager outlines the steps to be taken in moving the organization toward its objectives.

5. Control, in large part, is a function of obtaining useful _____ on how well the organization is doing.

6. In _____ _____ the manager attempts to make rational choices between alternatives.

7. The work of management can be summarized very nicely in a model known as the _____ and _____ cycle.

8. Responsibility relationships between managers are shown on the _____ _____.

9. A _____ department is one whose activities are directly related to the basic objectives of the organization.

10. Strategic planning in an organization is carried out by persons occupying _____ positions.

11. The accounting department has _____ authority over line departments in accounting matters.

12. The plans of management are often expressed as _____.

13. The manager generally is most interested in _____ of information drawn from accounting records, rather than in the details of transactions.

14. As compared to _____ accounting, _____ accounting places much more emphasis on the future.

15. _____ accounting draws heavily from other disciplines.

16. _____ means the delegation of decision-making authority throughout an organization by allowing managers at various operating levels to make key decisions relating to their area of responsibility.

Exercise

1.1 **Critical thought writing exercise:** Managerial accounting information is sometimes described as a means to an end, whereas financial accounting information is described as an end in itself. In what sense is this true?

_____

_____

_____

_____

_____

_____

_____

_____

_____

Chapter 1
Answers to Questions and Exercises

True or False

1. F The central purpose of managerial accounting is to provide information to managers. The information needs of stockholders are provided through financial accounting.

2. F An organization consists of people, not physical assets.

3. T The purpose of strategic planning is to outline the steps that must be followed in achieving an organization's objectives.

4. T As strategic planning takes place, policy is set for the organization.

5. F Controlling refers to the steps that must be taken to ensure that each part of the organization follows the plan that was outlined in the planning stage.

6. T A budget is a plan of action expressed in quantitative terms.

7. F Decision making is an integral part of the planning, organizing, and controlling functions.

8. T Feedback comes in many forms, one of which is a performance report.

9. F Staff departments provide support or services for line departments, but do not have direct authority over them.

10. T There are many similarities among organizations, as discussed in the text.

11. F Only a portion of the information needs of management are provided through the accounting system; information also comes from economists, marketing specialists, and others.

12. T The primary concern of managerial accounting is with the segments of an organization, rather than with the organization as a whole.

13. F International competition is increasing as trade barriers continue to fall. Firms are being forced to become "world class," rather than to stay at home.

14. F Ethical problems occur at all levels in an organization. These include the corporate level, the intracorporate level, the intercorporate level, the professional level, and the personal level.

15. T Codes of ethical conduct are widely used. A code title, **Guideline on Ethics for Professional Accountants** is designed for international use.

Multiple Choice

1. c The work of management follows the planning and control cycle, which is illustrated in Exhibit 1-1.

2. d Staff positions (such as Accounting) do appear on the organization chart, but they are neither superior nor equal in authority to line positions. They serve the needs of line positions by providing essential services.

3. c The three groups are: profit-oriented business enterprises; service-oriented agencies that are operated as nonprofit corporations; and service-oriented agencies that are created and controlled by governmental bodies.

4. a The controller has delegated authority from top management to specify accounting and reporting requirements that the line departments must follow.

5. c Managerial accounting draws from the behavioral sciences, statistics, and economics, as well as from other disciplines.

6. b Since it would be a waste of money to have two data collecting systems existing side by side, managerial accounting uses the data generated by the financial accounting system.

7. c The purpose of decentralization is to move all decisions to the lowest managerial level possible in an organization.

8. b By obtaining feedback, management can see how well an organization is moving toward its objectives and thus control is maintained.

Complete the Statements

1. organization
2. strategic planning
3. planning, organizing, directing, controlling, decision making
4. planning
5. feedback
6. decision making
7. planning, control
8. organization chart
9. line
10. line
11. delegated
12. budgets
13. summaries
14. financial, managerial
15. Managerial
16. Decentralization

Exercise

1-1. The purpose of financial accounting is to produce financial statements for stockholders and others. Once the financial statements have been produced, therefore, the purpose has been accomplished. Thus, the information is an end in itself. On the other hand, managerial accounting information is produced to help management in its planning, control, and decision making responsibilities. Thus, it functions as a means to accomplish these ends.

Chapter 2

Cost Terms, Concepts, and Classifications

Chapter Study Suggestions

This chapter introduces general cost terms which will be used throughout the remainder of the book. The chapter also gives a broad outline of the flow of costs in a manufacturing company. (Cost flow is treated in more depth in Chapter 3.) As you read the chapter, note each new term that is introduced and be sure you understand its meaning. Pay particular attention to the concepts of product cost, variable cost, fixed cost, direct cost, indirect cost, and differential cost.

Exhibit 2-3 presents the *schedule of cost of goods manufactured*. The format of this schedule should be put to memory, as well as the material in Exhibits 2-5 and 2-6. Learning the material in these exhibits will help you for Chapter 3 and also lay a foundation for many chapters which follow.

CHAPTER HIGHLIGHTS AND STUDY GUIDE

A.   Manufacturing costs are those costs involved in the manufacture of units of product. Manufacturing costs can be subdivided into three basic elements: direct materials, direct labor, and manufacturing overhead.

   1. Direct materials include those materials which become an integral part of a finished product, and which can be conveniently traced into it.

      a. An example of direct materials would be the steel used in manufacturing a file cabinet.

      b. Small materials items, such as glue, would be treated as indirect materials and added to manufacturing overhead.

   2. Direct labor consists of those labor costs which are physically traceable to the creation of products in a "hands on" sense.

      a. An example of direct labor cost would be the worker on an assembly line in a manufacturing plant.

      b. Other labor costs, such as supervisors and janitors, are treated as indirect labor and added to manufacturing overhead.

      c. Direct materials and direct labor together are known as prime cost.

   3. Manufacturing overhead consists of all costs of manufacturing except direct materials and direct labor.

      a. Synonymous terms for manufacturing overhead are: factory overhead, overhead, factory burden, indirect manufacturing costs, and manufacturing expense.

      b. Direct labor and manufacturing overhead together are known as conversion cost.

B.   Nonmanufacturing costs are those costs involved with selling and administrative activities.

   1. Selling costs include all costs associated with the marketing of finished products, including commissions, depreciation of delivery equipment, depreciation of finished goods warehouses, and advertising.

   2. Administrative costs include all costs associated with the general administration of an organization, including secretarial salaries, depreciation of general administrative facilities and equipment, and executive compensation.

C.   The costs of an organization can also be classified as being either product costs or period costs.

   1. Product costs and manufacturing costs are synonymous terms. Thus, product costs include direct materials, direct labor, and manufacturing overhead.

   2. Period costs and nonmanufacturing costs are synonymous terms. Thus, period costs include selling costs and administrative costs.

D.   The income statements and balance sheets prepared by manufacturing firms differ in important respects from those prepared by merchandising firms.

   1. The income statement of a manufacturing firm contains an element termed "cost of goods manufactured." You should study Exhibit 2–3 in the text very carefully; it shows how the cost of goods manufactured is computed.

   2. The balance sheet of a manufacturing firm contains three inventory accounts: Raw Materials, Work in Process, and Finished Goods. By contrast, the balance sheet of a merchandising firm contains only one inventory account—Merchandise Inventory.

      a. Raw Materials consists of materials on hand which will be used in the manufacture of units of product.

      b. Work in Process consists of units of product only partially completed at the end of a period.

      c. Finished Goods consists of units of product which are completed and ready for sale to customers.

E.   Manufacturing costs (direct materials, direct labor, and overhead) are also known as *inventoriable* costs.

   1. The term inventoriable costs arises since direct materials, direct labor, and overhead go into Work in Process and Finished Goods, which are *inventory* accounts. Therefore, direct materials, direct labor, and overhead can end up on the balance sheet as part of these inventory accounts (as assets) if goods are either not completed or not sold at the end of a period.

   2. You should study Exhibit 2–5 in the text with great care. It shows the conceptual flow of manufacturing costs through inventory accounts and the way these costs become an expense (cost of goods sold) on the income statement. *This is a key exhibit for Chapter 2.*

3. We can summarize manufacturing and non-manufacturing cost terms as follows:

Synonymous Cost Terms	Costs Involved
Manufacturing costs Product costs Inventoriable costs	Direct materials, direct labor, and manufacturing overhead
Nonmanufacturing costs Period costs	Selling and administrative expenses

F. For planning and control purposes, costs are classified as variable and fixed, direct and indirect, and controllable and noncontrollable.

1. Variable costs are those costs which vary, in total, in direct proportion to changes in the volume or level of activity within the relevant range. Variable cost behavior is illustrated in Exhibit 2-8.

a. Variable costs include, for example, direct materials, direct labor, commissions to salespersons, and cost of goods sold.

b. The relevant range is that range of activity within which the company normally operates and within which assumptions relative to cost behavior are valid.

2. Fixed costs are those costs which remain constant in total amount regardless of changes in the level of activity. They include, for example, depreciation, supervisory salaries, and rent. Fixed cost behavior is illustrated in Exhibit 2-8.

3. The terms direct cost and indirect cost have no meaning unless one first identifies some object or segment to which the costs are to be related.

a. A direct cost is a cost which can be obviously and physically traced to the object or segment under consideration. For example, if the object under consideration is a unit of product, then the materials and labor involved in its manufacture would both be direct costs.

b. An indirect cost is a cost which must be allocated in order to be assigned to the object or segment under consideration. For example, if the object under consideration is a unit of product, then the manufacturing overhead involved in its manufacture would be an indirect cost.

4. A cost is considered to be controllable at a particular level of management if that level has power to authorize the cost. If a manager has no power to authorize a particular cost, then the cost is not considered to be controllable by that manager.

G. The difference in costs between alternatives is known as differential cost. Differential costs include both cost increases and cost decreases.

1. Cost increases are also known as incremental costs.

2. Cost decreases are also known as decremental costs.

3. Differential costs can be either variable or fixed.

H. An opportunity cost is the potential benefit that is lost or sacrificed when the selection of one course of action makes it necessary to give up a competing course of action.

1. Every alternative facing a manager has opportunity costs attached to it.

2. Opportunity costs are not recorded on the books of an organization. They simply represent those benefits which are lost through giving up some competing course of action.

I. A sunk cost is a cost which has already been incurred and which cannot be changed by any decision made now or in the future. Sunk costs are never differential costs in decision making.

Appendix A: Further Classification of Labor Costs

A. Labor costs can be broken down into five main categories: direct labor, indirect labor, idle time, overtime premium, and labor fringe benefits.

1. Direct labor has already been discussed. As mentioned earlier, it consists of those factory labor costs which can be physically traced to the creation of products in a "hands on" sense.

2. Indirect labor consists of those factory labor costs which are supportive or supervisory in nature. These would include the labor costs of supervisors, superintendents, custodians, maintenance persons, and others whose services are essential to factory operations, but who do not work directly on the product.

3. Idle time represents the costs of direct labor workers who are unable to perform their assignments due to material shortages, power failures, and the like. Idle time is treated as part of manufacturing overhead.

4. Overtime premium consists of any amount paid above an employee's base hourly rate.

a. For example, if the base rate is $6 per hour and the employee is paid time-and-a-half for overtime, then the overtime premium would be $3 per hour (*not* $9 per hour).

b. Overtime premium is not charged to specific jobs, but rather is included as part of manufacturing overhead.

5. Labor fringe benefits include employment related costs paid by the employer, such as insurance programs, retirement plans, etc.

a. Many firms include *all* such costs as part of manufacturing overhead.

b. Other firms include only the labor fringe benefits relating to indirect labor as part of manufacturing overhead and treat those benefits relating to direct labor as added direct labor costs.

REVIEW AND SELF TEST
Questions and Exercises

True or False

For each of the following statements, enter a T or an F in the blank to indicate whether the statement is true or false.

____ 1. A manufacturing firm is more complex than most other types of organizations.

____ 2. Raw materials consist of basic natural resources, such as iron ore.

____ 3. A supervisor's salary would be considered direct labor if the supervisor works directly in the factory.

____ 4. Direct labor combined with direct materials is known as prime cost.

____ 5. Manufacturing overhead combined with direct materials is known as conversion cost.

____ 6. Nonmanufacturing costs consist of selling costs and administrative costs.

____ 7. All selling and administrative costs are period costs.

____ 8. The terms product cost and manufacturing cost are synonymous.

____ 9. The cost of goods manufactured is deducted from sales in order to derive gross profit in a manufacturing firm.

____ 10. Part of a cost such as factory depreciation can end up on the balance sheet as an asset if goods are uncompleted or unsold at the end of a period.

____ 11. Inventoriable costs and product costs are synonymous terms.

____ 12. A variable cost will change in total in proportion to changes in the level of activity.

____ 13. A fixed cost is constant per unit of product.

____ 14. Manufacturing overhead is an indirect cost with respect to units of product.

____ 15. The terms differential cost and incremental cost are used interchangeably, although technically differential cost is a broader concept.

____ 16. Sunk costs can be either variable or fixed.

____ 17. Property taxes and insurance on a factory building are examples of manufacturing overhead.

____ 18. (Appendix A) Overtime premium should be charged to the specific jobs worked on during overtime periods.

Multiple Choice

Choose the best answer or response by placing the identifying letter in the space provided.

____ 1. If the activity level increases, one would expect the variable costs per unit to: a) increase; b) decrease; c) remain unchanged; d) none of these.

____ 2. Which of the following costs would *not* be a period cost: a) indirect materials; b) advertising; c) administrative salaries; d) shipping costs; e) sales commissions.

____ 3. The term used to describe goods moving out of work in process into finished goods is: a) cost of goods sold; b) raw materials; c) period cost; d) cost of goods manufactured; e) none of these.

____ 4. "Manufacturing cost" is synonymous with all of the following terms except: a) product cost; b) inventoriable cost; c) period cost; d) all of the above are synonymous terms.

____ 5. If the activity level drops by 25 percent, one would expect the variable costs: a) to increase per unit of product; b) to drop in total by 25 percent; c) to remain constant in total; d) to decrease per unit of product.

____ 6. Which of the following appears as one element in the computation of cost of goods sold in a manufacturing company? a) direct materials; b) work in process; c) cost of goods manufactured; d) manufacturing overhead.

_____ 7. All of the following would be product costs except: a) indirect materials; b) advertising; c) rent on factory space; d) idle time; e) all of the above would be product costs.

_____ 8. (Appendix A) A machinist earns $10 per hour. During a given week he works 40 hours, of which he is idle 5 hours. For the week: a) $400 cost should be charged to direct labor; b) $50 cost should be charged to overtime premium; c) $50 cost should be charged to overhead; d) $425 cost should be charged to direct labor, and $25 cost should be charged to overhead.

Complete the Statements

Fill in the necessary words to complete the following statements.

1. The term "product costs" is synonymous with the terms _____ costs and _____ costs.

2. The opening finished goods inventory, plus the _____ _____ _____ _____, less the ending finished goods inventory equals the cost of goods sold in a manufacturing company.

3. Selling costs and administrative costs are also known as _____ costs.

4. From a cost behavior point of view, costs can be classified as being either _____ or _____.

5. Direct labor and manufacturing overhead added together are called _____ cost.

6. Cotter keys and other small items of materials used in auto manufacture would probably be classified as _____ _____, and added to manufacturing overhead.

7. _____ costs remain constant in total as the activity level fluctuates.

8. A sunk cost can never be a _____ cost in decision making.

9. Goods only partially completed at the end of a period are placed on the balance sheet as _____ _____ _____ inventory.

10. In terms of cost behavior, sales commissions would be classified as a _____ cost.

Exercises

2-1.   Classify each of the following costs as being either period costs or product costs. If a cost is a period cost, indicate whether it would be part of selling cost or part of administrative cost; if it is a product cost, indicate whether it would be direct or indirect to units of product.

		Period Cost		Product Cost	
		Selling	Admin.	Direct	Indirect
-	Example: Rent on a sales office	X			
-	Example: Direct materials			X	
a.	Sales commissions				
b.	Rent on a factory building				
c.	Secretarial salaries				
d.	Assembly line workers				
e.	Product advertising				
f.	Cherries in a cannery				
g.	Top management salaries				
h.	Lubricants for machines				
i.	Freight out				
j.	Overtime premium				
k.	Entertainment costs				
l.	Executive training program				
m.	Factory supervisory salaries				

2-2. From the following data, prepare a schedule of cost of goods manufactured.

Lubricants for machines	$ 4,500
Rent, factory building	16,000
Direct labor	90,000
Indirect materials	2,000
Sales commissions	24,600
Factory utilities	5,800
Insurance, factory	2,000
Purchases of raw materials	120,000
Finished goods, beginning	26,000
Finished goods, ending	31,000
Work in process, beginning	16,000
Work in process, ending	11,500
Advertising	72,000
Raw materials, beginning	15,000
Raw materials, ending	5,000
Depreciation of office equipment	4,000

2-3.   Harry has decided to produce and sell surfboards in his spare time. He has a garage which was constructed at a cost of $4,000 several years ago, and which will be used for production purposes. The garage will be depreciated over a 20-year life. Harry has determined that each surfboard will require $30 in wood. He will hire students to do most of the work and pay them $35 for each surfboard completed. He will rent tools needed at a cost of $200 per month. Harry has drawn money out of savings to provide the capital needed to get the operation going. The savings were earning interest at 6 percent annually. An ad agency will handle advertising at a cost of $100 per month. Harry will hire students to sell the surfboards and pay a commission of $20 per board.

Required:

From the foregoing information, identify all the examples you can of the following types of costs (a single item may be identified as more than one type of cost):

Variable cost: _____

_____

Fixed cost: _____

_____

Selling or administrative cost: _____

_____

Product cost: _____

_____

Manufacturing overhead cost: _____

_____

Sunk cost: _____

_____

Opportunity cost: _____

_____

Differential cost (between the alternatives of producing or not producing surfboards): _____

_____

_____

2-4. (Appendix A) Sally Anderson worked 47 hours last week. She was idle 3 hours and spent the remaining 44 hours working directly on the manufacture of finished products. Sally is paid $8 per hour and time-and-a-half for work in excess of 40 hours per week. Allocate her week's wages between direct labor and cost and manufacturing overhead.

Direct labor (   ) . . . . $

Manufacturing overhead:

   _____ (   ) . . . . $

   _____ (   ) . . . . _____ _____

Total earnings . . . . $_____

2-5. **Critical thought writing exercise:** Mary has just been hired by Acme Company. Mary's duties are such that the company is unsure whether to classify her salary as a period cost or as a product cost. From the point of view of the company's annual reported net income, explain why it does or does not matter how her salary cost is classified.

_____

_____

_____

_____

_____

_____

_____

_____

Chapter 2
Answers to Questions and Exercises

True or False

1. T A manufacturing firm is more complex because it must produce its goods as well as market them.

2. F Raw materials consist of any materials input into a product, and the finished goods of one company can become the raw materials of another company.

3. F Direct labor represents that labor which can be physically traced to the creation of products in a "hands on" sense. Supervisors do not work directly on products and therefore are not direct labor.

4. T This is the definition of prime cost.

5. F Manufacturing overhead combined with direct labor is known as conversion cost.

6. T Nonmanufacturing cost is a term synonymous with selling and administrative costs.

7. T Selling and administrative costs are period costs because they are charged against income in the period in which they are incurred, rather than being added to the cost of manufactured or purchased goods.

8. T These two terms are synonymous by definition.

9. F Cost of goods sold is deducted from sales in order to derive gross margin; the cost of goods manufactured is an element in the computation of cost of goods sold.

10. T Manufacturing costs "attach" or "cling" to units during production. If these units are not complete or not sold at the end of a period, then the manufacturing costs incurred to date are included as part of Work in Process or Finished Goods inventories (assets) on the balance sheet.

11. T These two terms are synonymous by definition.

12. T Since a variable cost is constant per unit, it will change in total in proportion to changes in the level of activity. If activity increases by 25 percent, then the total variable cost will also increase by 25 percent.

13. F A fixed cost is constant in total amount; on a per unit basis, it varies inversely with changes in the level of activity.

14. T Manufacturing overhead cost is an indirect cost, since it must be allocated in order to be assigned to units of product.

15. T Differential cost is a broader concept, since it relates to either increases or decreases in cost. Incremental cost relates only to increases in cost.

16. T A sunk cost is a cost that has already been incurred, and thus it can be variable as well as fixed. If direct materials have been purchased, for example, then the materials represent a sunk cost.

17. T Manufacturing overhead consists of all costs of production except direct materials and direct labor.

18. F Overtime premium should be added to manufacturing overhead cost and spread equally over all jobs worked on during the period.

Multiple Choice

1. c By definition, variable costs are constant per unit. Thus, if the activity level increases, they will remain unchanged although the variable cost *in total* will increase.

2. a Indirect materials would be part of manufacturing overhead, and thus it would be a product cost.

3. d Goods that are completed and ready for sale move out of work in process and into finished goods; such goods are termed cost of goods manufactured.

4. c A period cost represents a cost charged against the period in which the cost is incurred; it has nothing to do with the manufacture of a product and therefore it is not synonymous with manufacturing cost.

5. b By definition, total variable cost changes in proportion to changes in the activity level.

6. c The cost of goods manufactured is added to the beginning finished goods inventory to obtain the goods available for sale. The ending finished goods inventory is then deducted from the goods available for sale to get the cost of goods sold.

7. b Advertising is a period cost, rather than a product cost, since it is charged as an expense in the period in which it is incurred.

8. c All of the cost of idle time should be charged to manufacturing overhead. Thus, $10 per hour x 5 hours = $50.

Complete the Statements

1. manufacturing, inventoriable
2. cost of goods manufactured
3. period
4. variable, fixed
5. conversion
6. indirect material
7. Fixed
8. differential
9. work in process
10. variable

Exercises

2-1.

| | Period Cost | | Product Cost | |
	Selling	Admin.	Direct	Indirect
a.	X			
b.				X
c.		X		
d.			X	
e.	X			
f.			X	
g.		X		
h.				X
i.	X			
j.				X
k.	X			
l.		X		
m.				X

2-2. Direct materials:

Raw materials inventory, beginning	$ 15,000	
Add: Purchases of raw materials	120,000	
Raw materials available for use	135,000	
Deduct: Raw materials inventory, ending	5,000	
Raw materials used in production		$130,000
Direct labor		90,000
Manufacturing overhead:		
Lubricants for machines	$ 4,500	
Rent, factory building	16,000	
Indirect materials	2,000	
Factory utilities	5,800	
Insurance, factory	2,000	30,300
Total manufacturing costs		250,300
Add: Work in process, beginning		16,000
		266,300
Deduct: Work in process, ending		11,500
Cost of Goods Manufactured		$254,800

2-3. Variable cost: wood, $30; labor, $35; commission, $20.

Fixed cost: garage depreciation, $200; tool rent, $200; advertising, $100.

Selling or administrative cost: advertising, $100; commission, $20.

Product cost: garage depreciation, $200; wood, $30; labor, $35; tool rent, $200.

Manufacturing overhead cost: garage depreciation, $200; tool rent, $200.

Sunk cost: garage depreciation, $200 (the garage has already been purchased and therefore represents a sunk cost).

Opportunity cost: interest on the savings withdrawn.

Differential cost: all costs except the garage depreciation, since all costs except the depreciation could be avoided by not producing surfboards.

2-4.

Direct labor: (44 hours x $8)		$352
Manufacturing overhead:		
Idle time (3 hours x $8)........................	$24	
Overtime premium (7 hours x $4)	28	52
Total Earnings		$404

2-5. From the point of view of the company's annual reported net income, it does matter how Mary's salary cost is classified. If her salary is classified as a period cost, the entire amount of salary will appear as an expense on the company's income statement each year. If her salary is classified as a product cost, then it will go into Work in Process along with other production costs. If any goods are not completed at the end of the year, part of Mary's salary will remain in the Work in Process inventory account as part of the cost of these uncompleted goods. That portion of her salary that is attached to completed goods will go into the Finished Goods inventory account. If any of these goods are not sold at year-end, part of Mary's salary will remain in the Finished Goods inventory account as part of the cost of these unsold goods. Only that portion of Mary's salary that is attached to the goods that are completed and sold during the year will appear as an expense on the income statement (as part of Cost of Goods Sold).

Chapter 3

Systems Design: Job-Order Costing

This chapter expands on the concepts introduced in Chapter 2 by showing how costs are accumulated in manufacturing organizations for purposes of computing unit costs. The costing method illustrated in the chapter is known as *job-order costing.* Pay particular attention to the section early in the chapter titled "Application of Manufacturing Overhead." *Overhead application is a key concept in the chapter.* Exhibit 3-5 provides a bird's eye view of the overall flow of cost and documents in a job-order cost system.

Exhibits 3-6, 3-7, and 3-8 show how direct materials, direct labor, and overhead costs are added to units of product. Study these exhibits with particular care—the concepts they contain will show up often in the homework material. Exhibits 3-9 and 3-10 summarize the concepts and flows of costs up to that point. Notice from Exhibit 3-10 that the Schedule of Cost of Goods Manufactured has been expanded from that given in Chapter 2. *This schedule should be committed to memory.* Study and then *restudy* the section titled "Problems of Overhead Application," paying particular attention to how the under- and overapplied overhead figures are computed.

CHAPTER HIGHLIGHTS AND STUDY GUIDE

A.   Unit cost data are needed by managers for a variety of purposes.

   1. First, unit costs are needed to cost inventories on financial statements.

   2. Second, unit costs are needed for decision-making purposes. One of the most significant uses of unit cost data is in the setting of selling prices for products.

B.   There are two basic costing systems in use: process costing and job-order costing. These two systems have emerged in response to variations in how the manufacturing process can be carried out.

   1. Process costing is employed in those situations where manufacturing involves a single product, such as bricks, that is produced for long periods at a time.

   2. Job-order costing is used in those manufacturing situations where many different products or separate jobs are being produced each period. Examples would include special order printing and furniture manufacturing.

   3. Regardless of whether one is dealing with process costing or job-order costing, the problem of determining unit costs involves a need for averaging of some type. The essential difference between the two costing methods is the way this averaging is carried out.

C.   Before production can begin, raw materials must be acquired. Upon purchase, materials are placed in the Raw Materials inventory account, which is an asset.

   1. Materials are placed into production by means of the Materials Requisition Form. The journal entry is:

Work in Process (direct materials)   XXX
Manufacturing Overhead
   (indirect materials)   XXX
   Raw Materials   XXX

   2. If all of the materials used in production are direct materials, the entry is as follows:

Work in Process   XXX
   Raw Materials   XXX

   3. When materials are placed into production, they are recorded on a job cost sheet, which summarizes all production costs going into a particular job. This is illustrated in Exhibit 3-6 in the text.

D.   Labor costs are accumulated by means of time tickets or time sheets. The time tickets are then analyzed to determine the amount of time spent on various jobs and/or assignments.

   1. That labor time spent working directly on specific jobs is termed direct labor. That labor time spent working on supportive tasks (maintenance, janitorial) is termed indirect labor. The entry to record labor costs is:

Work in Process (direct labor)   XXXX
Manufacturing Overhead
   (indirect labor)   XXXX
   Salaries and Wages Payable   XXXX

   2. Direct labor costs are recorded on individual job cost sheets at the same time they are recorded in the formal accounts. This is illustrated in Exhibit 3-7 in the text.

E.   As explained in Chapter 2, manufacturing overhead is an *indirect* cost and therefore must be allocated in order to be assigned to units of product. This allocation is carried out through the *predetermined overhead rate*.

   1. The predetermined overhead rate is computed *before* a year begins and is based entirely on estimated data. The formula is:

$$\frac{\text{Estimated overhead costs}}{\text{Estimated base (machine-hours, etc.)}} = \begin{array}{l}\text{Predetermined} \\ \text{overhead rate}\end{array}$$

   2. In assigning overhead cost to units of product, the predetermined overhead rate is multiplied by the number of direct labor hours worked on a particular job and the amount of cost entered on the individual job cost sheet. The entry is:

Work in Process   XXXX
   Manufacturing Overhead   XXXX

Turn to Exhibit 3-8 in the text to see how overhead costs flow through the accounts and onto the job cost sheets.

3. The assigning of overhead to jobs is known as the application or absorption of overhead.

4. Notice from Exhibit 3-8 that the application of overhead to production and the incurrence of actual overhead costs represent two separate and distinct processes.

a. When incurred, actual overhead costs are *not* charged to work in process. Notice from the exhibit that they are entered into the manufacturing overhead account (see entries 2-6 in the exhibit).

b. The application of overhead comes later (see entry 7 in the exhibit), when the machine time on various jobs has been accumulated.

F. After direct materials, direct labor, and overhead costs have been added to jobs and the jobs are completed, they are transferred from Work in Process to Finished Goods to await sale.

1. The entry to record completed jobs is:

Finished Goods   XXXX
   Work in Process   XXXX

2. When completed jobs are later sold, the entry is:

   Cost of Goods Sold   XXXX
      Finished Goods   XXXX

3. Exhibits 3-9 and 3-10 are key exhibits in Chapter 3 since they summarize much of the material in the chapter. Study these exhibits with care. Notice particularly that the schedule of cost of goods manufactured in Exhibit 3-10 has been expanded somewhat from the format given in Chapter 2. *The format of this schedule should be put to memory.*

G. Generally there will be a difference between the amount of overhead cost *applied* to Work in Process and the amount of *actual* overhead cost for a period. This can be seen from the Manufacturing Overhead account in Exhibit 3-9, where there is a $5,000 difference between applied and actual overhead cost.

1. If more overhead cost is applied to Work in Process than has actually been incurred, then a situation of *overapplied* overhead exists.

2. If less overhead cost is applied to Work in Process than has actually been incurred, then a situation of *underapplied* overhead exists.

3. The formula for computing under- or overapplied overhead is:

Actual overhead costs .... $XXXX
Less overhead costs applied to
  work in process:
   Actual machine hours X
   predetermined overhead
   rate .... <u>XXXX</u>
Under- or overapplied
  overhead .... <u>$ XXX</u>

4. At the end of a period, under- or overapplied overhead usually is either closed out to Cost of Goods Sold or allocated between Work in Process, Finished Goods, and Cost of Goods Sold.

a. Closing any balance out to Cost of Goods Sold is simpler, since only one account is involved. The entry would be:

Cost of Goods Sold   XXXX
  Manufacturing Overhead   XXXX

This entry assumes that overhead was *underapplied*. The entry would be the reverse if overhead was *overapplied*.

b. Allocating any under- or overapplied overhead is more complex, but it is also more accurate from a costing point of view. The allocation is based on the ending balances in the Work in Process, Finished Goods, and Cost of Goods Sold accounts. Assuming that overhead is *underapplied*, the entry would be:

Work in Process   XXXX
Finished Goods   XXXX
Cost of Goods Sold   XXXX
  Manufacturing Overhead   XXXX

H.   In large companies, multiple overhead rates are often used rather than a single, "plant wide" rate. Overhead rates are set in various departments according to that base which most equitably allocates overhead cost to the various jobs.

1. As a unit of product moves along the production line, overhead cost is applied in each separate department where a predetermined overhead rate exists.

2. The total of all these different overhead applications represents the total overhead cost of the job.

REVIEW AND SELF TEST
Questions and Exercises

True or False

For each of the following statements, enter a T or an F in the blank to indicate whether the statement is true or false.

_____ 1. Product costs are historical figures and therefore are of little use to the manager.

_____ 2. A company producing furniture would probably use a job-order cost system.

_____ 3. Process costing systems are used in those situations where output is basically homogeneous.

_____ 4. Both job-order and process costing systems utilize averaging concepts in computing unit costs.

_____ 5. Most factory overhead costs are direct costs and therefore can be easily identified with specific jobs.

_____ 6. The predetermined overhead rate is computed using estimates of cost and activity.

_____ 7. The predetermined overhead rate is generally computed on a monthly basis rather than on an annual basis to increase the accuracy of unit costs.

_____ 8. The cost of indirect materials used in production is added to the Manufacturing Overhead account rather than added directly to Work in Process.

_____ 9. The job cost sheet is used to accumulate the costs chargeable to a particular job.

_____ 10. Actual manufacturing overhead costs are charged directly to the Work in Process account as the costs are incurred.

_____ 11. Selling and administrative expenses should be added to the Manufacturing Overhead account.

_____ 12. If more overhead is applied to Work in Process than is actually incurred, then overhead will be overapplied.

_____ 13. All of the raw materials purchased during a period are included in the cost of goods manufactured figure.

_____ 14. More accurate unit cost figures can be obtained by using departmental overhead rates to assign overhead cost to products than can be obtained by using activity-based costing.

_____ 15. A debit balance in the Manufacturing Overhead account at the end of a period would mean that overhead was underapplied for the period.

_____ 16. Any balance in the Work in Process ac-count at the end of a period should be closed to Cost of Goods Sold.

_____ 17. On the Schedule of Cost of Goods Manufactured, any underapplied overhead should be deducted from the actual overhead costs in order to determine the amount of overhead cost applied to Work in Process.

_____ 18. Once production is completed, the job cost sheet can be discarded.

_____ 19. Allocating any under- or overapplied overhead cost between Work in Process, Finished Goods, and Cost of Goods Sold is a more accurate costing approach than closing the entire under- or overapplied amount to Cost of Goods Sold.

_____ 20. Under- or overapplied overhead is computed by finding the difference between actual overhead costs and the amount of overhead cost applied to Work in Process.

Multiple Choice

Choose the best answer or response by placing the identifying letter in the space provided.

_____ 1. For 19x1, a company reported estimated overhead, $100,000; actual overhead, $90,000; and applied overhead, $92,000. The company's overhead cost for the year would be: a) underapplied, $10,000; b) underapplied, $8,000; c) overapplied, $2,000; d) overapplied, $10,000.

_____ 2. In a job-order cost system, the basic document for accumulating costs by individual job is: a) the materials requisition form; b) the job cost sheet; c) the Work in Process control account; d) the labor time ticket; e) none of these.

_____ 3. The most common treatment of under- or overapplied overhead is to close it out to: a) Work in Process; b) Retained Earnings; c) Cost of Goods Sold; d) Finished Goods; e) none of these.

_____ 4. Apple Company bases its predetermined overhead rates on machine hours. Its estimates for 19x2 were: overhead, $60,000; machine hours, 40,000. Actual operating data for 19x2 were: overhead, $65,100; machine hours, 42,000. Under- or overapplied overhead for the year would be: a) underapplied, $2,100; b) overapplied, $3,000; c) underapplied, $3,000; d) overapplied, $5,100; e) none of these.

_____ 5. The Work in Process account is a control account supported by detailed cost information contained in: a) the Finished Goods inventory account; b) the Cost of Goods Sold account; c) the job cost sheets of uncompleted jobs; d) the Manufacturing Overhead account; e) none of these.

_____ 6. On January 1, Hessler Company's Work in Process account had a balance of $18,000. During the year, raw materials costing $40,000 were purchased, and raw materials costing $35,000 were placed into production. Factory labor cost for the year totaled $70,000, of which $60,000 was direct labor. The predetermined overhead rate for the year was set at 150 percent of direct labor cost. Actual overhead costs for the year totaled $92,000. Jobs costing $190,000 to manufacture were completed during the year. On December 31, the balance in the Work in Process inventory account was: a) $13,000; b) $18,000; c) $15,000; d) none of these.

_____ 7. On the schedule of cost of goods manufactured, the final cost of goods manufactured figure: a) represents the amount of cost charged to Work in Process during the period; b) represents the amount transferred from Work in Process to Finished Goods during the period; c) represents the amount of cost placed into production during the period; d) none of these.

_____ 8. If overhead is overapplied for a period, it means that: a) the predetermined overhead rate used to apply overhead cost to Work in Process was too low; b) the company incurred more overhead cost than it charged to Work in Process; c) too much cost has been assigned to units of product; d) none of these.

_____ 9. Marvel Company's Manufacturing Overhead account showed a $10,000 underapplied overhead balance on December 31. Other accounts showed the following balances on that date:

Raw Materials	$ 50,000
Work in Process	40,000
Finished Goods	60,000
Cost of Goods Sold	100,000

If the company allocates the underapplied overhead, the amount allocated to Work in Process would be: a) $2,000; b) $4,000; c) $1,600; d) none of these.

Complete the Statements

Fill in the necessary words to complete the following statements.

1. A company doing special order printing would very likely use _____ _____ _____, rather than process costing.

2. Raw materials are drawn from the storeroom on presentation of a _____ _____ _____

3. The predetermined overhead rate is computed by dividing estimated _____ _____ by estimated _____ _____ hours or some other activity base.

4. The _____ _____ _____ is used to summarize all of the costs chargeable to a particular job.

5. Applied manufacturing overhead cost should be debited to the _____ _____ _____ inventory account, and credited to the _____ _____ account.

6. The process of assigning overhead cost to jobs is known as the _____ or _____ of overhead.

7. If the amount of overhead cost applied to Work in Process is less than the actual overhead costs of a period, then overhead is _____.

8. The most accurate way to dispose of under- or overapplied overhead is to allocate it between _____, _____, and _____.

9. The most accurate way to assign overhead cost to products is by use of _____ _____ _____.

10. A debit balance in the Manufacturing Overhead account indicates that overhead was _____, and a credit balance indicates that overhead was _____.

11. Only _____ materials cost and _____ labor cost are charged to Work in Process; _____ materials cost and _____ labor cost are charged to manufacturing overhead.

12.   Labor costs are charged to various jobs by means of a document known as a _____ _____, which shows an hour-by-hour summary of an employee's work.

13.   Manufacturing overhead is an _____ cost to units of product, and thus must be allocated in order to be assigned to jobs.

14.   Actual overhead costs incurred during a period are charged to the _____ _____ account, rather than charged to work in process.

15.   An overhead rate established before a period begins is known as a _____ _____ rate.

Exercises

3-1. Bartle Company uses a job-order cost system. Estimated cost and activity data for 19x5 were: manufacturing overhead, $150,000; direct labor hours, 100,000. At the end of 19x5, cost records revealed that actual overhead costs of $160,000 had been incurred and that 105,000 direct labor hours had been worked.

a.   The predetermined overhead rate for 19x5 would be .... $_____ .

b.   Manufacturing overhead cost applied to work in process for 19x5 would be .... $_____ .

c.   The amount of underapplied or overapplied overhead cost for 19x5 would be .... (underapplied/overapplied) $_____ .

3-2. The following selected account balances are taken from the books of Pardoe Company as of June 1, 19x6, the start of the current year:

Cash		Work in Process		Accounts Payable			
12,000		40,000			75,000		

Accounts Receivable		Finished Goods		Salaries and Wages Payable			
48,000		100,000			12,000		

Prepaid Insurance		Accumulated Depreciation		Sales			
8,000			120,000				

Raw Materials		Manufacturing Overhead		Cost of Goods Sold			
30,000							

The following data relate to the activities of Pardoe Company for the fiscal year ending May 31, 19x7:

1. Raw materials purchased on account, $150,000.
2. Raw materials issued to production, $145,000 (all direct materials).
3. Advertising cost incurred for the year, $50,000.
4. Utilities cost incurred for the factory, $35,000.
5. Salaries and wages costs incurred: direct labor, $250,000 (30,000 hours); indirect labor, $75,000; selling and administrative, $140,000.
6. Depreciation recorded for the year, $20,000, of which 75 percent related to the factory and 25 percent related to selling and administrative functions.
7. Other factory overhead costs incurred for the year, $30,000 (credit accounts payable).
8. Other selling and administrative expenses incurred for the year, $25,000 (credit accounts payable).
9. The prepaid insurance relates to factory operations. One-half of the amount expired during the current year.
10. The company applies overhead cost to production on a basis of direct labor hours, at $5.50 per hour.
11. Goods completed (cost of goods manufactured) for the year totaled $550,000.
12. Goods which had a manufactured cost of $540,000 were sold on account for $800,000.
13. Collections on account from customers during the year totaled $790,000.
14. Cash disbursed during the year: on accounts payable, $300,000; for salaries and wages, $460,000.

Required:

1. Post the entries above directly into Pardoe Company's T-accounts. Key your entries with the numbers 1-14 above.
2. Compute the ending balance in each T-account.
3. Is overhead underapplied or overapplied for the year?_____ Close the balance into Cost of Goods Sold. (Key the entry as #15.)
4. Prepare an income statement for the year.

PARDOE COMPANY
Income Statement
For the Year Ended May 31, 19x7

_____
_____
_____
_____
_____
_____
_____
_____
_____
_____
_____
_____
_____
_____

3-3. From the following data, compute the amount of raw materials used in production during the year:

Direct labor cost	$240,000
Raw materials inventory, 12/31/x5	15,000
Indirect labor cost	90,000
Raw materials inventory, 1/1/x5	10,000
Work in process inventory, 12/31/x5	75,000
Work in process inventory, 1/1/x5	60,000
Purchases of raw materials	145,000

_____

_____

_____

_____

_____

_____

3-4. **Critical thought writing exercise:** Quality Foods, Inc., is a major producer of canned vegetables, fruits, and other goods. In 19x3 the company planned a normal year of producing canned goods and set its predetermined overhead rate the same as in other years. However, during the year a major freeze in key growing areas wiped out much of the expected fruit crop and the company was able to do little canning of fruit. A large amount of the manufacturing overhead cost associated with producing canned goods consists of depreciation and other fixed costs. Would you expect Quality Foods, Inc., to have underapplied or overapplied manufacturing overhead cost for 19x3? Explain.

_____

_____

_____

_____

_____

_____

_____

_____

Chapter 3
Answers to Questions and Exercises

True or False

1. F   Product costs are of great usefulness to the manager in determining the profits for a period, the value of inventories on the balance sheet, and the selling price for goods.

2. T   Job-order costing is used in those situations where units of product are not homogeneous.

3. T   By definition, process costing is used when output is homogeneous.

4. T   Averaging is involved in both costing systems, since costs such as depreciation, rent, and salaries must be assigned to products.

5. F   Only direct materials and direct labor are direct costs; manufacturing overhead, which may be the largest category of cost, is indirect.

6. T   Estimates are used since a rate must be developed before the period begins.

7. F   The predetermined overhead rate is computed on an annual basis in order to smooth out month-by-month variations in cost and activity.

8. T   Costs of production other than direct materials and direct labor are charged to the Manufacturing Overhead account.

9. T   A separate job cost sheet is prepared for each job entered into production, and used to accumulate costs as they are charged to the job.

10. F   Actual manufacturing overhead costs are charged to the Manufacturing Overhead account—not to Work in Process.

11. F   Selling and administrative expenses are period costs, not product costs; thus, they are deducted as expenses on the income statement in the period they are incurred.

12. T   If more overhead is applied to Work in Process than is actually incurred, then a credit balance will exist in the Manufacturing Overhead account. A credit balance represents overapplied overhead.

13. F   Only the raw materials used in production are included in the cost of goods manufactured figure. Some materials purchased during a period may remain in the Raw Materials inventory account.

14. F   Activity-based costing is a more accurate method of assigning overhead cost to products than either departmental overhead rates or plantwide overhead rates.

15. T   A debit balance in the Manufacturing Overhead account would mean that more overhead cost was incurred than was allocated to Work in Process. Thus, manufacturing overhead would be underapplied.

16. F   Any balance in the *Manufacturing Overhead* account (not Work in Process) should be closed to Cost of Goods Sold. Work in Process is an inventory account that appears on the balance sheet at the end of a period.

17. T   If overhead is underapplied, then less overhead cost was added to Work in Process than was incurred during the period. Thus, the underapplied overhead must be deducted from actual overhead costs to show the proper amount of cost added to Work in Process. See Exhibit 3-10.

18. F   The job cost sheet becomes the control document for determining the number of units still on hand and the number of units shipped to customers; thus, it is not discarded but rather kept on file.

19. T   Allocation is more accurate, since it shows where the overhead cost would have gone if overhead rates had been completely accurate.

20. T   By definition, this is how under- or overapplied overhead cost is computed, as shown in Exhibit 3-11.

Multiple Choice

1. c   Under- or overapplied overhead represents the difference between actual overhead cost and applied overhead cost (see Exhibit 3-11). Thus, the computation in this case would be:

Actual overhead cost	$90,000
Applied overhead cost	92,000
Overapplied overhead cost	$(2,000)

2. b   The job cost sheet is used to accumulate direct materials, direct labor, and overhead costs, as illustrated in Exhibits 3-6, 3-7, and 3-8.

3. c   Since under- or overapplied overhead represents a cost adjustment item, it must eventually flow through Cost of Goods Sold. The simplest procedure is to close any under- or overapplied balance directly to the Cost of Goods Sold account at the end of a period.

4. a   The predetermined overhead rate would be: $60,000 ÷ 40,000 hours = $1.50/hr.

Actual overhead cost	$65,100
Applied overhead cost ($1.50 × 42,000 hours)	63,000
Underapplied overhead cost	$ 2,100

5. c   By definition, the job cost sheets constitute a subsidiary ledger that is controlled by the Work in Process account.

6. a   The solution would be:

Work in Process

Balance	18,000	190,000	Goods
Direct materials	35,000		completed
Direct labor	60,000		
Overhead applied	90,000*		
Balance	13,000		

*$60,000 × 150% = $90,000

7. b   The cost of goods manufactured represents goods completed during a period; thus, it is the amount transferred from Work in Process to Finished Goods.

8. c   If overhead is overapplied, then more overhead cost has been added to products than has been incurred. Therefore, too much overhead cost will have been assigned to units of product.

9. a   The computations would be:

Work in Process	$ 40,000	20%
Finished Goods	60,000	30
Cost of Goods Sold	100,000	50
Total cost	$200,000	100%

20% × $10,000 = $2,000.

Complete the Statements

1. job-order costing
2. materials requisition form
3. manufacturing overhead, direct labor
4. job cost sheet
5. Work in Process, Manufacturing Overhead
6. application, absorption
7. underapplied
8. Work in Process, Finished Goods, Cost of
    Goods Sold

9. activity-based costing
10. underapplied, overapplied
11. direct, direct, indirect, indirect
12. time ticket
13. indirect
14. Manufacturing Overhead
15. predetermined overhead

Exercises

3-1. a. $\dfrac{\$150,000}{100,000} = \$1.50/\text{direct labor hour}$

b. 105,000 direct labor hours $\times$ \$1.50 = \$157,500 applied

c.
Actual overhead cost \$160,000
Applied overhead cost 157,500
Underapplied overhead cost . . . . \$ 2,500

3-2. The answers to parts 1 and 2 are on the following page.

3. Overhead is overapplied by \$6,000.

4.

PARDOE COMPANY
Income Statement
For the Year Ended May 31, 19x7

Sales		\$800,000
Less cost of goods sold		534,000
Gross margin		266,000
Less operating expenses:		
Advertising expense	\$ 50,000	
Salaries expense	140,000	
Depreciation expense	5,000	
Other expenses	25,000	220,000
Net Income		\$ 46,000

3-3.
Raw materials inventory, 1/1/x5	\$ 10,000
Add purchases of raw materials	145,000
Total	155,000
Deduct raw materials inventory, 12/31/x5	15,000
Raw Materials Used in Production	\$140,000

3-4. Quality Foods, Inc. would probably have underapplied manufacturing overhead cost for the year. Since a large amount of the manufacturing overhead cost associated with producing canned goods is fixed, the company's **actual** manufacturing overhead costs would be about as plannned. However, the company's **applied** manufacturing overhead costs would be less than planned since less productive activity would take place in the plant due to the loss of the fruit crop. Thus, with a large amount of **actual** overhead cost and less than planned **applied** overhead cost, the company would end the year with an underapplied balance in its Manufacturing Overhead account.

(Exercise 3-2) 1. and 2.

Cash			Work in Process			Accounts Payable			Advertising Expense	
12,000	760,000(14)		40,000	550,000(11)		(14)300,000	75,000		(3) 50,000	
(13)790,000			(2)145,000				150,000	(1)		
--- ---	--- ---		(5)250,000				50,000	(3)		
42,000			(10)165,000				35,000	(4)		
							30,000	(7)		
			--- ---	--- ---			25,000	(8)		
			50,000			--- ---	--- ---			
							65,000			

Accounts Receivable			Finished Goods			Salaries and Wages Payable			Salaries Expense	
48,000	790,000(13)		100,000	540,000(12b)		(14)460,000	12,000		(5)140,000	
(12a)800,000			(11)550,000				465,000	(5)		
--- ---	--- ---		--- ---	--- ---		--- ---	--- ---			
58,000			110,000				17,000			

Prepaid Insurance			Accumulated Depreciation			Sales			Depreciation Expense	
8,000	4,000 (9)			120,000			800,000(12a)		(6) 5,000	
--- ---	--- ---			20,000 (6)						
4,000			--- ---	--- ---						
				140,000						

Raw Materials			Manufacturing Overhead			Cost of Goods Sold			Other Selling and Administrative Expense	
30,000	145,000 (2)		(4) 35,000	165,000(10)		(12b)540,000	6,000(15)		(8) 25,000	
(1)150,000			(5) 75,000							
--- ---	--- ---		(6) 15,000							
35,000			(7) 30,000							
			(9) 4,000							
			--- ---	--- ---						
			(15) 6,000	6,000						

Chapter 4

Systems Design: Process Costing

Chapter Study Suggestions

The chapter is divided into six main parts. The first part is a comparison of job-order and process costing. Exhibit 4-1, which outlines the differences between the two costing methods, is the key item in this part. The second part gives a perspective of cost flows in a process costing system. Study Exhibits 4-3 and 4-4 carefully, as well as the journal entries that follow.

The third part deals with a concept known as *equivalent units of production*. This part will require special effort in order to grasp the concept of equivalent units. Pay particular attention to the computations in Exhibits 4-5, 4-6, and 4-7.

The fourth part illustrates the preparation of a production report under the weighted-average method. The production report is the single most important concept in the chapter. Thus, you will need to focus a large portion of your time on learning how it is constructed. A detailed example is provided in Exhibit 4-10. The fifth part of the chapter provides a discussion of innovations in costing systems. The most important of these concerns a hybrid system called *operation costing*, which is widely used in actual practice.

The final part of the chapter is contained in Appendix B, which illustrates the preparation of a production report under the FIFO method. Pay particular attention to Exhibit B-1 on the format of a production report when FIFO is used, and Exhibit B-2 which compares the weighted-average and FIFO methods.

CHAPTER HIGHLIGHTS AND STUDY GUIDE

A. Process costing is used in those industries which produce basically homogeneous products such as bricks, flour, and cement. The method is also employed in assembly-type operations, as well as in utilities producing gas, water, and electricity.

B. Process costing is similar to job-order costing in three ways.

1. The same basic purposes exist in both systems, which are: (a) to assign material, labor, and overhead costs to products; (b) to provide a mechanism for computing unit costs; and (c) to provide data essential for planning, control, and decision making.

2. Both systems maintain and use the same basic manufacturing accounts, including Manufacturing Overhead, Raw Materials, Work in Process, and Finished Goods.

3. Cost flows through the manufacturing accounts in (2) move in basicially the same way in both systems.

C. Process costing differs from job-order costing in four ways.

1. A single product is produced on a continuous basis, and each unit is identical.

2. Costs are accumulated by department, rather than by job.

3. The department production report (rather than the job cost sheet) is the key document showing the accumulation and disposition of cost.

4. Unit costs are computed by department (rather than by job). This computation is made on the department production report.

D. A processing department is any location in the factory where work is performed on a product and where materials, labor, and overhead costs are added to it.

1. All processing departments have two essential features. First, the activity performed in the department is performed uniformly on all units passing through it. And second, the output of the department is homogeneous.

2. Processing departments can be organized in either a sequential or a parallel pattern. A sequential pattern is where all units go through all departments.

A parallel pattern is where not all units go through all departments. Some units may be going through one department while other units are going through other departments, in a parallel fashion.

E. Cost accumulation is simpler in a process costing system than in a job-order costing system. The reason is that costs only need to be identified with a few processing departments rather than with hundreds (or even thousands) of individual jobs.

F. Exhibit 4-4 provides a T-account model of cost flows in a process costing system. A separate Work in Process account is maintained for each processing department. With this separate account, materials, labor, and overhead costs can be entered directly into any processing department—not just the first.

G. Once costs have been accumulated, a department's output must be determined so that unit costs can be computed. A department's output is always stated in terms of equivalent units of production.

1. Equivalent units can be defined as the number of units which would have been produced during a period if all of a department's efforts had resulted in completed units of product.

2. Equivalent units can be computed either by the weighted-averaged method or by the FIFO method.

a. The formula for computing equivalent units by the weighted-average method is:

Units completed and transferred out	XXX
Equivalent units completed in the ending inventory	XXX
Equivalent units of production	XXX

Under the weighted-average method, units in the *beginning* Work in Process inventory are not used in computing the equivalent units figure. The reason is that these units are treated as if they were started and completed during the current period.

b. The formula for computing equivalent units by the FIFO method is:

Equivalent units to complete the beginning inventory	XXX
Units started and completed this year	XXX
Equivalent units completed in the ending inventory	XXX
Equivalent units of production	XXX

3. Since separate unit costs are computed for both materials cost and conversion cost, an equivalent units figure must be computed for each of these cost items.

H. The purpose of the production report is to summarize for the manager all of the activity that takes place in a department's Work in Process account for a period. This activity includes the units which flow through the Work in Process account as well as the costs which flow through it. A production report has three parts:

1. A quantity schedule, which shows the flow of units through a department, and a computation of equivalent units.

2. A computation of total and unit costs.

3. A reconciliation of all cost flows into and out of a department during a period.

I. The purpose of a quantity schedule is to show the flow of units through a department. The schedule is self-balancing in nature, in that it shows the number of units to be accounted for in a department and it shows how those units have been accounted for.

1. The format of the schedule under the weighted-average method is:

Units to be accounted for:	
Work in process, beginning	XXX
Started into production	XXX
Total units to account for	XXX
Units accounted for as follows:	
Transferred out*	XXX
Work in process, ending	XXX
Total units accounted for	XXX

*Transferred to the next department or to Finished Goods.

2. The quantity schedule deals with whole units, not with equivalent units, although the stage of completion is always shown parenthetically.

J. The second step in a production report is to compute unit costs. A computation of unit costs under the weighted-average method is shown in Exhibit 4-10.

Note that costs in the beginning Work in Process inventory are added in with current period costs in computing the unit costs for the period.

K. The final step in a production report is to prepare a reconciliation of all costs for the period.

1. Costs which must be accounted for consist of (a) costs in the beginning Work in Process inventory and (b) costs which have been added by the department during the period.

2. Costs are accounted for as being either (a) transferred out during the period or (b) assigned to the ending Work in Process inventory.

3. In transferring out costs under the weighted-average method, no distinction is made between units in the beginning Work in Process inventory and units started and completed during the period. This procedure is shown in Exhibit 4-10.

L. Operation costing is a hybrid system containing elements of both job-order and process costing. It is used when products have some common characteristics and some individual characteristics.

1. Products are typically handled in batches, with each batch charged with the specific materials used in its production. In this sense, operation costing is similar to job-order costing.

2. Labor and overhead costs are accumulated by department, and these costs are assigned to batches on an average per unit basis, as done in process costing.

APPENDIX B: PRODUCTION REPORT—FIFO METHOD

A. The format of the quantity schedule under the FIFO method follows:

Units to be accounted for:

Work in process, beginning	XXX
Started into production	XXX
Total units to account for	XXX

Units accounted for as follows:
Transferred out:

Units from the beginning inventory	XXX
Units started and completed	XXX
Work in process, ending	XXX
Total units accounted for	XXX

B. After preparing the quantity schedule and computing the equivalent units, unit costs must be computed. Exhibit B-1 contains a computation of unit costs under the FIFO method.

1. Note that unit costs under the FIFO method are computed *only* on costs added during the period.

2. As shown on Exhibit B-1, the unit costs are added together to get the cost of a whole unit of product.

C. The final step in the production report is to prepare a reconciliation of all costs for the period.

1. As in the case of the weighted-average method, the costs that must be accounted for consist of (a) costs in the beginning Work in Process inventory and (b) costs that have been added by the department during the period.

2. The costs in (1) above are accounted for as being either (a) transferred out during the period or (b) assigned to the ending Work in Process inventory.

3. In computing the cost of units transferred out under the FIFO method, the units in the beginning Work in Process inventory must be kept separate from the units started and completed during the current period. An example of a completed production report showing this procedure under the FIFO method is provided in Exhibit B-1. *Study this exhibit with great care, since the material it (and Exhibit 4-10) contains represents the heart of the chapter.*

D. In comparing the weighted-average and FIFO methods, three points can be noted:

1. In most situations, the two methods will produce unit costs which are nearly the same. Any difference is likely to be traceable to raw material prices.

2. From a standpoint of cost control, the FIFO method is superior to the weighted-average method.

3. Although the FIFO method is more complex to apply than is the weighted-average method, this complexity is not a significant factor due to the advent of the computer.

REVIEW AND SELF TEST
Questions and Exercises

True or False

For each of the following statements, enter a T or an F in the blank to indicate whether the statement is true or false.

_____ 1. A utility such as the water company would typically use a process costing system.

_____ 2. Under process costing it is important to identify the materials, labor, and overhead costs associated with a particular customer's order, the same as with job-order costing.

_____ 3. If processing departments are arranged in a parallel manner, all units will go through all departments.

_____ 4. In a process costing system, the production report takes the place of the job cost sheet.

_____ 5. Costing is more difficult in a process costing system than it is in a job-order costing system.

_____ 6. Process and job-order costing are similar in that costs are accumulated (and unit costs are computed) for each separate customer order.

_____ 7. In a process costing system, a Work in Process account is maintained for each department.

_____ 8. It is important to identify labor costs with each customer order in a process costing system.

_____ 9. Operation costing employs aspects of both job-order and process costing systems.

_____ 10. Since costs are accumulated by department, there is no need for a Finished Goods inventory account in a process costing system.

_____ 11. In a process costing system, costs incurred in one department remain there rather than being transferred on to the next department.

_____ 12. If the opening Work in Process inventory contains 500 units that are 60 percent complete, then the inventory contains 300 equivalent units.

_____ 13. Under the FIFO method of computing equivalent units, costs in the opening Work in Process inventory are kept separate from current period costs.

_____ 14. The purpose of the quantity schedule is to show the equivalent units for the period.

_____ 15. Under the FIFO method of computing equivalent units, units in the opening Work in Process inventory are treated as if they were started and completed during the current period.

_____ 16. (Appendix B) Under the FIFO method, units are transferred out in separate blocks—one block consisting of the units in the opening inventory, and the other block consisting of the units started and completed during the period.

_____ 17. (Appendix B) The weighted-average and FIFO methods will typically produce widely different unit costs.

_____ 18. (Appendix B) From a standpoint of cost control, the weighted-average method is superior to the FIFO method.

Multiple Choice

Choose the best answer or response by placing the identifying letter in the space provided.

_____ 1. Apple Company started 4,800 units into process during 19x1. Five hundred units were in the opening inventory and 300 units were in the ending inventory. How many units were completed and transferred out during the period? a) 5,000; b) 4,600; c) 5,300; d) 5,100; e) none of these.

_____ 2. During 19x5 Eager Company started 8,000 units into production. The company had 2,000 units in process on January 1 of that year, which were 60 percent complete, and 3,000 units in process on December 31 which were 50 percent complete. 7,000 units were completed and transferred to the next department during the year. Using the weighted-average method, the equivalent units for the year would be: a) 8,200; b) 8,500; c) 9,200; d) 9,500; e) none of these.

_____ 3. (Appendix B) Refer to the data in question 2 above. Using the FIFO method, the equivalent units for the year would be: a) 8,300; b) 7,700; c) 7,300; d) 6,700; e) none of these.

_____ 4. Costs in the opening Work in Process inventory are added in with costs of the current period when making unit cost calculations by: a) the FIFO cost method; b) the weighted-average cost method; c) the quantity schedule method; d) none of these.

_____ 5. Under the weighted-average cost method: a) completed units are transferred out in two separate blocks; b) units in the ending inventory are not considered in making equivalent units computations; c) units in the opening inventory are treated as if they were started and completed during the current period.

_____ 6. If all units do not go through all processing departments, then the departments are probably arranged in a: a) sequential pattern; b) linear pattern; c) homogeneous pattern; d) parallel pattern; e) none of these.

_____ 7. Doley Company uses the weighted-average method. It had $8,000 of conversion cost in the beginning Work in Process inventory and added $64,000 of conversion cost during 19x1. The company completed 40,000 equivalent units (for conversion costs) during the year. If the company had 10,000 units in the ending Work in Process inventory that were 30 percent complete as to conversion cost, the amount of cost assigned to these units would be: a) $12,600; b) $4,800; c) $11,200; d) $5,400.

_____ 8. The costing method used when products have some common characteristics and some individual characteristics is called: a) job-order costing; b) flexible manufacturing system; c) process costing; d) operation costing.

_____ 9. (Appendix B) Mercer Company had $6,000 cost in its beginning Work in Process inventory for materials and the company added $75,000 in cost for materials during the period. The company completed 20,000 equivalent units for materials and it uses the FIFO method. The unit cost for materials would be: a) $3.75; b) $4.05; c) $0.30; d) none of these.

Complete the Statements

Fill in the necessary words to complete the following statements.

1. Processing departments might be organized in either a _____ processing pattern or a _____ processing pattern.

2. Rather than using job cost sheets, in a process costing system a document known as a _____ _____ is prepared for each department.

3. In a process costing system, costs are accumulated by _____ rather than by job.

4. A separate _____ _____ _____ account is maintained for each department in a process costing system.

5. A department's output is measured in terms of _____ _____ of production.

6. Under the _____ _____ method, units in the beginning Work in Process inventory are treated as if they were started and completed during the current period.

7. The purpose of the _____ _____ is to account for the physical flow of units through a department during a period.

8. On a production report, labor and overhead costs are often added together and called _____ costs.

9. (Appendix B) Under the _____ method, units in the beginning Work in Process inventory are kept separate from units started and completed during the current period.

10. (Appendix B) From a standpoint of cost control, the _____ method is superior to the _____ method.

Exercises

4-1. Diebold Company has a process costing system. Data relating to activities in the Mixing Department for March 19x6 follow:

		Percent Completed	
	Units	Materials	Conversion
Work in process, March 1	5,000	100	60
Units started into production	80,000		
Work in process, March 31	2,000	100	50

Using the weighted-average method, prepare a quantity schedule and a computation of equivalent units for the month:

	Quantity Schedule	Equivalent Units — Materials	Conversion
Units to be accounted for:			
Units accounted for as follows:			

(Appendix B) Using the FIFO method, prepare a quantity schedule and a computation of equivalent units for the month:

	Quantity Schedule	Equivalent Units — Materials	Conversion
Units to be accounted for:			
Units accounted for as follows:			

4-2. Minden Company has a process costing system and uses the weighted-average method. Complete the production report below for the company's Mixing Department by showing how the $470,000 in cost charged to the department for the period is to be accounted for.

Production Report, Mixing Department

Quantity schedule and equivalent units

	Quantity Schedule	Equivalent Units — Materials	Labor	Overhead
Units to be accounted for:				
Work in process, beginning (all materials, 20% labor and overhead added last month)	5,000	(Work done last month)		
Started into production	75,000			
Total units	80,000			

	Quantity Schedule	Equivalent Units		
		Materials	Labor	Overhead
Units accounted for as follows:				
Transferred out	72,000	72,000	72,000	72,000
Work in process, ending (all materials, 75% labor and overhead added this month)	8,000	8,000	6,000	6,000
Total units	80,000	80,000	78,000	78,000

Total and Unit costs

	Total Cost	Materials	Labor	Overhead	Whole Unit
Cost to be accounted for:					
Work in process, beginning	$ 9,500	$ 4,500	$ 3,000	$ 2,000	
Cost added by the department	460,500	75,500	231,000	154,000	
Total cost (a)	$470,000	$ 80,000	$234,000	$156,000	
Equivalent units (b)	--	80,000	78,000	78,000	
Unit cost (a) ÷ (b)	--	$1.00 +	$3.00 +	$2.00 =	$6.00

Cost reconciliation

		Equivalent Units (above)		
		Materials	Labor	Overhead
Cost accounted for as follows:				
Transferred out ( )	$	___	___	___
Work in process, ending:		___		
Materials ( )				
Labor ( )			___	
Overhead ( )				___
Total work in process, ending	___			
Total cost	$470,000			

4-3. (Appendix B) Sinclair Company uses a process costing system. Complete the production report below for the company's Cooking Depoartment by showing how the $277,300 in cost charged to the department for the period is to be account for. The company uses the FIFO cost method.

Production Report, Cooking Department

Quantity schedule and unit costs

	Quantity Schedule	Equivalent Units		
		Materials	Labor	Overhead
Units to be accounted for:				
Work in process, beginning (all materials, 25% labor and overhead added last month)	8,000	(Work done last month)		
Started into production	62,000			
Total units	70,000			

	Quantity Schedule	Equivalent Units		
		Materials	Labor	Overhead
Units accounted for as follows:				
Transferred out:				
Units from the beginning inventory	8,000	—	6,000	6,000
Units started and completed this month	57,000	57,000	57,000	57,000
Work in process, ending (all materials, 80% labor and overhead added this month)	5,000	5,000	4,000	4,000
Total units	70,000	62,000	67,000	67,000

Total and Unit costs	Total Cost	Materials	Labor	Overhead	Whole Unit
Cost to be accounted for:					
Work in process, beginning	$ 16,800				
Added by the department(s)	260,500	$93,000	$134,00	$33,500	
Total cost	$277,300				
Equivalent units (b)	--	62,000	67,000	67,000	
Unit cost, (a) ÷ (b)	--	$ 1.50 +	$ 2.00 +	$ 0.50 =	$ 4.00

Cost reconciliation	Total Cost	Equivalent Units (above)		
		Materials	Labor	Overhead
Cost accounted for as follows:				
Transferred out:				
Units from the beginning inventory:				
Cost in the beginning inventory	$			
Cost to complete these units:				
Materials ( )		_____		
Labor ( )			_____	
Overhead ( )	_____			_____
Total cost				
Units started an completed during the month ( )	_____	_____	_____	_____
Total cost transferred out	_____			
Work in process, ending:				
Materials ( )		_____		
Labor ( )			_____	
Overhead ( )	_____			_____
Total work in process, ending				
Total cost	$277,300			

4-4. Critical thought writing exercise: Dover Company is increasing its production and sales of Product A each year. The ending work in process inventory is maintained at about five percent of total annual production. If the company uses the weighted-average method of computing equivalent units, would you expect the equivalent units figure in a given year to be higher or lower than if the FIFO method was being used? Explain.

_____

_____

_____

_____

_____

_____

_____

Chapter 4
Answers to Questions and Exercises

True or False

1. T   Process costing is widely used by utilities since their units of output (water, gas, electricity) are homogeneous.

2. F   Since units are indistinguishable from each other, there is no need to identify materials, labor, and overhead costs by customer order.

3. F   Under parallel processing, some units go through one set of departments and other units go through a different set of departments.

4. T   See the discussion in Exhibit 4-1.

5. F   Costing is easier in a process costing system since costs are accumulated by department rather than by individual job.

6. F   Costs are accumulated by department in a process costing system; see Exhibit 4-1.

7. T   Each department is responsible for its own costs; thus, a Work in Process account is maintained for each department.

8. F   Again, costs are accumulated by department in a process costing system.

9. T   This statement is true by definition.

10. F   A Finished Goods inventory account is needed in a process costing system to carry unsold units, the same as in a job-order costing system.

11. F   As goods move from one department to another, the costs that have been incurred to that point are transferred with the goods. This point is illustrated in Exhibit 4-4.

12. T   The computation is:

    500 units $\times$ 60% = 300 equivalent units.

13. T   Costs in the opening Work in Process inventory are kept separate from current period costs so that unit costs will be reflective only of current period activities.

14. F   The purpose of the quantity schedule is to show the flow of units through a department.

15. F   Under the *weighted-average* method (not the FIFO method) this statement would be true.

16. T   This point is illustrated in Exhibit B-1.

17. F   Unit costs will tend to be very close, with any difference in unit cost traceable for the most part to changes in materials prices from period to period.

18. F   The reverse is true—from a standpoint of cost control, the FIFO method is superior to the weighted-average method.

Multiple Choice

1. a   The computations are:

Beginning inventory	500
Add: Units started into process	4,800
Total units	5,300
Less ending inventory	300
Completed and transferred	5,000

2. b.   The computations are:

Units completed and transferred	7,000
Work in process, ending:	
3,000 units × 50%	1,500
Equivalent units of production	8,500

3. c   The computations are:

Work in process, beginning:	
2,000 units × 40%*	800
Units started and completed	5,000**
Work in process, ending:	
3,000 units × 50%	1,500
Equivalent units of production	7,300

*100% − 60% = 40%.
**7,000 units − 2,000 units = 5,000 units.

4. b   Units in the beginning Work in Process inventory are treated as if they were started and completed during the current period; thus, costs in the beginning inventory are added in with current period costs when making unit cost computations.

5. c   This point was just made in question (4) above.

6. d   By definition, some units go through different departments than other units in a parallel processing situation.

7. d   The computations are:

Cost in the beginning Work in Process	$ 8,000
Cost added during the year	64,000
Total cost (a)	$72,000
Equivalent units (b)	40,000
Unit cost (a) ÷ (b)	$1.80

10,000 units × 30% = 3,000 units;
3,000 units × $1.80 = $5,400.

8. d   Operation costing is used for such items as shoes and jewelry, where some work is done in common (e.g., sewing or stamping) and some work is individual (e.g., materials used).

9. a   The computations are:

$75,000 ÷ 20,000 units = $3.75 per unit.

Complete the Statements

1. sequential, parallel
2. production report
3. department
4. Work in Process
5. equivalent units
6. weighted-average
7. quantity schedule
8. conversion
9. FIFO
10. FIFO, weighted-average

Exercises

4-1. *Weighted-average method:*

	Quantity Schedule	Equivalent Units Materials	Conversion
Units to be accounted for:			
Work in process, beginning (all materials; 60% conversion cost added last month)	5,000	(Work done last month)	
Started into production	80,000		
Total units to account for	85,000		
Units accounted for as follows:			
Transferred out during the month	83,000	83,000	83,000
Work in process, ending (all materials; 50% conversion cost added this month)	2,000	2,000	1,000
Total units accounted for	85,000	85,000	84,000

FIFO method:

	Quantity Schedule	Equivalent Units Materials	Conversion
Units to be accounted for:			
Work in process, beginning (all materials; 60% conversion cost added last month)	5,000	(Work done last month)	
Started into production	80,000		
Total units to account for	85,000		
Units accounted for as follows:			
Transferred out during the month:			
Units from the beginning inventory	5,000	—	2,000
Units started and completed during the month	78,000	78,000	78,000
Work in process, ending (all materials; 50% conversion cost added this month)	2,000	2,000	1,000
Total units accounted for	85,000	80,000	81,000

	Total Cost	Equivalent Units Materials	Labor	Overhead
4-2				
Cost accounted for as follows:				
Transferred out: 72,000 units x $6	$432,000	72,000	72,000	72,000
Work in process, ending:				
Materials cost, at $1 per EU	8,000	8,000		
Labor cost, at $3 per EU	18,000		6,000	
Overhead cost, at $2 per EU	12,000			6,000
Total work in process, ending	38,000			
Total cost	$470,000			

	Total Cost	Equivalent Units		
		Materials	Labor	Overhead
4-3.				
Cost accounted for as follows:				
Transferred out:				
Units from the beginning inventory:				
Cost in the beginning inventory	$ 16,800			
Cost to complete these units:				
Materials, at $1.50 per EU	–	–		
Labor, at $2.00 per EU	12,000		6,000	
Overhead, at $0.50 per EU	3,000			6,000
Total cost	31,800			
Units started and completed during the				
month: 57,000 x $4.00	228,000	57,000	57,000	57,000
Total cost transferred out	259,800			
Work in process, ending:				
Materials cost, at $1.50 per EU	7,500	5,000		
Labor cost, at $2.00 per EU	8,000		4,000	
Overhead cost, at $0.50 per EU	2,000			4,000
Total work in process, ending	17,500			
Total cost	$277,300			

4-4. You would expect the equivalent units figure to be higher under the weighted-average method. The reason is because the weighted-average method treats all units in the beginning work in process inventory (which is the same as the ending work in process inventory from the prior year) as if they were started and completed during the current year. By contrast, the FIFO method includes as part of the current year's equivalent units only the actual work done on units in the beginning work in process inventory. Thus, whenever a beginning work in process inventory exists, one would **always** expect the weighted-average method to show the highest equivalent units figure.

Chapter 5

Systems Design:
JIT and Activity-Based Costing

Chapter Study Suggestions

The chapter is divided into two parts. The first part covers just-in-time (JIT) inventory systems. Study Exhibit 5-1 carefully; it illustrates the "pull" approach to manufacturing that is followed under JIT. Also, study with care the section titled "Expansion of the JIT Concept." The ideas in this section are referred to many times in remaining chapters. Exhibit 5-8 provides an overview of the JIT management system.

The second part of the chapter focuses on activity-based costing. Exhibits 5-13, 5-14, and 5-15 are the key exhibits to study.

Exhibit 5-15 contains many detailed computations that you *must* understand. This exhibit is the key to much of the homework material. The review problem at the end of the chapter provides added help with the computations involved in activity-based costing.

CHAPTER HIGHLIGHTS AND STUDY GUIDE

A. In an effort to reduce or eliminate inventories, just-in-time inventory systems are coming into use.

1. "Just in time" means that raw materials are received *just in time* to go into production, manufactured parts are completed *just in time* to be assembled into products, and products are completed *just in time* to be shipped to customers.

2. In a JIT environment, the flow of goods is controlled by a "pull" approach to the manufacture of products. Under the pull approach, work is initiated at the final assembly stage.

a. At the final assembly stage, a signal is sent to preceding workstations as to the exact amounts of parts and materials that will be needed *over the next few hours* for the assembly of products.

b. Under conventional systems, parts and material are "pushed" forward to the next workstation, regardless of need. The result is a needless buildup of inventory.

B. Five key elements are involved in the operation of a JIT system.

1. A company must learn to rely on a few suppliers who are willing to make frequent (even daily) deliveries in small lots.

2. A company must improve its product flow lines by creating an individual flow line for each separate product.

3. A company must reduce the setup time between production runs. One way to do this is through employee training. Another way is through automation by creating a flexible manufacturing system (FMS).

a. An FMS gives a company the power to manufacture a whole family of products on a single product flow line, with minimal setup time between products.

b. An FMS is just one part of the overall concept of computer-integrated manufacturing, in which a company's business functions are integrated with its manufacturing functions.

4. A company must develop a system of total quality control (TQC) over its parts and materials. In the absence of TQC, it would be impossible to successfully implement a JIT system.

a. TQC starts with suppliers, who must inspect good before they are shipped to ensure that the goods are free of defects.

b. A company's own employees also have TQC responsibilities. Employees are responsible to inspect their own work before sending partially completed units on to the next workstation.

5. A company must develop a flexible work force. Since the plant layout in a JIT environment is different from that of a conventional factory, workers must be multiskilled.

a. In addition to being able to operate all of the machines in a cell, workers must also be able to perform routine maintenance on these machines.

b. Having a flexible workforce reduces the number of job descriptions that a company must carry and simplifies work assignments.

C. Many benefits accrue from a JIT system. The reader should review the benefits listed in the text.

D. Over the last two decades JIT has expanded from simple inventory control into what is termed *the JIT philosophy*. This philosophy says that management should focus its efforts on *simplification* and *elimination of waste*. Three ideas are pivotal of this philosophy.

1. All activities should be eliminated that do not add value to a product or service. Activities that do not add value are called non-value-added activities. Manufacturing time for a product can be expressed as follows:

Manufacturing time =
> Process time + Inspection time
> + Move time + Queue time

The only one of these activities that adds value to products is process time

2. A commitment must be made to achieve and maintain high levels of quality in all aspects of a company's activities.

3. A commitment must be made to continuous improvement in all of a company's activities and in the usefulness of data generated for its management. *Continuous improvement* is the constant pursuit of ever-greater value being provided for the customer.

E. JIT affects process costing in two ways.

1. First, it eliminates the differences in unit costs between the weighted-average and FIFO methods. Differences in unit costs are eliminated because there are no work in process inventories under JIT.

2. Second, it allows companies that previously used job-order costing to use process costing instead. This is because of improved plant layouts and reduction in setup times.

F. Predetermined overhead rates can be computed at three levels in a company. Level One is known as a *plantwide overhead rate.*

1. A plantwide overhead rate encompasses all parts of a company, and it is typically based on direct labor-hours.

2. In an automated environment, plantwide overhead rates generally result in distorted unit costs since they do not properly trace overhead costs to different products.

G. Level Two uses a "two stage" allocation process that involves *departmental overhead rates.*

1. In the first stage, overhead costs are assigned to cost pools, such as individual departments or operations.

2. In the second stage, costs are allocated from the cost pools (departments) to individual jobs. These second stage allocations are made on various bases, according to the nature of the work being performed in the department.

3. As a job moves along the production line, overhead is applied in each department according to the various overhead rates that have been set.

4. However, even departmental rates will not correctly assign overhead costs to products in situations where the products differ in volume, lot size, or complexity of production.

H. Level Three also uses a "two stage" allocation process, but this approach involves *activity-based costing*. Level Three is considered to be the most accurate overhead costing method.

1. In the first stage, overhead costs are again assigned to cost pools, but these pools represent activities, such as setups required, purchase orders issued, and so forth.

2. In the second stage, overhead costs are assigned to jobs according to the number of these activities required in their completion.

3. An "activity" is any event or transaction that is a cost driver—that is, that acts as a causal factor in the incurrence of cost in an organization. The number of activities is a function of the complexity of operations.

I. Four steps are involved in the design of an activity-based costing system. These steps are process value analysis, identifying activity centers, tracing costs to activity centers, and selecting cost drivers.

1. Process value analysis consists of systemically analyzing the activities required to make a product, and eliminating any activities that are non-value-added.

2. Activity-based costing recognizes four general levels of activity centers, as follows:

a. *Unit-level activities*, which are performed each time a unit is produced.

b. *Batch-level activities*, which are performed each time a batch of goods is handled or processed.

c. *Product-level activities*, which are performed as needed to support production of each different type of product.

d. *Facility-level activities*, which simply sustain a facility's general manufacturing process.

3. The most accurate way to assign costs to activity centers is to trace them directly. If a resource, such as plant space, is shared by several activity centers, the costs of the resource will have to be assigned on some basis such as space occupied.

4. Two factors must be considered when selecting a cost driver for an activity center. These factors are:

a. The ease of obtaining data relating to the cost driver.

b. The degree to which the cost driver measures actual consumption by products of the activity involved.

J. The reader should study the example of activity-based costing in Exhibit 5-15.

K. Activity-based costing improves the costing systems of organizations in three ways.

1. It increases the number of cost pools used to accumulate overhead costs.

2. It changes the base used to assign overhead costs to products. Rather than use direct labor, activity-based costing uses those factors (such as setups and purchase orders) that were the cost drivers in the incurrence of overhead.

3. It changes the nature of many overhead costs, in that costs that were formerly treated as indirect are recognized as being directly traceable to products.

L. Activity-based costing has two major limitations.

1. To the extent that facility-level costs are involved, activity-based costing still allows some costs to be assigned to products on an arbitrary, volume basis.

2. Activity-based costing is expensive to install and operate, due to the complexity of the system.

APPENDIX C: COST FLOWS IN AN ACTIVITY-BASED SYSTEM

A. The flow of costs through Raw Materials, Work in Process, and other accounts is the same under activity-based costing as was illustrated in Chapter 3.

1. Although the flow of costs is the same, a company must compute several predetermined overhead rates when activity-based costing is used. This complicates the journal entries and T-accounts somewhat.

2. See the numeric example in the appendix for an illustration of journal entries and T-accounts.

B. When a company uses JIT inventory methods, its cost flows can be simplified. Typically, only two inventory accounts are used.

1. One is a new account titled, *Raw and In-Process Inventory*. This account is a combination of the Raw Materials and Work in Process inventory accounts.

2. The other account is the Finished Goods inventory account that we have used before.

C. Several things can be done under JIT to simplify cost flows.

1. Under JIT, purchase and issue of materials into production occur simultaneously. All materials purchased can therefore go directly into the Raw and In-Process inventory account.

2. In a JIT system, job cost sheets, work orders, issue slips, and so forth are sometimes not used. This greatly reduces the amount of detailed entries needed to operate the system.

3. Adding material and conversion costs to products can be deferred until the products are completely and ready for shipment. This is referred to as *backflush costing*.

a. However, backflush costing should not be used unless a company employs a true JIT system.

b. In the absence of a true JIT system, backflush costing can result in less accurate and more expensive data.

REVIEW AND SELF TEST
Questions and Exercises

True or False

For each of the following statements, enter a T or an F in the blank to indicate whether the statement is true or false.

____ 1. One purpose of a JIT inventory system is to have goods ready just when the customer needs them.

____ 2. Under JIT, materials are "pushed" from one workstation to another to ensure timely completion of finished products.

____ 3. A company will typically have fewer suppliers under JIT than under a conventional system.

____ 4. For JIT to operate successfully, all similar pieces of equipment (such as lathes or drill presses) must be grouped together.

____ 5. One way to reduce inventories is to reduce the setup time needed between production runs.

____ 6. The most effective way to achieve total quality control is to have an Inspection Department that inspects all incoming raw materials and that inspects goods as they move along the product flow line.

____ 7. In a JIT environment, workers are expected to be cross-trained and work as a team.

____ 8. Under JIT, process time and queue time would both be considered value-added activities.

____ 9. If a company employs a JIT inventory system and process costing is being used, unit costs will be the same regardless of whether the FIFO or weighted-average method is in use.

____ 10. If direct labor is used as a base for overhead cost assignment, the result will always be distorted product costs.

____ 11. Where product diversity exists, even departmental overhead rates will not correctly assign overhead costs to products.

____ 12. Activity-based costing involves a one-stage allocation process.

____ 13. The key concept underlying activity-based costing is that resources are consumed by activities, and activities are consumed by products and services.

____ 14. Process value analysis (PVA) means that a company must choose between a process costing system and a job-order costing system in the manufacture of its products.

____ 15. Not every activity identified in the manufacture of a product needs to be treated as a separate activity center under activity-based costing.

____ 16. Batch-level activities would include issuing purchase orders, issuing production orders, and performing machine setups.

____ 17. Quality inspections, product testing, and maintaining parts inventories would be all unit-level activities.

____ 18. A major drawback of activity-based costing is the difficulty involved in gathering data relating to activities and cost drivers.

____ 19. One of the benefits of activity-based costing is that it changes how a manager perceives overhead costs in that costs that were formerly considered indirect are identified with specific activities and thereby recognized as being traceable to individual products.

____ 20. (Appendix C) When activity-based costing is used, a company will have only one predetermined overhead rate although it may have several activity centers.

Multiple Choice

Choose the best answer or response by placing the identifying letter in the space provided.

_____ 1. All of the following are non-valued-added activities except: a) move time; b) queue time; c) process time; d) inspection time.

_____ 2. Under JIT, the plant floor: a) is laid out in a functional format with similar machines grouped together; b) is laid out in multiple product flow lines; c) is laid out in a single flow line through which all products pass; d) is usually cluttered with excessive work in process goods.

_____ 3. Which of the following is not a characteristic of a of a flexible manufacturing system: a) an FMS gives a company the power to manufacture a whole family of similar products on a single flow line; b) an FMS can greatly reduce the setup time required for product; c) an FMS is part of the concept of computer-integrated manufacturing; d) an FMS is typically dedicated to a single product.

_____ 4. Which of the following is a true statement regarding the workforce under JIT: a) it must be multiskilled and operate as a team; b) it must be trained in a single task in order to increase the efficiency of production; c) it is not required to perform maintenance work on equipment; d) it has less responsibility for quality control than in a conventional production system.

_____ 5. Product-level activities: a) are performed each time a unit is produced; b) are performed as needed to support the production of each different type of product; c) simply sustain a facility's general manufacturing process; d) are performed each time a batch of goods is handled or processed.

_____ 6. Product testing would be a: a) product-level activity; b) batch-level activity; c) unit-level activity; d) facility-level activity.

_____ 7. The issue of a purchase order would be a: a) unit-level activity; b) product-level activity; c) batch-level activity; d) facility-level activity.

_____ 8. Plant occupancy would be a: a) facility-level activity; b) unit-level activity; c) batch-level activity; d) product-level activity.

_____ 9. The cost to Acme Company to issue a purchase order is $60. During 19x1, the company issued 400 purchase orders to purchase material for product A, and manufactured 12,000 units of product. The cost per unit for purchase orders for product A is: a) $30; b) $15; c) $2; d) $0.15.

_____ 10. Which of the following is not a benefit of activity-based costing: a) it increases the number of cost pools used to accumulate overhead costs; b) it is relatively easy to develop and implement; c) it changes the base used to assign overhead costs to products; d) it changes how a manager perceives overhead costs in that costs that were formerly viewed as being indirect are recognized as being traceable to products and services.

Complete the Statements

Fill in the necessary words to complete the following statements.

1. In a JIT environment, the flow of goods is controlled by what is described as a _____ approach to the manufacture of products.

2. The _____ _____ is the physical path taken by a product as it moves through the manufacturing process.

3. The _____ _____ is the length of time required to turn materials into products.

4. The time involved in changing equipment and getting jigs and forms in place to accommodate the production of a different item is known as the _____ _____ .

5. The JIT philosophy says that management should focus its efforts on _____ and on _____ ___ _____ .

6. Only _____ time is a value-added activity in a company.

7. If a company uses a _____-_____ allocation process, it first assigns overhead costs to cost pools and then it applies overhead costs from the pools to jobs and products.

8. The first step in designing an activity-based costing system is to perform a _____ _____ _____ , which consists of systematically analyzing the activities required to make a product.

9. _____-_____ activities are those that arise as a result of the total volume of production going through a facility.

10. An _____ _____ is a part of the production process for which management wants a separate accumulation and reporting of production costs.

Exercises

5-1. The steps listed below are followed in the manufacture of one of Warren Company's Products. Classify each step as process time, inspection time, move time, or queue time by Placing an X under the proper heading.

Step	Process Time	Inspection Time	Move Time	Queue Time
a. Materials are received at the company's warehouse and checked to be sure that they are free of defects.				
b. Materials are kept in the warehouse while waiting use in production				
c. A materials requisition form is prepared and materials are transferred to the production line.				
d. Materials are cut into proper pieces and sizes.				
e. Cut materials are inspected for accuracy of work.				
f. Cut materials are transferred to the sewing area.				
g. Materials are sewed into proper form.				
h. Sewed materials are inspected for defects.				
i. Completed products are transferred to a finished goods warehouse.				

5-2. Listed below are several activity centers that might be found in a company using activity-based costing. For each activity, place an X under the proper heading to indicate whether the activity center would be unit-level, batch-level, and so forth.

Activity Center	Unit-Level Activity	Batch-Level Activity	Product-Level Activity	Facility Level Activity
a. Parts inventory management				
b. Labor-related				
c. Plant occupancy				
d. Purchase orders				
e. Machine-related				
f. General factory				
g. Product testing				
h. Production orders				
i. Product design				
j. Machine setup				
k. Personnel administration				

5-3. Kozales Company uses activity-based costing and manufactures two products, the Regular Model and the Super Model. During the coming year the company expects to produce 20,000 units of the Regular Model and 5,000 units of the Super Model. Below are listed other selected data relating to the coming year. Complete the schedules below by filling in the missing data.

Basic Data

Activity Center and Cost Driver	Traceable Costs	Expected Number of Events or Transactions		
		Total	Regular	Super
Labor related (direct labor-hours)	$ 80,000	10,000	8,000	2,000
Machine setups (number of setups)	420,000	1,400	500	900
Product testing (number of tests)	600,000	8,000	6,400	1,600
General factory (machine-hours)	900,000	45,000	30,000	15,000
Total cost	$2,000,000			

Overhead Rates by Activity Center

Activity Center	(a) Traceable Costs	(b) Total Events or Transaction	(a) ÷ (b) Rate per Event or Transaction)
Labor related			
Machine setups			
Product testing			
General factory			

Overhead Cost per Unit of Product

	Regular Product		Super Product	
	Events or Transactions	Amount	Events or Transactions	Amount
Labor related, at _____		$		$
Machine setups, at _____				
Product testing, at _____				
General factory, at _____				
Total overhead cost assigned (a)		$		$
Number of units produced (b)				
Overhead cost per unit (a) ÷ (b)		$		$

5-4. **Critical thought writing exercise:** Whitney Company manufactures 40,000 units of Product A and only 5,000 units of Product B each year. In prior years, the company has used direct labor-hours to apply overhead costs to its products, but in the current year it has used activity-based costing. The switch to activity-based costing has caused the per unit cost of the low volume product to increase dramatically. Explain the probable causes of the increase in per unit costs for the low volume product.

_____

_____

_____

_____

_____

_____

_____

_____

_____

_____

Chapter 5
Answers to Questions and Exercises

True or False

1. T   Under JIT, goods are shipped as soon as they are completed.

2. F   JIT operates under a "pull" approach in which goods are produced only as requested by the final assembly stage.

3. T   Under JIT, a company uses only a few suppliers who are bound under firm contracts to deliver materials on a frequent basis.

4. F   All of the different pieces of equipment needed to manufacture a product are placed on a single flow line, thus breaking up groupings of similar equipment.

5. T   By reducing setup time, it is possible to produce in smaller lot sizes, thereby reducing the level of inventory on hand.

6. F   The most effective way to achieve total quality control is to have workers perform their own inspections before sending goods to the next workstation.

7. T   A key element of JIT is to have a flexible workforce that is trained to perform any task needed in a cell and that works together as a team.

8. F   Only process time is value-added time.

9. T   Since there are no work in process inventories under JIT, both equivalent units and total cost will be the same under the two costing methods. Thus, unit costs will also be the same.

10. F   Distorted product costs will result only if there is no correlation between direct labor and the incurrence of overhead cost, and if other factors exist that have a significant effect on the amount of overhead cost incurred during a period.

11. T   If products differ in volume, lot size, and complexity of design, departmental rates will not ensure accurate product costs.

12. F   Activity-based costing involves a two-stage costing process.

13. T   This statement is true by definition.

14. F   Process value analysis is a systematic method of identifying value-added and non-value-added activities.

15. T   Several activities are often combined into one activity center.

16. T   These activities are batch-level by definition. See Exhibit 5-13.

17. F   These would be product-level activities. See Exhibit 5-13.

18. T   Gathering data is the key weakness of the activity-based costing approach.

19. T   Since costs are associated with activities under activity-based costing, these costs can be traced directly to products rather than treated as indirect costs.

20. F   Under activity-based costing, a company will have a predetermined overhead rate for each activity center.

Multiple Choice

1. c   Only process time is a value-added activity.

2. b   Under JIT, the plant floor is laid out into many product flow lines—one for each family of products.

3. d   One of the strengths of a flexible manufacturing system is that it can accommodate the manufacture of many products.

4. a   Under JIT, the workforce performs many tasks; it does perform maintenance work, and it has more responsibility for quality control.

5. b   This statement is true by definition.

6. a   See the data in Exhibit 5-13.

7. c   See the data in Exhibit 5-13.

8. a   See the data in Exhibit 5-13.

9. c   The computations are:

   12,000 units
       ÷ 400 orders = 30 units/order

   $60/order ÷ 30 units/order = $2/unit

10. b   Activity-based costing is relatively difficult and costly to implement.

Complete the Statements

1. pull
2. flow line
3. throughput time
4. setup time
5. simplicity, elimination of waste
6. process
7. two-state
8. process value analysis
9. Unit-level
10. activity center

Exercises

5-1.

Step	Process Time	Inspection Time	Move Time	Queue Time
a. Materials are received at the company's warehouse and checked to be sure that they are free of defects		X		
b. Materials are kept in the warehouse while waiting use in production.				X
c. A materials requisition form is prepared and materials are transferred to the production line.			X	
d. Materials are cut into proper pieces and sizes.	X			
e. Cut materials are inspected for accuracy of work.		X		
f. Cut materials are transferred to the sewing area.			X	
g. Materials are sewed into proper form.	X			
h. Sewed materials are inspected for defects.		X		
i. Completed products are transferred to a finished goods warehouse.			X*	X*

*Note that both move time and queue time are involved in this step.

5-2.

Activity Center	Unit-Level Activity	Batch-Level Activity	Product-Level Activity	Facility Level Activity
a. Parts inventory management			X	
b. Labor-related	X			
c. Plant occupancy				X
d. Purchase orders		X		
e. Machine-related	X			
f. General factory				X
g. Product testing			X	
h. Production orders		X		
i. Product design			X	
j. Machine setup	X			
k. Personnel administration				X

5-3.

Basic Data

Activity Center and Cost Driver	Traceable Costs	Expected Number of Events or Transactions		
		Total	Regular	Super
Labor related (direct labor-hours)	$ 80,000	10,000	8,000	2,000
Machine setups (number of setups)	420,000	1,400	500	900
Product testing (number of tests)	600,000	8,000	6,400	1,600
General factory (machine-hours)	900,000	45,000	30,000	15,000
Total cost	$2,000,000			

Overhead Rates by Activity Center

Activity Center	(a) Traceable Costs	(b) Total Events or Transaction	(a) ÷ (b) Rate per Event or Transaction
Labor related	$ 80,000	10,000	$8/DLH
Machine setups	420,000	1,400	$300/setup
Product testing	600,000	8,000	$75/test
General factory	900,000	45,000	$20/MH

Overhead Cost per Unit of Product

	Regular Product		Super Product	
	Events or Transactions	Amount	Events or Transactions	Amount
Labor related, at $8/DLH	8,000	$ 64,000	2,000	$ 16,000
Machine setups, at $300/setup	500	150,000	900	270,000
Product testing, at $75/test	6,400	480,000	1,600	120,000
General factory, at $20/MH	30,000	600,000	15,000	300,000
Total overhead cost assigned (a)		$1,294,000		$706,000
Number of units produced (b)		20,000		5,000
Overhead cost per unit (a) ÷ (b)		$64.70		$141.20

5-4. The increase in per unit costs for the low volume product is probably the result of two factors. First, rather than treating overhead cost as a lump amount and spreading it uniformly over both products, activity-based costing has traced the overhead costs to specific products. Since low volume products often require special equipment, special handling, and so forth, they typically are responsible for the incurrence of a disproportionately large amount of overhead cost. As this cost is traced to the low volume products, it drives their unit costs upward. Second, many overhead costs are incurred at the batch level. Since low volume products typically have fewer units processed per batch than high volume products, their average processing cost per unit is higher.

Chapter 6

Cost Behavior: Analysis and Use

Chapter Study Suggestions

Chapter 6 expands on the discussion of fixed and variable costs which was started in Chapter 2. In addition, the chapter introduces a new cost concept—mixed costs—and shows how mixed costs can be broken down into their basic fixed and variable elements. Focus the bulk of your study time on the section titled, "The Analysis of Mixed Costs," which is found midway through the chapter. Pay particular attention to how a *cost formula* is derived from the data in Exhibits 6-9 and 6-10 and how these cost formulas are used to predict future costs at various levels.

Commit to memory the elements of the equation: $Y = a + bX$. An understanding of this equation is needed to complete most of the homework exercises and problems. The section titled "The Least Squares Method" shows how this equation can be used to predict the amount of total cost at various activity levels. At the end of the chapter, a new format to the income statement called the "contribution approach" is introduced, which gears the income statement to cost behavior. The format of the contribution income statement is found in Exhibit 6-12. *This format should be put to memory immediately*—you will be using it throughout the rest of the book.

Appendix D at the end of the chapter contains additional material on the least squares method of cost analysis. Note that the least squares method employs two simultaneous linear equations to determine a cost formula.

CHAPTER HIGHLIGHTS AND STUDY GUIDE

A. A variable cost is a cost which varies, in total, in direct proportion to changes in the activity level. Variable costs are constant on a *per unit basis*.

1. Variable costs are shown graphically in Exhibit 6-1. Notice that the relationship between cost and activity is *linear*. This is a key idea which is discussed in more detail a little later.

2. Variable costs vary according to some activity base. The most common activity bases are hours worked, units produced, and units sold. Other activity bases include miles driven by salespersons, the number of beds in a hospital, and the number of letters typed by a secretary.

3. Direct materials and direct labor are both variable costs. Manufacturing overhead consists of both variable and fixed costs.

4. Variable costs may be either true variable or step variable.

a. A true variable cost is one which varies in direct proportion to changes in activity. Direct materials is an example of such a variable cost.

b. A step variable cost is one which is obtainable only in fairly large chunks and which increases or decreases only in response to fairly wide changes in the activity level. The labor cost of maintenance persons is such a variable cost.

c. The behavior patterns of true variable and step variable costs are shown graphically in Exhibit 6-3.

5. The accountant assumes a strictly linear relationship between cost and volume when dealing with variable costs.

a. Many variable costs actually behave in a curvilinear fashion, such as illustrated in Exhibit 6-4.

b. Although the accountant recognizes that many costs behave in a curvilinear fashion, he or she concentrates on their behavior within the band of activity known as the relevant range.

c. Within the relevant range, the relationship between cost and activity is basically linear.

B. A fixed cost is a cost which remains constant in total, regardless of changes in the activity level. When expressed on a per unit basis, fixed costs vary inversely with changes in the activity level. As the activity level rises, fixed costs per unit fall; as the activity level falls, fixed costs per unit rise.

1. Fixed costs are becoming more significant due to automation and trends toward stabilization of employee salaries.

2. Fixed costs can generally be classified into two categories: committed and discretionary.

a. Committed fixed costs are those costs which relate to the investment in plant, equipment, and the basic organization of a firm.

b. Discretionary fixed costs arise from annual decisions by management to spend in certain fixed costs areas, such as advertising, research, and management development programs.

c. There generally is more flexibility in the year-to-year control of discretionary fixed costs than there is in the control of committed fixed costs. Committed fixed costs tend to be very inflexible.

3. The concept of the relevant range also has application in dealing with fixed costs, particularly those of a discretionary nature. This is illustrated in Exhibit 6-6.

C. A mixed cost is a cost which contains both variable and fixed cost elements. Mixed costs are sometimes known as semivariable costs. The behavior pattern of a mixed cost is shown graphically in Exhibit 6-7.

1. Mixed costs are generally made up of manufacturing overhead. Examples of mixed costs include electricity, heat, repairs, and maintenance.

2. The fixed portion of a mixed cost represents the basic, minimum charge for having the service involved ready and available for use. The variable portion represents the charge made for actual consumption of the service.

3. Several methods are available for breaking a mixed cost down into its basic variable and fixed cost elements. These methods include the high-low method, the scattergraph method, and the least squares method.

D. The high-low method requires that costs be observed both at high and at low levels of activity within the relevant range.

1. The difference in cost observed at the two extremes is divided by the change in activity in order to determine the amount of variable cost involved. The formula is:

$$\frac{\text{Change in cost}}{\text{Change in activity}} = \text{Variable rate}$$

2. Once the variable rate has been determined, it can be used to determine the amount of fixed cost involved in the mixed costs:

Total cost observed at the "high" activity
level .... $XXXX
Less variable portion:
Variable rate X "high" level of activity   XXX
Fixed portion of the mixed cost .... $ XX

3. The fixed and variable cost elements can be expressed in a *cost formula*, which can be used to predict costs at other levels of activity within the relevant range.

4. In a cost formula, cost represents the *dependent* variable, and activity represents the *independent* variable.

5. The high-low method is the least accurate method of analyzing mixed costs. This is because the high and low points may not be representative of costs throughout the *entire* relevant range. The high and low points simply represent extremes.

E. The scattergraph method plots all observed costs at various activity levels on a graph. A *regression line* is then fitted to the plotted points by visual inspection.

1. The slope of the regression line represents the variable cost rate. The point where the regression line cuts the cost axis represents total fixed cost.

2. The scattergraph method is more accurate than the high-low method, since it considers all observed points in computing a cost formula rather than just the high and low points.

F. The least squares method fits a regression line to scattergraph data by means of statistical analysis. Thus, it is the most accurate method available for analyzing mixed costs.

1. A cost formula can be expressed in the form of an equation for a straight line, which is:

$$Y = a + bX$$

where:

Y = dependent variable (the total mixed cost observed).

a = vertical intercept of the line (the total fixed cost).

b = slope of the line (the variable rate).

X = independent variable (the activity level observed).

2. By determining the expected activity level (X), the variable rate (b), and the total fixed cost (a), a manager can compute the expected amount of total cost (Y).

G. If there is more than one basis of variability in a mixed cost, then *multiple regression analysis* must be used to separate the fixed and variable elements.

H. Internally, the manager generally organizes costs on the income statement according to cost behavior in what is known as the *contribution format*.

1. Variable expenses are deducted from sales to yield the contribution margin. Contribution margin can be defined as the amount remaining from sales after variable expenses have been deducted which is available to contribute toward covering fixed costs, and then toward profits.

2. Fixed costs are then deducted from the contribution margin, and the remainder represents the profits of the period.

3. The format of the contribution income statement is given in Exhibit 6-12. This format should be put to memory.

APPENDIX D: THE LEAST SQUARES METHOD

A. The least squares method is based on two simultaneous linear equations, which can be employed to determine the fixed and variable elements of a mixed cost. The formulas are:

$$\Sigma XY = a\Sigma X + b\Sigma X^2$$
$$\Sigma Y = na + b\Sigma X$$

where: a = fixed cost, b = variable rate, n = number of observations, X = activity measure (hours, etc.), Y = total mixed cost observed.

1. Four steps are involved in determining the variable rate and the total fixed cost elements. These steps are:

a. Compute ΣY, ΣX, ΣXY, ΣX^2, and n.

b. Insert the values computed in step one into the simultaneous equations.

c. Solve the simultaneous equations for the variable rate.

d. Solve one of the equations for the total fixed cost.

2. With the variable rate and total fixed cost available, the linear equation Y = a + bX can be used to predict total cost at various activity levels.

REVIEW AND SELF TEST
Questions and Exercises

True or False

For each of the following statements, enter a T or an F in the blank to indicate whether the statement is true or false.

____ 1. Variable costs are costs which change, in total, in direct proportion to changes in the activity level.

____ 2. In cost analysis work, activity is known as the dependent variable.

____ 3. Within the relevant range, the higher the activity level, the lower the fixed costs will be when these costs are expressed on a per unit basis.

____ 4. Mixed costs are also known as semivariable costs.

____ 5. Contribution margin and gross margin are synonymous terms.

____ 6. Contribution margin is the difference between sales and variable expenses.

____ 7. Discretionary fixed costs arise from annual decisions by management to spend in certain program areas.

____ 8. Advertising would be an example of a committed fixed cost.

____ 9. Mixed costs can be defined as costs which contain both manufacturing and nonmanufacturing cost elements.

____ 10. The accountant assumes a linear relationship between cost and activity within the relevant range, so far as variable costs are concerned.

____ 11. In order for a cost to be a variable, it must vary with either units produced or units sold.

____ 12. The relevant range has no significance so far as fixed costs are concerned.

____ 13. There is a strong trend in industry today toward more fixed costs.

____ 14. The cost formula produced by the high-low method and the scattergraph method would generally be the same.

____ 15. A regression line is a line of averages, with the average variable cost per unit represented by the slope of the line.

____ 16. The contribution approach to the income statement organizes costs according to behavior, rather than according to function.

Multiple Choice

Choose the best answer or response by placing the identifying letter in the space provided.

____ 1. Sparks Company's cost formula for maintenance is: $Y = \$4,000 + \$3X$, based on machine hours. During a period, 2,000 machine hours were worked. The expected cost for maintenance would be: a) $12,000; b) $6,000; c) $10,000; d) none of these.

____ 2. The costs associated with a company's basic plant, equipment, and organization are known as: a) committed costs; b) discretionary costs; c) linear costs; d) variable costs; e) none of these.

____ 3. For 19x5, Barker Company's sales were $240,000, its fixed costs were $50,000, and its variable costs were $2 per unit. During the year, 80,000 units were sold. The contribution margin for 19x5 was: a) $200,000; b) $240,000; c) $30,000; d) $80,000; e) none of these.

____ 4. The regression line derived by the least squares equation: a) is curvilinear; b) is the best possible fit of a regression line to the data; c) generally has a downward slope; d) can be represented by the equation $Y = ab + X$; e) none of these.

____ 5. An example of a discretionary fixed cost would be: a) depreciation on equipment; b) rent on a factory building; c) salaries of top management; d) items *a, b,* and *c* are all discretionary fixed costs; e) none of these.

____ 6. Fixed costs are most easily (and most safely) dealt with: a) on a per unit basis; b) on a total basis; c) on a contribution margin basis; d) on a manufacturing basis; e) none of these.

____ 7. Given the cost formula: $Y = \$70,000 + \$5X$, at what activity level will total cost equal $110,000? a) 14,000 units; b) 22,000 units; c) 8,000 units; d) none of these.

____ 8. An analysis of utility costs for Hart Company shows that utility costs will be $0.40 per hour at an activity level of 9,000 machine hours and $0.25 per hour at an activity level of 18,000 machine hours. What will be the total utility costs at 13,000 machine hours? a) $4,000; b) $5,200; c) $6,000; d) $3,250.

Complete the Statements

Fill in the necessary words to complete the following statements.

1. A variable cost is _____ per unit, but varies _____ _____ in direct proportion to changes in the activity level.

2. Variable costs can be divided into two classes, true variable costs and _____ variable costs.

3. The accountant concentrates on the behavior of costs within a narrow band of activity called the _____ _____.

4. Fixed costs can be divided into two categories, _____ and _____.

5. In analyzing mixed costs, the _____ method is probably the least accurate of the three methods available.

6. In analyzing mixed costs, the scattergraph method fits a _____ line to plotted points by visual inspection.

7. The expression "$5,000 fixed costs, plus $10 per hour" would be called a cost _____.

8. A straight line can be expressed in equation form as _____.

9. The contribution approach gears the income statement to _____ _____.

10. Contribution margin is the difference between _____ and _____ _____.

11. The traditional income statement organizes costs in a _____ format.

Exercises

6-1. Doughby Company has observed its electrical costs as follows over the relevant range of 5,000 to 8,000 machine hours:

6,800 hrs.	$1,770
6,000 hrs.	1,650
5,400 hrs.	1,560
7,900 hrs.	1,935

a. Using the high-low method, what is the variable rate per machine hour? .... $_____

	Cost	Machine Hours
High activity level		
Low activity level		
Difference	_____	_____

$$\frac{\text{Change in Cost}}{\text{Change in Activity}} = \text{_____} = \text{\_\_\_\_ / Machine Hour}$$

b. What is the total fixed cost? .... $_____

Total cost at the "high" activity level ....$_____
Less variable cost element:

_____ .... _____
Fixed cost element ....$_____

c. Express the cost formula for electrical costs:

_____

_____

_____

_____

_____

6-2. (Apprndix D) Data on a week's activity in the shipping department of Osan, Inc. are given below:

Day	Units Shipped (X)	Shipping Cost (Y)	XY	X²
Monday	12	$ 580	$ 6,960	144
Tuesday	17	655	11,135	289
Wednesday	10	550	5,500	100
Thursday	7	505	3,535	49
Friday	9	535	4,815	81
Saturday	5	475	2,375	25
	60	$3,300	$34,320	688

a. Using the least squares method, determine the variable rate per unit shipped:

Equation (1): $\Sigma XY = a\Sigma X + b\Sigma X^2$
Equation (2): $\Sigma Y = na + b\Sigma X$

Equation (1) data:
Equation (2) data:

Multiply equation (1) by _____:
Multiply equation (2) by _____: _____
Subtract (2) from (1):
Variable rate

b. Determine the fixed cost per day:

Equation (2) data from above:

Substitute the variable rate for the "b" term in equation (2):

Solve equation (2) for term "a":

c. Express the cost formula for shipping costs in the form $Y = a + bX$:

6-3. During July 19x3, Simple Company (a merchandising firm) sold 500 units of product. The company's income statement for the month follows:

SIMPLE COMPANY
Income Statement
For the Month Ended July 31, 19x3

Sales ($100/unit)		$50,000
Less cost of goods sold ($60/unit)		30,000
Gross margin		20,000
Less operating expenses:		
Commissions ($6/unit)	$3,000	
Salaries	8,000	
Advertising	6,000	
Shipping ($2/unit)	1,000	18,000
Net Income		$ 2,000

Redo the company's income statement for the month, by presenting it in the contribution format:

SIMPLE COMPANY
Income Statement
For the Month Ended July 31, 19x3

_____

_____

_____

_____

_____

_____

_____

_____

_____

_____

_____

_____

6-4. **Critical thought writing exercise:** "The concept of the relevant range has no application to fixed costs." Explain why you do or do not agree with this statement.

_____

_____

_____

_____

_____

_____

_____

_____

Chapter 6
Answers to Questions and Exercises

True or False

1. T   The statement represents a straightforward definition of a variable cost.

2. F   Activity is the independent variable.

3. T   When expressed on a per unit basis, fixed costs vary inversely with changes in activity.

4. T   A mixed cost contains both fixed and variable cost elements, and thus is sometimes called a semivariable cost.

5. F   Contribution margin is sales less variable expenses; gross margin is sales less cost of goods sold.

6. T   The statement represents a straightforward definition of contribution margin.

7. T   Discretionary fixed costs consist of costs that are re-evaluated each year by management.

8. F   Advertising would be a discretionary fixed cost since the advertising program is typically re-evaluated on an annual basis.

9. F   Mixed costs are costs that contain both variable and fixed cost elements.

10. T   This statement is true since variable costs are considered to be constant per unit within the relevant range.

11. F   There can be many measures of activity besides units produced and units sold. Other measures include miles driven, number of occupied beds in a hospital, number of flight hours, and so forth.

12. F   The relevant range has significance so far as fixed costs are concerned, as shown in Exhibit 6-6.

13. T   This trend toward more fixed costs is a result of the move toward greater automation.

14. F   The cost formula produced by the high-low method tends to be quite inaccurate since the high-low method utilizes only two points from a group of data. The scatter-graph method, by contrast, utilizes all points of data in developing a cost formula.

15. T   A regression line is a line of averages, by definition; thus, the slope of the line represents the average variable cost per unit.

16. T   The contribution approach groups variable costs together and then groups fixed costs together; thus, the income statement is organized according to cost behavior.

Multiple Choice

1. c   The computation is:

Fixed cost	$ 4,000
Variable cost: $3 × 2,000 hours	6,000
Total cost	$10,000

2. a   By definition, committed fixed costs relate to a company's basic plant, equipment, and organization.

3. d   The computation is:

Sales	$240,000
Less variable costs:	
$2 × 80,000 units	160,000
Contribution margin	$ 80,000

4. b   The least squares method provides the best fit of a regression line to the data since the line is fit to the data by statistical analysis.

5. e   All of the costs listed are committed fixed costs.

6. b   Fixed costs are most easily dealt with on a total basis since per unit fixed costs are not stable and therefore may be misleading or confusing to managers.

7. c   The computations are:

$110,000 − $70,000 = $40,000; $40,000 ÷ $5 = 8,000 units.

8. a   The computations are:

$0.25 × 18,000 hours $4,500
  0.40 × 9,000 hours $3,600

	Hours	Cost
High activity level	18,000	$4,500
Low activity level	9,000	3,600
Difference	9,000	$ 900

$900 ÷ 9,000 hours = $0.10 per hour variable rate.
$4,500 − ($0.10 × 18,000 hours) = $2,700 fixed.

Fixed cost	$2,700
Variable cost:	
$0.10 × 13,000 hours	1,300
Total cost	$4,000

Complete the Statements

1. constant, in total
2. step
3. relevant range
4. committed, discretionary
5. high-low
6. regression

7. formula
8. $Y = a + bX$
9. cost behavior
10. sales, variable expenses
11. functional

Exercises

6-1. a.   Variable rate: $.15 per machine hour.

	Cost	Machine Hours
High activity level	$1,935	7,900
Low activity level	1,560	5,400
Difference	$ 375	2,500

$$\frac{\text{Change in cost} \quad \$375}{\text{Change in activity} \quad 2,500 \text{ hours}} = \$.15 \text{ per machine hour}$$

b. Total fixed cost: $750 per period.

Total cost at the "high" activity level $1,935
Less variable cost element:
  7,900 hours × $.15 per hour 1,185
Fixed Cost Element .... $ 750

c. Cost formula for electrical costs: $750 per period, plus $.15 per machine hour.

6-2. a. Equation (1) data: $34,320 = 60a + 688b
Equation (2) data: $ 3,300 = 6a + 60b

Multiply equation (1) by 1: $34,320 = 60a + 688b
Multiply equation (2) by 10: $33,000 = 60a + 600b
Subtract (2) from (1): $ 1,320 =   88b
Variable rate: $ 15 = b

b. Equation (2) data from above: $3,300 = 6a + 60b
Substitute the variable rate for
  the "b" term in equation (2): $3,300 = 6a + 60 ($15)
Solve equation (2) for term "a": $3,300 = 6a + $900
                                     $2,400 = 6a
                                     $ 400 = a

c. Y = $400 + $15X

6-3.
                    SIMPLE COMPANY
                    Income Statement
               For the Month Ended July 31, 19x3

Sales $50,000
Less variable expenses:
  Cost of goods sold ($60/unit) $30,000
  Commissions ($6/unit) 3,000
  Shipping ($2/unit) 1,000   34,000
Contribution margin   16,000
Less fixed expenses:
  Salaries 8,000
  Advertising 6,000   14,000
Net Income .... $ 2,000

6-4. The concept of the relevant range does have application to fixed costs. As the activity level increases and decreases, both discretionary and committed fixed costs can also increase and decrease over time. Discretionary fixed costs such as advertising can be increased year by year as a company attempts to expand its sales, and committed fixed costs such as depreciation will increase as a company expands the size of its plant. These increases and decreases in fixed costs come in steps as the activity level rises and falls, and the *width* of these steps is generally quite large. That is, the width of the steps may be measured in terms of *thousands* or even *tens of thousands* of hours of activity, whereas a variable cost may increase or decrease with each hour of activity.

Cost-Volume-Profit Relationships

Chapter Study Suggestions

Chapter 7 can be described as one of the "key" chapters in the book. What you do in many chapters ahead will depend on concepts developed here. In your study, there are several sections in the chapter that should be given particular attention. The first of these is the section early in the chapter titled, "Contribution Margin." Notice the relationship illustrated here between contribution margin and net income and how the latter is affected by the former. The next section to be studied with particular care is the one titled, "Contribution Margin Ratio." The CM ratio discussed there is used in most of the analytical work in the chapter.

Another section to be given particular attention is the one titled, "Some Applications of CVP Concepts." Much of the homework material is drawn from this section, so be sure you understand the examples given. The section titled, "Break-Even Analysis" is also drawn from heavily in the homework material. *You should commit the break-even formulas given in this section to memory.* Finally, the latter part of the chapter contains a section titled, "The Concept of Sales Mix," which shows the impact of CVP concepts on multiple-product firms. Notice particularly how the break-even point is computed if a company has more than one product line.

In studying the material in the chapter, try especially hard to understand the *logic* behind solutions given. Keep in mind that CVP analysis represents a *way of thinking,* rather than a mechanical set of procedures.

CHAPTER HIGHLIGHTS AND STUDY GUIDE

A. It is very helpful to the manager to think of contribution margin in *per unit* terms, as well as in total amount.

1. Each unit sold will generate a fixed amount of contribution margin—the difference between the unit's selling price and its variable expenses.

2. Total contribution margin can be computed by multiplying the contribution margin per unit times the number of units sold.

   a. Contribution margin is first applied to cover the fixed costs.

   b. The break-even point is reached when the contribution margin generated on sales just equals the fixed costs.

   c. Once the break-even point is reached, net income will increase by the unit contribution margin for each additional unit sold.

3. The concept contained in part 2 *c.* above provides the manager with a very powerful planning tool. It gives him or her the ability to predict what profits will be at various activity levels without the necessity of preparing detailed income statements.

B. The percentage of contribution margin to total sales is known as the contribution margin ratio (CM ratio) or as the profit/volume ratio (P/V ratio). It shows how contribution margin will be affected by a given dollar change in sales.

1. The formula for computing the impact on contribution margin of a change in sales is:

Dollar increase or decrease in sales $\times$ CM ratio = Dollar increase or decrease in contribution margin

2. Any increase in contribution margin will be reflected dollar-for-dollar in increased net income, if the fixed costs do not change.

3. The CM ratio is often of more use to the manager than the unit contribution margin figure, particularly when a company has multiple product lines.

   a. The reason the CM ratio is more useful is because it is in ratio form, which makes it easier to compare product lines as to relative profitability.

b. Generally, a company should concentrate its sales efforts on the product lines that have the highest CM ratio figures.

C. There are many applications of CVP concepts in day-to-day decision making in an organization. Study carefully the examples given under the heading "Some Applications of CVP Concepts" in the early part of the chapter.

1. Notice that each example makes use of either the unit contribution margin figure or the CM ratio in arriving at an answer. This underscores the importance of these two concepts.

2. Also notice that several of the examples employ a technique known as *incremental analysis*. An incremental analysis is based only on those items of cost or revenue that will *change* as between alternatives.

3. These examples show clearly that the purpose of CVP analysis is to help the manager to find the most profitable combination of variable costs, fixed costs, selling price, and sales volume.

   a. The effect on the contribution margin is a major consideration in deciding on the most profitable combination of these factors.

   b. There is no magic formula that applies to all organizations, in terms of the mix of costs, selling price, and sales volume. Each organization must determine that mix which maximizes its profits.

D. The break-even point can be defined either (1) as the point where total sales equal total expenses, variable and fixed, or (2) as the point where total contribution margin equals total fixed expenses.

1. These two definitions show the two ways the break-even point can be computed. For definition (1) above, the break-even formula is:

$$\text{Sales} = \frac{\text{Variable expenses} + \text{Fixed expenses} + \text{Profits}}{}$$

   a. A zero figure for "profits" is entered into the formula when the break-even point is being computed.

   b. This formula can also be used to compute the activity level at which a *target net profit* figure will be realized. This is done by inserting the target net profit figure into the "profits" part of the formula.

2. For definition (2) above, the break-even formula is:

$$\frac{\text{Total fixed expenses}}{\text{Unit contribution margin}} = \begin{array}{c}\text{Break-even point}\\\text{(in units)}\end{array}$$

or

$$\frac{\text{Total fixed expenses}}{\text{CM ratio}} = \begin{array}{c}\text{Break-even point}\\\text{(in dollars)}\end{array}$$

a. This is known as the "unit contribution method." It actually is just a variation of the equation method given above.

b. These formulas can also be used to compute the activity level at which a target net profit figure will be realized. This is done by adding the target net profit figure to the "total fixed expenses" figure in the formulas above.

E. Break-even analysis can also be done graphically. Exhibits 7-1 through 7-5 show how the appropriate graphs are prepared.

1. Exhibits 7-1 and 7-2 relate to the conventional cost-volume-profit graph. This is also known as a "break-even chart." *Study carefully how the graph is prepared and how it is interpreted.*

a. This graph is called a cost-volume-profit graph because it shows more than just a break-even point. It shows the relationships between sales, costs, and volume throughout wide ranges of activity.

2. Exhibit 7-3 shows an alternate format to the cost-volume-profit graph that is preferred by some managers. This format shows the fixed expenses on top of the variable expenses—the reverse of the conventional graph in Exhibit 7-2. It also shows the contribution margin.

3. Exhibits 7-4 and 7-5 relate to the "profit-graph." It is preferred by some managers because it shows how profits change with changes in the sales volume.

F. CVP formulas can be used to determine the sales volume needed to achieve a target net profit figure.

1. One approach is to use the CVP equation and insert a target profit figure in the "profits" portion of the formula.

$$\text{Sales} = \begin{array}{c}\text{Variable}\\\text{Expenses}\end{array} + \begin{array}{c}\text{Fixed}\\\text{Expenses}\end{array} + \text{Profits}$$

2. Another approach is to expand the unit contribution formula to include a target net profit figure.

$$\frac{\begin{array}{c}\text{Fixed}\\\text{expenses + Profits}\end{array}}{\begin{array}{c}\text{Unit contribution}\\\text{margin}\end{array}} = \begin{array}{c}\text{Target}\\\text{sales}\end{array}$$

G. The margin of safety (MS) can be defined as the excess of budgeted (or actual) sales over the break-even volume of sales. It states the amount by which sales can drop before losses begin to be incurred in a company.

1. The formula for computing the margin of safety is: Total sales − Break-even sales = Margin of safety.

2. The margin of safety can also be expressed in percentage form, by dividing the margin of safety in dollars by total sales:

$$\frac{\text{Margin of safety in dollars}}{\text{Total sales}} = \begin{array}{c}\text{Margin of safety}\\\text{percentage}\end{array}$$

H. A company often has some latitude in trading off between fixed and variable costs. There is no categorical answer to the question as to whether it is beneficial to make such trade-offs.

1. A company with low fixed costs and high variable costs (a low CM ratio) will enjoy greater stability in net income, but will do so at the risk of losing substantial profits if sales trend sharply upward over time.

2. A company with high fixed costs and low variable costs (a high CM ratio) will experience wider movements in net income as sales fluctuate up and down, but will reap greater profits if sales trend sharply upward over time.

I. Operating leverage measures the change in net income which will result from a given change in sales volume.

1. The formula for computing operating leverage is:

$$\frac{\text{Contribution margin}}{\text{Net income}} = \text{Degree of operating leverage}$$

2. The operating leverage figure is multiplied times the anticipated percentage increase in sales, to obtain the anticipated *percentage* increase in net income, e.g., if the degree of operating leverage is 5, and sales are expected to increase by 10 percent, then net income should increase by:

$$5 \times 10\% = 50\%$$

3. The degree of operating leverage decreases in amount the further a company moves away from its break-even point.

J. Commissions to salespersons are often based on the total contribution margin which the salespersons are able to generate, rather than on total sales. This has the beneficial effect of encouraging the salespersons to focus their efforts on selling those products which will maximize total contribution margin, rather than total sales.

K. Sales mix is defined as the relative proportion of total units sold (or total sales dollars) which is represented by each of a company's several product lines.

1. When a company has more than one product line, the break-even point must be computed by using the *overall* CM ratio, considering the mix of products being sold. The formula is:

$$\frac{\text{Total fixed expenses}}{\text{Overall CM ratio}} = \text{Company break-even point}$$

2. As the mix of products being sold changes, *the overall CM ratio will also change*. If the shift in mix is toward the less profitable products, then the overall CM ratio will fall; if the shift is toward the more profitable products, then the overall CM ratio will rise. The break-even point will change inversely with changes in the overall CM ratio.

L. There are five limiting assumptions in cost-volume-profit analysis:

1. That the behavior of both revenues and expenses is linear throughout the entire relevant range.

2. That expenses can be accurately divided into variable and fixed categories.

3. That the sales mix is constant.

4. That inventories do not change in break-even computations.

5. That worker productivity and efficiency do not change.

REVIEW AND SELF TEST
Questions and Exercises

True or False

For each of the following statements, enter a T or an F in the blank to indicate whether the statement is true or false.

_____ 1. If product A has a higher unit contribution margin than product B, then product A will always have a higher CM ratio than product B.

_____ 2. The break-even point occurs where the contribution margin is equal to total variable expenses.

_____ 3. One of the assumptions of break-even analysis is that there is no change in inventories.

_____ 4. The break-even point can be expressed either in terms of units sold or in terms of total sales dollars.

_____ 5. If the product mix changes, a break-even point that was valid in the past may no longer be valid.

_____ 6. As sales exceed the break-even point, a high CM ratio will result in lower profits than will a low CM ratio.

_____ 7. A firm with a high CM ratio will have greater operating leverage at a given level of sales than will a firm with a low CM ratio.

_____ 8. If sales increase by 8 percent, and the degree of operating leverage is 4, then profits can be expected to increase by 12 percent.

_____ 9. The degree of operating leverage for a given firm remains the same at all levels of sales activity.

_____ 10. Once the break-even point has been reached, net income will increase by the unit contribution margin for each additional unit sold.

_____ 11. A shift in sales mix toward less profitable products will cause the overall break-even point to fall.

_____ 12. An incremental analysis will focus on changes in costs between two alternatives.

_____ 13. If a company's cost structure shifts toward greater fixed costs, one would expect the company's CM ratio to fall.

_____ 14. One of the major conceptual lessons in this chapter is that the effect on the contribution margin is a key consideration in most cost/revenue decisions.

_____ 15. One way to compute the break-even point is to divide total sales by the CM ratio.

_____ 16. Basing sales commissions on contribution margin is generally less desirable from the company's standpoint than basing sales commissions on gross sales.

_____ 17. A key assumption in break-even analysis is that the sales mix will not change.

_____ 18. One approach to the cost-volume-profit graph is to place the fixed expenses on top of the variable expenses, so that the contribution margin can be shown.

Multiple Choice

Choose the best answer or response by placing the identifying letter in the space provided.

_____ 1. Product A has a selling price of $50 per unit and variable expenses of $30 per unit. If the company is past its break-even point and sales increase by $200,000, one would expect net income to increase by: a) $120,000; b) $40,000; c) $80,000; d) None of these.

_____ 2. The break-even point in a given situation would be decreased by an increase in: a) the ratio of variable costs to sales; b) the CM ratio; c) total fixed costs; d) the mix of less profitable products sold; e) none of these.

_____ 3. If the total contribution margin increases and fixed costs do not change, then net income can be expected: a) to increase by an equal amount; b) to decrease by an equal amount; c) to increase by an amount equal to the increase in contribution margin times the CM ratio; d) none of these.

_____ 4. In multiple product firms, a shift in the sales mix from less profitable products to more profitable products will cause the company's break-even point to: a) increase; b) decrease; c) there will be no change in the break-even point; d) none of these.

_____ 5. The most important use of the cost-volume-profit graph is to show: a) the break-even point; b) the CM ratio at various levels of sales activity; c) the relationship between volume, costs, and revenues over wide ranges of activity; d) none of these.

_____ 6. As a company moves further from its break-even point, one would expect the degree of operating leverage to: a) decrease; b) increase; c) remain unchanged; d) vary in direct proportion to changes in the activity level; e) none of these.

_____ 7. The following figures are taken from Parker Company's income statement: Net income, $30,000; Fixed costs, $90,000; Sales, $200,000; and CM ratio, 60 percent. The company's margin of safety in dollars is: a) $150,000; b) $30,000; c) $50,000; d) none of these.

_____ 8. Refer to the data in question 7 above. The margin of safety in percentage form is: a) 60 percent; b) 75 percent; c) 40 percent; d) 25 percent; e) none of these.

_____ 9. If sales increase from $400,000 to $450,000, and if the degree of operating leverage is 6, one would expect net income to increase by: a) 12.5 percent; b) 75 percent; c) 67 percent; d) none of these.

_____ 10. Given the following data: selling price, $60; CM ratio, 30%; and fixed costs, $150,000; the total variable expenses at the break-even point would be: a) $350,000; b) $150,000; c) $500,000; d) none of these.

Complete the Statements

Fill in the necessary words to complete the following statements.

1. Product X sells for $10 per unit and requires variable expenses of $6.50 per unit. Product Y sells for $8 per unit and requires variable expenses of $2.40 per unit. For Product X, the unit contribution margin is $_____, and the contribution margin ratio is _____. For Product Y, the unit contribution margin is $_____, and the contribution margin ratio is _____.

2. Refer to the data in question 1 above. At a given level of sales, one would expect Product _____ to have the highest degree of operating leverage.

3. Refer again to the data in question 1 above. Assuming that total fixed costs will be the same to produce and sell either product, Product _____ will have the lowest break-even point.

4. Any increase in contribution margin will be reflected dollar-for-dollar in increased net income, so long as the _____ _____ do not change.

5. The relative proportion of various products represented in a company's total sales is called the _____ _____.

6. The cost-volume-profit equation is: Sales = _____ _____ + _____ _____ + _____.

7. Some companies feel that the way to maximize overall profits is to base sales commissions on _____ _____ rather than on gross sales.

8. Other things equal, managers should seek out and promote those products which have the highest _____ _____ _____.

9. On a CVP graph, the break-even point is where the total revenue line crosses the _____ _____ line.

10. At a given level of sales, the contribution margin divided by the net income yields a figure known as the _____ _____.

Exercises

7-1. Hardee Company sells a single product. The selling price is $30 per unit and the variable expenses are $18 per unit. The company's most recent income statement is given below:

Sales (4,500 units)	$135,000
Less variable expenses	81,000
Contribution margin	54,000
Less fixed expenses.........................	48,000
Net Income	$ 6,000

a. Compute the contribution margin per unit .... $_____

b. Compute the CM ratio .... _____%

c. Compute the break-even point in sales dollars .... $_____

d. Compute the break-even point in units sold .... _____ units

e. How many units must be sold next year to double the company's profits? ..... _____ units

f. Compute the company's degree of operating leverage .... _____

g. Sales for next year (in units) are expected to increase by 5 percent. Using the operating leverage concept, net income should increase by .... _____%

h. Prove your answer to part *g* by preparing a contribution income statement showing a 5 percent increase in sales.

_____

_____

_____

_____

_____

7-2. From the data below, construct a cost-volume-profit graph like the one in Exhibit 7-2 in the text:

Sales: 15,000 units at $10 each.
Variable expenses: $6 per unit.
Fixed expenses: $40,000 total.

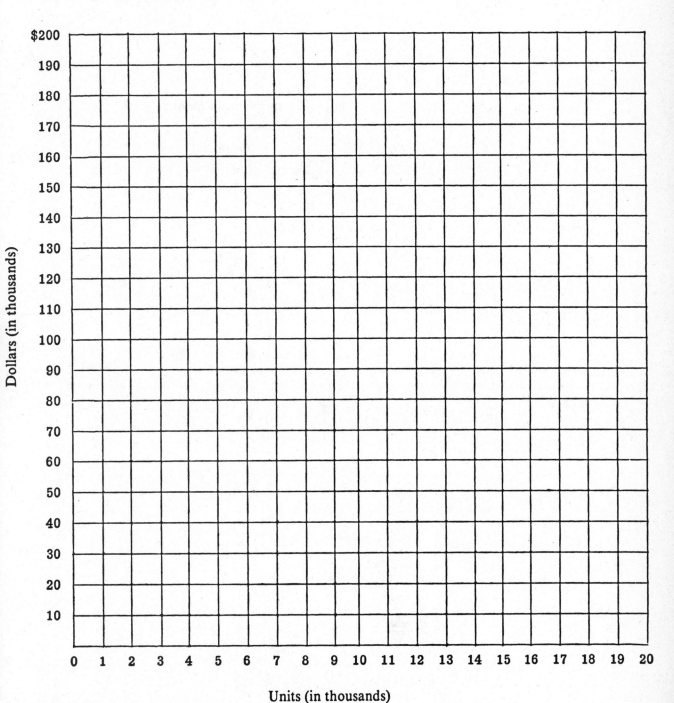

Units (in thousands)

What is the break-even point:

In units? _____

In total sales dollars? _____

7-3. Seaver Company produces and sells two products, X and Y. Cost and revenue data on the products follow:

	Product X	Product Y
Selling price per unit	$10	$12
Variable expenses per unit	6	3
Contribution margin per unit	$ 4	$ 9

In the most recent month, the company sold 400 units of Product X and 600 units of Product Y. Fixed expenses are $5,000 per month.

a. Complete the following income statement for the most recent month (carry percentages to one decimal point):

	Product X		Product Y		Total	
	Amount	%	Amount	%	Amount	%
Sales	$		$		$	
Less variable expenses	_____	__	_____	__	_____	__
Contribution margin	$		$			
Less fixed expenses					_____	
Net income (loss)					$	

b. Compute the company's overall monthly break-even point in sales dollars ...... $_____

c. If the company continues to sell 1,000 units, in total, each month, but the sales mix shifts so that an equal number of units of each product is being sold, would you expect monthly net income to rise or fall? Explain.

_____

_____

_____

_____

d. Refer to the data in part c above. If the sales mix shifts as explained, would you expect the company's monthly break-even point to rise or fall? Explain.

_____

_____

_____

_____

7.4. Critical thought writing exercise: Able Company and Baker Company are competing firms that sell a product at the same price. Both companies are operating above the break-even point. Able Company's cost structure includes costs that are mostly variable, whereas Baker Company's cost structure includes costs that are mostly fixed. In a time of increasing sales which company will tend to realize the most rapid increase in net income? Explain your answer.

_____

_____

_____

_____

_____

_____

_____

_____

Chapter 7
Answers to Questions and Exercises

True or False

1. F   The CM ratio depends on the relationship between selling price and contribution margin. One company might have a higher unit contribution than another, but its selling price may be so high that its CM ratio is lower than the other company's.

2. F   The break-even point occurs where the contribution margin is equal to fixed expenses.

3. T   This is one of the basic assumptions about break-even analysis that makes the concept usable in a manufacturing company. (This point is considered further in Chapter 8 following.)

4. T   The break-even point is computed in terms of both units sold and total sales dollars in the examples in the chapter.

5. T   A change in product mix usually means a change in the average CM ratio for the company as a whole. The effect of a change in the average CM ratio is illustrated in Exhibits 7-8 and 7-9 in the chapter.

6. F   The reverse is true—a high CM ratio will result in *greater* profits than will a low CM ratio.

7. T   A high CM ratio means that contribution margin is also high in relation to sales. Thus, if one company has a higher contribution margin figure than another, then one would expect it to also have a higher operating leverage figure (since operating leverage is computed by dividing contribution margin by net income). See the section of the chapter titled "Operating Leverage."

8. F   Profits can be expected to increase by: $4 \times 8\% = 32\%$.

9. F   The degree of operating leverage decreases as a firm moves further and further from its break-even point.

10. T   This is because at the break-even point all fixed costs have been covered, and therefore all contribution margin generated from that point forward can go directly into net income.

11. F   The reverse is true—the overall break-even point will rise since the average CM ratio will be lower as a result of selling less profitable products.

12. T   By definition, an incremental analysis deals only with changes between alternatives.

13. F   The reverse is true—one would expect the company's CM ratio to rise. The reason is that the fixed costs would be replacing variable costs (such as machinery replacing workers); thus, variable costs would be lower and the CM ratio would be higher.

14. T   The effect on the contribution margin is the key consideration in most cost/revenue decisions because it is the contribution margin that covers the fixed costs and generates the net income of a company.

15. F   The break-even point is computed by dividing total *fixed costs* by the CM ratio.

16. F   The opposite is true—basing sales commissions on contribution margin is more desirable from the company's standpoint. This is because using contribution margin as a base encourages the sales staff to focus their attention on maximizing total contribution margin rather than maximizing total sales.

17. T   This is a key assumption since a change in the sales mix will change the break-even point.

18. T   A break-even graph prepared in this manner is illustrated in Exhibit 7-3.

Multiple Choice

1. c   The computations are:

Sales price	$50	100%
Variable expenses	30	60
Contribution margin	$20	40%

40% × $200,000 = $80,000

2. b   As the CM ratio increases, more is available from each dollar of sales to cover the fixed expenses. Thus, an increase in the CM ratio would man a decrease in the amount of sales needed to reach the break-even point.

3. a   After the break-even point has been reached, any increase in contribution margin goes directly into net income.

4. b   A shift to more profitable products would result in an increase in the average CM ratio. Thus, less sales would be needed to cover the fixed costs and the break-even point would therefore decrease.

5. c   The manager needs to know more than just the break-even point and the CM ratio. He or she needs to know CVP relationships at various levels of activity.

6. a   The degree of operating leverage decreases because net income becomes less and less sensitive to changes in total sales.

7. c   The computations are:

$90,000 fixed costs ÷ 60% = $150,000 break-even point; $200,000 total sales − $150,000 = $50,000.

8. d $50,000 ÷ $200,000 = 25%.

9. b   The computations are:

$50,000 sales increase ÷ $400,000 sales = 12.5% increase; 6 × 12.5% = 75%.

10. a   The computations are:

$150,000 fixed costs ÷ 30% CM ratio = $500,000 break-even sales; $500,000 × (100% − 30%) = $350,000.

Complete the Statements

1. $3.50, 35%, $5.60, 70%
2. Y
3. Y
4. fixed costs
5. sales mix
6. variable expenses, fixed expenses, profits
7. contribution margin
8. contribution margin ratio
9. total expenses
10. operating leverage

Exercises

7-1. a.

	Unit	
Selling price	$30	100%
Less variable expenses	18	60
Contribution Margin	$12	40%

b. $\dfrac{\text{Contribution Margin} \quad \$12}{\text{Selling Price} \qquad\qquad \$30} = 40\%$ CM Ratio

c.   Sales = Variable Expenses + Fixed Expenses + Profits

$$X = .60X + \$48,000 + \$\text{-0-}$$
$$.40X = \$\ 48,000$$
$$X = \$120,000$$

Alternate solution:

$$\frac{\text{Total Fixed Expenses} \quad \$48,000}{\text{CM Ratio} \qquad\qquad\quad .40} = \$120,000$$

d.   Sales = Variable Expenses + Fixed Expenses + Profits

$$\$30X = \$18X + \$48,000 + \$-0-$$
$$\$12X = \$48,000$$
$$X = 4,000 \text{ units}$$

Alternate solution:

$$\frac{\text{Total Fixed Expenses}}{\text{Unit Contribution Margin}} \quad \frac{\$48,000}{\$12} = 4,000 \text{ units}$$

e.   Sales = Variable Expenses + Fixed Expenses + Profits

$$\$30X = \$18X + \$48,000 + \$12,000$$
$$\$12X = \$60,000$$
$$X = 5,000 \text{ units}$$

Alternate solution:

$$\frac{\text{Total Fixed Expenses} + \text{Target Net Income}}{\text{Unit Contribution Margin}} \quad \frac{\$48,000 + \$12,000}{\$12} = 5,000 \text{ units}$$

f. $\dfrac{\text{Contribution Margin} \quad \$54,000}{\text{Net Income} \qquad \$\,6,000} = 9$

g. $5\% \times 9 = 45\%$

h.   New sales volume: 4,500 units $\times$ 105% = 4,725 units

Sales (4,725 units)	$141,750
Less variable expenses (4,725 units)	85,050
Contribution margin	56,700
Less fixed expenses	48,000
Net Income	$ 8,700
Present net income......................	$ 6,000
Expected increase: $6,000 × 45%	2,700
Expected Net Income (as above)	$ 8,700

7-2. The completed CVP graph:

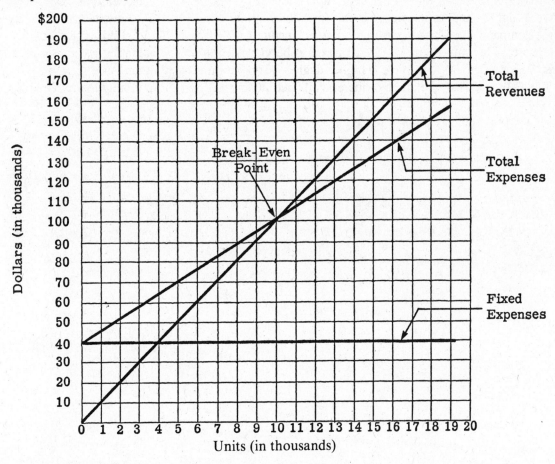

The break-even point in units: 10,000. The break-even point in dollars: $100,000.

7-3. a. The completed income statement:

	Product X		Product Y		Total	
	Amount	%	Amount	%	Amount	%
Sales	$4,000	100	$7,200	100	$11,200	100.0
Less variable expenses	2,400	60	1,800	25	4,200	37.5
Contribution margin	$1,600	40	$5,400	75	7,000	62.5
Less fixed expenses					5,000	
Net income					$ 2,000	

b. $\dfrac{\text{Fixed Expenses} \quad \$5,000}{\text{Overall CM Ratio 62.5\%}}$ = $8,000 in sales to break even.

c. Monthly net income will fall. The shift in sales mix will mean that less of Product Y is being sold and more of Product X is being sold. Since Product Y has a higher contribution margin per unit than does Product X, this means that less contribution margin *in total* will be available, and profits will therefore fall.

d. The monthly break-even point will rise. As explained above, the shift in sales mix will be toward the less profitable Product X, which has a CM ratio of only 40 percent as compared to 75 percent for Product Y. Thus, the company's *average* CM ratio will fall, and the break-even point will rise since less contribution margin will be available per unit to cover the fixed costs.

7-4. Baker Company will realize the most rapid increase in net income. The reason is that Baker Company will have a higher contribution margin ratio (and contribution margin per unit) due to its lower variable costs. Thus, the company's contribution margin (and net income) will increase more rapidly than Able Company's as sales increase. The impact on net income can also be viewed in terms of operating leverage. At a given level of sales, Baker Company will have a higher degree of operating leverage than Able Company because of its higher fixed costs. Therefore, as sales increase, its net income will rise more rapidly than will Able Company's.

Chapter 8

Variable Costing—
A Tool for Management

Chapter Study Suggestions

This chapter introduces a new method of costing products called *variable costing*. Throughout the chapter we compare variable costing with absorption costing, which you studied in Chapter 3.

In your study, note that the difference between the two costing methods centers on the handling of the fixed portion of manufacturing overhead cost. This point is shown in graphic form in Exhibit 8-1. Exhibits 8-2 through 8-6 are the heart of the chapter; these exhibits show how to compute unit costs under both variable and absorption costing, and they show the impact of the two methods on net income. Spend the bulk of your study time on these exhibits, and be sure you understand the computations they contain. You must understand these computations in order to complete the homework assignment material.

CHAPTER HIGHLIGHTS AND STUDY GUIDE

A. Two methods are available for determining the cost of a unit of product. These methods are absorption costing and variable costing.

1. Under absorption costing, all manufacturing costs, both variable and fixed, are added to units or product.

2. Under variable costing, only variable manufacturing costs—which consist of direct materials, direct labor, and variable overhead—are added to units of product.

a. Variable costing focuses on *cost behavior* in computing unit costs. One of the strengths of this costing method is that it harmonizes fully with both the contribution approach and the cost-volume-profit concepts discussed in Chapter 7.

b. Under the variable costing method, fixed manufacturing costs are treated as *period* costs and, like selling and administrative expenses, are charged against revenues in the time period in which they are incurred.

c. Variable costing is sometimes referred to as *direct costing* or *marginal costing*.

B. In sum, under absorption costing fixed manufacturing overhead is treated *as a product cost*, whereas under variable costing it is treated *as a period cost*. Essentially, the difference in the way absorption costing and variable costing handle fixed manufacturing overhead centers on a matter of timing.

1. Advocates of variable costing argue that fixed manufacturing costs relate to the *capacity* to produce, rather than to the production of specific units of product in any given year. Thus, they argue that fixed manufacturing overhead costs should be charged against the period, and not added to the cost of units produced.

2. Advocates of absorption costing argue that all manufacturing costs—variable and fixed—are essential to the production process and therefore can't be ignored when costing units of product. Thus, to be fully costed, each unit of product must bear and equitable portion of *all* manufacturing costs.

C. Under absorption costing, it is possible to defer a portion of the fixed overhead costs of the current period to future periods through the inventory account.

1. Such a deferral is known as *fixed overhead cost deferred in inventory*.

2. The deferral occurs because units of product going into inventory carry a portion of the fixed manufacturing overhead costs of the period with them. This portion of the period's fixed overhead costs is not charged against revenues, but rather is held (or deferred) in inventory until the units are sold in some future period.

D. Exhibit 8-3 is a key exhibit illustrating the differences between variable and absorption costing. *Study this exhibit carefully before going on.* Several important generalizations relative to variable and absorption costing can be drawn from the data in this exhibit.

1. When production and sales (in units) are equal, the same net income will be reported under either variable or absorption costing.

2. When production exceeds sales (in units), greater net income will be reported under absorption costing than under variable costing.

a. Net income will be greater under absorption costing because fixed overhead cost will be deferred in inventory when production exceeds sales.

b. The amount of fixed overhead cost deferred will be equal to the excess production times the fixed overhead cost per unit.

3. When production is less than sales (in units), less net income will be reported under absorption costing than under variable costing.

a. Net income will be less under absorption costing because fixed overhead costs will be released from inventory when production is less than sales.

b. The amount of fixed overhead cost released will be equal to the excess units sold times the fixed overhead cost per unit.

4. Over an *extended* period of time, the net income reported by the two costing methods will tend to be the same.

a. The reason net income will tend to be the same is that over the long run sales can't exceed production, nor can production much exceed sales.

b. The shorter the time period, the more the net income figures will tend to differ.

E. The following format, which is illustrated in Exhibit 8-4, can be used to reconcile the variable and absorption costing net income figures.

Direct costing net income $XX

Add: Fixed overhead costs deferred in
    inventory under absorption costing   XX
Deduct: Fixed overhead costs released
    from inventory under absorption costing (XX)
Absorption costing net income $XX

F. Exhibit 8-6 shows the effect of changes in production on net income under both variable and absorption costing.

1, Net income under variable costing is not affected by changes in production. It is affected only by changes in the number of units sold.

2. Net income under absorption costing is affected by changes in production.

a. Net income will increase as production increases, and decrease as production decreases.

b. These changes in net income are a major criticism of absorption costing, since a company can increase its reported net income by simply increasing production.

G. Several factors should be considered by the manager in choosing between the variable and absorption costing methods.

1. A weakness of the absorption costing method is its inability to dovetail well with CVP analysis. It is not possible, for example, to compute a break-even point under the absorption costing method unless an assumption is made that inventory levels will not change.

2. Advocates of variable costing argue that it provides more useful cost information for pricing decisions than does absorption costing.

3. For external reporting purposes and in preparing income tax returns, a company is required to cost units of product by the absorption costing method. Variable costing is limited to *internal use* in a company.

H. When companies employ JIT inventory methods, problems with net income under absorption costing are either eliminated or reduced to insignificant proportions.

1. The reason is that the erratic movement of net income under absorption costing, and the differences in net income between absorption and variable costing, arise because of changing levels of inventory. Under JIT, goods are produced strictly to customers' orders, so inventories are either eliminated or held constant from period to period.

2. With no changes in inventories, there is no opportunity for fixed overhead costs to be shifted between periods under absorption costing. Thus, net income will be the same between variable and absorption costing, and the erratic movement in net income under absorption costing will be eliminated.

REVIEW AND SELF TEST
Questions and Exercises

True or False

For each of the following statements, enter a T or an F in the blank to indicate whether the statement is true or false.

____ 1. Variable costing focuses on cost behavior in computing unit costs.

____ 2. Under variable costing, variable selling and administrative expenses are treated as product costs.

____ 3. The cost of a unit of product under the absorption costing method consists of direct materials, direct labor, and both variable and fixed overhead.

____ 4. Selling and administrative expenses are treated as period costs under both the variable costing and absorption costing methods.

____ 5. Fixed manufacturing overhead costs are treated the same way under both the variable costing and absorption costing methods.

____ 6. Advocates of variable costing argue that fixed overhead costs relate to the capacity to produce rather than to the actual production of units of product in a given year.

____ 7. Under the absorption costing method it is possible to defer a portion of the fixed overhead costs of the current period to future periods through the inventory account.

____ 8. Advocates of variable costing argue that fixed overhead costs should be expensed as incurred (that is, treated as period costs) since fixed overhead costs have no future service potential.

____ 9. Variable costing will always produce a higher net income figure than will absorption costing.

____ 10. When production and sales are equal the same net income will be reported regardless of whether variable costing or absorption costing is being used.

____ 11. When production exceeds sales, the net income reported under absorption costing will generally be greater than the net income reported under variable costing.

____ 12. When production is less than sales, the net income reported under absorption costing will generally be less than the net income reported under variable costing.

____ 13. When production exceeds sales, fixed overhead costs are released from inventory under absorption costing.

____ 14. When sales exceed production, fixed overhead costs are released from inventory under absorption costing.

____ 15. Changes in the level of production do not affect net income under the variable costing method.

____ 16. When sales are constant but the level of production fluctuates, the absorption costing method will produce a more stable net income pattern than will the variable costing method.

____ 17. The variable costing method is not acceptable for external reporting or for income tax purposes.

____ 18. Absorption costing data are generally better suited for cost-volume-profit analysis than variable costing data.

Multiple Choice

Choose the best answer or response by placing the identifying letter in the space provided.

_____ 1. White Company manufactures a product called a Zet. The following unit costs are associated with Zet:

Direct materials	$3
Direct labor	4
Variable overhead	1
Variable selling and admin. expense	2

In addition, fixed manufacturing overhead costs total $100,000 each period. The company normally produces 20,000 Zets each period. The cost of a single Zet under the absorption costing method would be: a) $10; b) $13; c) $15; d) none of these.

_____ 2. Refer to the data in question 1 above. The cost of a single Zet under the variable costing method would be: a) $8; b) $10; c) $13; d) none of these.

_____ 3. If production exceeds sales, one would expect net income under the variable costing method to be: a) the same as net income under the absorption costing method; b) less than net income under the absorption costing method; c) greater than net income under the absorption costing method.

_____ 4. If sales exceed production, one would expect net income under the variable costing method to be: a) the same as net income under the absorption costing method; b) less than net income under the absorption costing method; c) greater than net income under the absorption costing method.

_____ 5. Which of the following costs are treated as period costs under the variable costing method: a) fixed manufacturing overhead and both variable and fixed selling and administrative expenses; b) both variable and fixed manufacturing overhead; c) only fixed manufacturing overhead and fixed selling and administrative expenses.

_____ 6. When production exceeds sales, fixed manufacturing overhead costs: a) are released from inventory under absorption costing; b) are deferred in inventory under absorption costing; c) are released from inventory under variable costing; d) are deferred in inventory under variable costing.

_____ 7. When sales are constant but production fluctuates: a) net income will be erratic under variable costing; b) absorption costing will always show a net loss; c) variable costing will always show a net income; d) net income will be erratic under absorption costing.

_____ 8. During 19X2, Peck Company produced 10,000 units and sold 9,000 units. Fixed overhead costs total $20,000 annually, and variable overhead costs are $3 per unit. For 19X2, one would expect net income under the absorption costing method to be: a) $2,000 more than net income under the variable costing method; b) $5,000 more than net income under the variable costing method; c) $2,000 less than net income under the variable costing method; d) $5,000 less than net income under the variable costing method.

Complete the Statements

1. Only _____ manufacturing costs are treated as product costs under the variable costing method.

2. Variable costing is also known as _____ or _____ costing.

3. The inventory carrying value under absorption costing will always be _____ in dollar amount than the inventory carrying value under variable costing.

4. If sales exceed production, fixed overhead costs are _____ _____ inventory under absorption costing.

5. If production exceeds sales, fixed overhead costs are _____ _____ inventory under absorption costing.

6. If sales are constant and production fluctuates from period to period, net income will tend to be erratic under the _____ costing method.

7. Net income is not affected by changes in production under the _____ costing method.

8. Total assets on the balance sheet will be higher under the _____ costing method than under the _____ costing method.

9. Advocates of _____ costing argue that it provides more useful cost information for pricing decisions than does _____ costing.

10. For external reporting on financial statements, a company is required to cost units of product by the _____ costing method.

8-1. Selected data relating to the operations of Dole Company for 19x1 are given below:

Units produced	40,000
Units sold	35,000
Fixed costs:	
Manufacturing overhead	$160,000
Selling and administration	140,000
Variable costs per unit:	
Direct materials	7
Direct labor	6
Manufacturing overhead	3
Selling and administration	2

a. Assume that the company uses absorption costing. Compute the cost to produce one unit of product .... $ _____

Determine the value of the ending inventory .... $ _____

b. Assume that the company uses variable costing. Compute the cost to produce one unit of product .... $ _____

Determine the value of the ending inventory .... $ _____

c. Which method would show the highest net income for 19x1? (Variable costing/absorption costing) By how much? ...... $ _____

8-2. The Hodex Company was organized just one month ago. The company manufactures and sells a unique product that has been quickly accepted by consumers. The results of the company's first month of operations are shown below (absorption costing basis):

Sales (10,000 units @ $20)	$200,000
Less cost of goods sold (10,000 units @ $14)	140,000
Gross margin	60,000
Less selling and administrative expenses	45,000
Net Income	$ 15,000

Variable selling and administrative expenses are $2 per unit. The company produced 12,000 units during the month. Variable manufacturing costs total $10 per unit, and fixed manufacturing overhead costs total $48,000 per month.

a. Redo the company's income statement in the contribution format, using variable costing.

_____

_____

_____

_____

_____

_____

_____

_____

_____

_____

_____

_____

_____

_____

b.   Reconcile the variable costing and absorption costing net income figures:

Variable costing net income ································· $

Absorption costing net income ···························· $15,000

8-3. **Critical thought writing exercise:** Lake Company uses absorption costing in preparing statements for its annual report to stockholders. For 19x5, the company had $10,000,000 in sales and reported a $400,000 loss in its annual report. According to a CVP analysis prepared for management's use (using variable costing) $10,000,000 in sales is the break-even point for the company. Based on these data, did the company's inventory level for the 19x5 increase, decrease, or remain unchanged? Explain your answer.

_____

_____

_____

_____

_____

_____

_____

_____

_____

Chapter 8
Answers to Questions and Exercises

True or False

1. T   Variable costing includes direct materials, direct labor, and variable overhead as product costs. Thus, this costing method does focus on cost behavior in computing unit costs.

2. F   Both variable and fixed selling and administrative expenses are treated as period costs under variable costing, the same as under absorption costing *The only difference between the two costing methods lies in their treatment of fixed manufacturing overhead costs.*

3. T   All manufacturing costs are included as product costs under absorption costing.

4. T   Selling and administrative expenses are never treated as product costs under either costing method.

5. F   Under variable costing, fixed overhead costs are treated as period costs; under absorption costing, fixed overhead costs are treated as product costs.

6. T   Since fixed overhead costs remain constant regardless of the level of production, they are viewed as relating to the *capacity* to produce, rather than to actual production under the variable costing method.

7. T   Fixed overhead costs will be deferred to the future under absorption costing whenever production exceeds sales.

8. T   Fixed overhead costs are viewed as having no future service potential since the incurrence of such costs in one year will not affect the incurrence of the same costs in a following year.

9. F   Variable costing will produce a higher net income figure than absorption costing only when sales exceed production.

10. T   The reason is that when sales and production are equal, there is no chance for fixed overhead cost to be deferred in (or released from) inventory under absorption costing.

11. T   When production exceeds sales, fixed overhead cost is deferred in inventory under absorption costing, thus causing net income to be higher than under variable costing.

12. T   When production is less than sales, fixed overhead cost is released from inventory under absorption costing, thus causing net income to be lower than under variable costing.

13. F   When production exceeds sales, fixed overhead costs are *deferred* in inventory under absorption costing as units of product are added to the inventory account. This point is illustrated in Year 2 in Exhibit 8-3 (under the absorption costing part of the exhibit).

14. T   When sales exceed production, *units are taken out of inventory*, thus releasing fixed overhead costs that were previously deferred. This point is illustrated in Year 3 in Exhibit 8-3 (under the absorption costing part of the exhibit).

15. T   Only changes in the number of units sold can affect net income under the variable costing method.

16. F   If production fluctuates, the absorption costing method will produce an erratic net income pattern. The reason is that fixed overhead cost will be shifted into and out of inventory as production goes up and down.

17. T   Variable costing is used internally by the manager for planning and decision making purposes.

18. F The reverse is true—variable costing data are better suited for CVP analysis than absorption costing data.

Multiple Choice

1. b The computations are:

Variable manufacturing costs
($3 + $4 +$1) $8
Fixed manufacturing costs
($100,000 ÷ 20,000 units)   5
Total manufacturing costs $13

2. a Only the variable manufacturing costs are treated as product costs under the variable costing method. Thus, $3 + $4 + $1 = $8.

3. b If production exceeds sales, fixed overhead cost will be deferred in inventory under absorption costing. Thus, a higher net income will be reported under that method than under variable costing. This point is illustrated in Year 2 in Exhibit 8-3.

4. c If sales exceed production, fixed overhead cost will be released from inventory under absorption costing. Thus, a lower net income will be reported under that method than under variable costing. This point is illustrated in Year 3 in Exhibit 8-3.

5. a Fixed manufacturing overhead cost is expensed as incurred under variable costing. Also, both variable and fixed selling and administrative expenses are *always* treated as period costs under both variable or absorption costing.

6. b When production exceeds sales, units are added to inventory. Thus, fixed overhead costs are deferred in inventory under absorption costing. See Year 2 in Exhibit 8-3.

7. d When production fluctuates, net income will be erratic under absorption costing since fixed overhead costs will be shifted into and out of inventory as production goes up and down.

8. a Under the absorption costing method, fixed overhead cost per unit will be:
$20,000 ÷ 10,000 units produced = $2. If only 9,000 units are sold, then 1,000 units will go into inventory. Thus, under the absorption costing method, $2,000 in fixed overhead cost will be deferred in inventory ($2 x 1,000 units = $2,000). Net income will therefore be $2,000 more under absorption costing than under variable costing.

Complete the Statements

1. variable
2. direct, marginal
3. greater
4. released from
5. deferred in
6. absorption
7. variable
8. absorption, variable
9. variable, absorption
10. absorption

8-1. a.

Direct materials	$ 7
Direct labor	6
Variable overhead	3
Fixed overhead ($160,000 ÷ 40,000 units) ...	4
Total Cost per Unit	$20

Ending Inventory: 5,000 units × $20   = $100,000

b.

Direct materials	$ 7
Direct labor	6
Variable overhead	3
Total Cost per Unit	$16

Ending Inventory: 5,000 units × $16   = $80,000

c.   Absorption costing would show the highest net income, by $20,000. The reason is that the inventory has increased by 5,000 units, and each unit has taken $4 of fixed overhead cost into inventory with it, thus relieving these costs from the income statement.

8-2. a.

Sales (10,000 units @ $20)		$200,000
Less variable expenses:		
Variable cost of goods sold @ $10	$100,000	
Selling and administrative @ $2	20,000	
Total variable expenses		120,000
Contribution margin		80,000
Less fixed expenses:		
Manufacturing overhead	48,000	
Selling and administrative	25,000*	
Total fixed expenses		73,000
Net Income		$ 7,000

*$45,000 − (10,000 units × $2) = $25,000

b.

Variable costing net income	$ 7,000
Add: fixed manufacturing overhead cost deferred in inventory under absorption costing:	
2,000 units x $4*	8,000
Absorption Costing Net Income	$ 15,000

*$48,000 ÷ 12,000 units produced = $4 per unit.

8-3. The company's inventory level for the year decreased. When inventory levels decrease, fixed overhead costs are released from inventory under absorption costing. Since Lake Company reported a loss when its sales were at the break-even level (as computed by the variable costing approach), it must have had fixed overhead costs released from inventory for the year under the absorption costing approach. Thus, the fixed overhead costs released from inventory would have resulted in a loss for the year, even though from a variable costing point of view the company should have broken even.

Chapter 9

Profit Planning

Chapter Study Suggestions

Before reading the chapter material, turn to Exhibit 9-2 and study the flow of budget data as depicted there. This will provide you with an overview of what the chapter contains. Notice particularly how all budgets eventually impact on the cash budget. As suggested by this exhibit, the cash budget is a "key" budget and serves to tie together much of the budget data in an organization. Schedule 8 contains a numerical illustration of a cash budget; it will be helpful to review the contents of this schedule before proceeding with the chapter reading.

Schedules 1 and 2, containing the sales and production budgets, are also of particular importance in understanding the overall budgeting process. As you proceed through the chapter, you will see that all other budgets depend in some way on the sales budget in Schedule 1. Notice that the sales budget is accompanied with a "Schedule of Expected Cash Collections." An understanding of how this schedule is constructed is essential to being able to complete the homework material. The format of the production budget, contained in Schedule 2, should be put to memory.

CHAPTER HIGHLIGHTS AND STUDY GUIDE

A. Profit planning is accomplished through the preparation of a series of documents known as *budgets*. A budget can be defined as a plan for the future expressed in formal quantitative terms.

1. The master budget is a summary of all phases of a company's plans and goals for the future. It sets specific targets for sales, production, distribution, and financing, and outlines how these targets are to be met.

2. There are two steps in the budgeting process—planning and control.

a. Planning involves the development of future objectives and the formulation of steps to achieve these objectives.

b. Control involves the means by which management ensures that all parts of the organization function properly and attain the objectives set down at the planning stage.

3. There are several benefits to be gained through the use of budgeting in an organization. These benefits include:

a. It forces managers to *think ahead* by requiring them to *formalize* their planning efforts.

b. It provides definite goals and objectives which serve as *benchmarks* for evaluating subsequent performance.

c. It uncovers potential *bottlenecks* before they occur.

d. It *coordinates* the activities of the entire organization by *integrating* the plans and objectives of the various parts.

e. It provides a vehicle for *communicating* management's plans throughout the entire organization.

B. Much of budgeting rests on the concept of responsibility accounting. Each manager is charged with the control of those costs under his or her care, and his or her performance is measured by how well budgeted goals are met.

1. Responsibility accounting personalizes accounting information by looking at costs from a *personal control* standpoint, rather than an *institutional* standpoint. This concept is central to any effective planning and control system.

2. A basic premise of the responsibility accounting idea is that effective budget data can be generated as a basis for evaluating managerial performance. The basic purpose of this chapter is to illustrate the steps involved in budget preparation.

C. Budget preparation is a complex task requiring the cooperative effort of all levels of management.

1. One of the first steps is the choice of a budget period. Operating budgets (the budgets discussed in this chapter) are ordinarily set to cover a one-year period.

a. The budget year is generally divided into quarters, with the quarters subdivided into months. As the year progresses, budget data are continually reviewed and refined.

b. These budgets are often set on a continuous or perpetual basis. This is where a new month is constantly being added on the end as the current month is completed. This stabilizes the planning horizon by keeping the budget set at a full 12 months ahead.

2. Capital budgets, involving the purchase of plant and equipment, have a longer planning horizon, going two or three decades into the future.

3. The most successful budget programs are those which permit managers to assist in setting the budget data on which their performance is to be evaluated.

a. When managers participate in this manner, their budgets are said to be *self-imposed* in nature. The major advantage of a self-imposed budget is its positive motivational characteristics. A manager is more apt to work at meeting a budget if he or she has played a central role in its development.

b. Notice from Exhibit 9-1 that the flow of budget data in an organization is *upward,* rather than from top management downward.

4. A key element in a successful budgeting program is how top management *uses* budgeted data.

a. Employees will not be supportive of a budgeting program if it is used as a way of finding someone to "blame" for a problem.

b. The budget must be used as a positive instrument for aiding the company in setting objectives, in measuring results, and in working toward short- and long-range goals.

c. In the past, managers have often been preoccupied with the technical aspects of the budget program to the exclusion of the human aspects. Accountants particularly are open to criticism in this regard.

5. A budget committee, consisting of key executives from the various functional areas, generally has responsibility for overall policy matters relating to the budget program.

D. The master budget is a network consisting of many separate budgets that are interdependent. This network is illustrated in Exhibit 9-2. Study this exhibit carefully before going on.

1. The sales budget is the beginning point in the budgeting process. The sales budget is derived from the *sales forecast.*

a. The sales forecast is broader than the sales budget, generally encompassing potential sales in the entire industry.

b. The sales budget is supported by a "Schedule of Expected Cash Collections," which shows the anticipated cash inflow for the budget period. This is illustrated in Schedule 1 in the text.

2. The sales budget is followed by the production budget, which shows what must be produced to meet both sales needs and inventory needs for the budget period. The formula for the production budget is:

Expected sales in units XXX
Add: Desired ending inventory in units ... XXX
  Total needs XXX
Deduct: Opening inventory in units XXX
Required production in units XXX

The production budget deals with units of *finished goods,* rather than raw materials. Watch this point carefully; it often trips students up as they attempt the homework problems.

3. The direct materials budget follows the production budget, to show the amount of materials which must be acquired to support production and to provide for adequate inventories. The formula for the direct materials budget is:

Raw materials needed to meet the
  production schedule XXXX
Add: Desired ending inventory of
    raw materials XXXX
  Total raw materials needs XXXX
Less: Beginning inventory of raw
    materials XXXX
Raw materials to be purchased XXXX

The direct materials budget should be accompanied by a schedule showing the expected cash disbursements for raw materials for the period.

4. All items of cash inflow or cash outflow appearing on the various budgets are summarized on the cash budget. The cash budget contains four major sections:

The cash receipts section
The cash disbursements section
The cash excess or deficiency section
The financing section

a. The cash budget is one of the key budgets in the planning process. Study the numerical illustrations provided in Schedule 8 with care, noting particularly how the financing section is handled.

b. Notice that the "Year" column begins with the cash balance from the first quarter and ends with the cash balance from the fourth quarter.

5. The culmination of the budgeting process is the preparation of an income statement and a balance sheet.

E. It is important to make a distinction between JIT production and JIT purchasing.

1. JIT production can only be used by manufacturing companies, since it focuses on the manufacture of goods.

2. JIT purchasing can be used by any organization—retail, wholesale, distribution, or manufacturing—since it focuses on the acquisition of goods.

3. There are five key features of JIT purchasing.

a. Goods are delivered immediately before demand or use.

b. The number of suppliers is greatly reduced.

c. Long-term agreements are signed with suppliers, and these agreements stipulate the delivery schedule, the quality of the goods, and the price to be paid.

d. Little or no inspection is made as to the quantity of goods received in a shipment, nor is the shipment inspected for defects.

e. Payments are not made for each individual shipment; rather, payments are "batched" for each supplier.

4. The adoption of JIT purchasing does not require that a retail or distribution company eliminate *all* inventories. But the amount of time that a good spends on the shelf or in a warehouse can be greatly reduced through the JIT approach.

F. Zero-based budgeting is so named because managers using this system are required to start at zero budget levels every year and justify all costs as if the programs involved were being initiated for the first time.

1. This is done in a series of "decision packages" in which the manager ranks all of the activities in his/her department according to relative importance.

2. Opponents of the zero-base approach argue that a zero-base review every year soon becomes mechanical and leads to less cost control, rather than to more cost control.

Appendix E: Economic Order Quantity and the Reorder Point

A. There are three groups of costs associated with inventory. They are: the costs of ordering inventory, the costs of carrying inventory, and the costs of not carrying sufficient inventory. In a broad, conceptual sense, the "right" inventory level is that level which will minimize the total of these three classes of costs.

1. Inventory cost minimization has two dimensions—how much to order and how often to do it. The "how much to order" is referred to as the *economic order quantity*.

a. Computing the economic order quantity is a matter of minimizing the first two classes of costs above (the costs of ordering inventory and the costs of carrying inventory).

b. The more frequently orders are placed, the higher the total ordering costs will be, but the lower the total carrying costs will be (since the average inventory balance on hand will be smaller). The reverse will be true if orders are placed less frequently.

c. The formula for finding the order quantity which will minimize ordering and carrying costs is:

$$E = \sqrt{\frac{2QP}{C}}$$

where: E = the order size in units; Q = the annual quantity used in units; P = the cost of placing one order; and C = the annual cost of carrying one unit in stock.

d. The economic production run size can be found by inserting the set-up costs for a new production run in place of the "cost of placing one order" in the formula above.

2. The "how often to place orders" dimension of inventory cost minimization seeks to minimize the total of the second two classes of costs above (the costs of carrying inventory and the costs of not carrying sufficient inventory).

    a. This is known as determining the *reorder point*. The formula is:

$$\text{Reorder point} = \frac{\text{Lead time} \times \text{Average daily}}{\text{or weekly usage}}$$

    b. The lead time can be defined as the interval between when an order is placed and when the order is finally received from the supplier.

    c. If usage during the lead time is not constant, then a *safety stock* must be carried. The safety stock is computed as follows:

Maximum expected usage per day (or week)	XX units
Average usage per day (or week)	XX units
Excess	XX units
Multiply by the lead time	x days (or weeks)
Safety stock	XX units

    d. With the safety stock considered, the new formula for computing the reorder point becomes:

$$\text{Reorder point} = \begin{array}{c}(\text{Lead time} \times \text{Average daily} \\ \text{or weekly usage}) + \text{Safety} \\ \text{stock}\end{array}$$

    e. The reorder point and the safety stock are both shown graphically in Exhibit E-3

REVIEW AND SELF TEST
Questions and Exercises

True or False

For each of the following statements, enter a T or an F in the blank to indicate whether the statement is true or false.

_____ 1. The best way to establish budget figures is to use last year's actual cost and activity data as this year's budget estimates.

_____ 2. Budgeting is generally of little value to smaller organizations.

_____ 3. The usual starting point in budgeting is to make a forecast of industry sales.

_____ 4. A sales budget is different from a sales forecast.

_____ 5. A self-imposed budget is one prepared by top management and imposed on other management levels as it is passed downward through an organization.

_____ 6. Budgets are essentially planning devices, rather than control devices.

_____ 7. The basic idea behind responsibility accounting is that each manager's performance should be judged by how well he or she manages those items directly under his or her control.

_____ 8. Depreciation is not included as part of a cash budget.

_____ 9. One of the premises underlying the responsibility accounting concept is that effective budget data can be generated as a basis for evaluating performance.

_____ 10. Operating budgets generally have long time horizons and may extend 30 years or more into the future.

_____ 11. A continuous or perpetual budget is one that maintains a constant 12-month planning horizon.

_____ 12. Budget data are generally prepared by top management and distributed downward in an organization.

_____ 13. The budget committee is responsible for preparing detailed budget figures in an organization.

_____ 14. Nearly all other parts of the master budget are dependent in some way on the sales budget.

_____ 15. Ending inventories are primarily a function of an organization not being able to sell all that it had planned to sell during a period.

_____ 16. The primary purpose of the cash budget is to show the expected cash balance at the end of the budget period.

_____ 17. JIT purchasing is used only by manufacturing companies.

____ 18. (Appendix E) As inventory levels increase, the costs of carrying inventory will decrease.

____ 19. (Appendix E) In computing the economic order quantity, the manager tries to balance off the costs of ordering inventory and the costs of carrying inventory.

____ 20. (Appendix E) The lead time is a critical factor in computing the reorder point.

Multiple Choice

Choose the best answer or response by placing identifying letter in the space provided.

____ 1. Detailed budget data are generally prepared by: a) the accounting department; b) top management; c) lower levels of management; d) the budget committee; e) none of these.

____ 2. Most other budgets are dependent in some way on the: a) cash budget; b) income statement; c) direct materials budget; d) sales budget.

____ 3. If the beginning cash balance is $15,000, the required ending cash balance is $12,000, cash disbursements are $125,000, and cash collections from customers are $90,000, the company must: a) borrow $32,000; b) borrow $20,000; c) borrow $8,000; d) borrow $38,000; e) none of these.

____ 4. Archer Company has budgeted sales of 30,000 units in April, 40,000 units in May, and 60,000 units in June. The company has 6,000 units on hand on April 1. If the company requires an ending inventory equal to 20 percent of the following month's sales, production during May should equal: a) 32,000 units; b) 44,000 units; c) 36,000 units; d) none of these.

____ 5. Refer to the data for Archer Company in question 4. Each unit requires 3 pounds of material X. Some 24,000 pounds of material X were on hand April 1, and the company requires materials on hand at the end of each month equal to 25 percent of the following month's production needs. For April, the company should purchase how many pounds of material X? a) 105,000; b) 19,000; c) 87,000; d) none of these.

____ 6. Actual sales in Ward Company were: June, $30,000; July, $50,000; and August, $70,000. Sales in September are expected to be $60,000. If 30 percent of a month's sales are collected in the month of sale, 50 percent in the first month after sale, and 15 percent in the second month after sale, then cash receipts for September are budgeted to be: a) $60,500; b) $62,000; c) $57,000; d) none of these.

____ 7. A planning horizon of 30 years or more is generally used in preparing a(n): a) cash budget; b) operating budget; c) zero-based budget; d) capital budget.

____ 8. (Appendix E) In computing the reorder point, the manager seeks to minimize the costs of carrying inventory and: a) ordering inventory; b) not carrying sufficient inventory; c) carrying a safety stock; d) not carrying a safety stock; e) none of these.

____ 9. (Appendix E) The lead time is used in computing the: a) economic order quantity; b) reorder point; c) safety stock; d) responses a, b, and c are all correct; e) responses b and c are both correct.

____ 10. (Appendix E) Wynn Company has been ordering in amounts greater than the economic order quantity. This would result in: a) carrying costs being less than ordering costs; b) more frequent reorder points; c) carrying costs being greater than ordering costs; d) safety stocks being unneeded; e) none of these.

Complete the Statements

Fill in the necessary words to complete the following statements.

1. In a budgeting program, _____ involves the setting of goals and objectives, and _____ involves the steps taken to assure that the organization meets these goals.

2. Budgeting provides management with a vehicle for _____ its plans in an orderly way throughout the entire organization.

3. The accounting concept which looks at costs from a personal control standpoint is called _____.

4. A _____ or _____ budget maintains a constant 12-month planning horizon, adding a new month on the end when the current month is completed.

5. A _____-_____ budget contains its own unique system of control, in that if an individual is not able to meet budget specifications, he only has himself to blame.

6. A standing_____ _____is charged with overall responsibility for policy matters relating to the budget program.

7. The sales budget is derived from the _____ _____.

8. All of the operating budgets, including the sales budget, have an impact of some type on the _____ budget.

9. Production must be adequate to provide for both sales needs and _____ needs.

10. (Appendix E) There are three groups of costs associated with inventory. These are the costs of _____ inventory, the costs of _____ inventory, and the costs of _____ _____ _____ inventory.

11. (Appendix E) In a broad, conceptual sense, the "right" level of inventory to carry is that which will _____ the total of the three classes of costs in part 10 above.

12. (Appendix E) In order to protect itself against stockouts, an organization should carry an adequate _____ _____, which is computed by taking the difference between average and maximum usage during the lead time.

Exercises

9-1. Billings Company produces and sells a single product. Expected sales for the next four months are given below:

	Sales in Units
April	10,000
May	12,000
June	15,000
July	9,000

The company needs a production budget for the second quarter. Past experience indicates that end-of-month inventories must equal at least 10 percent of the following month's sales in units. At the end of March, 1,000 units were on hand. Complete the following production budget for the quarter:

	April	*May*	*June*	*Second Quarter*
Budgeted sales				
Add: Desired ending inventory	___	___	___	___
Total needs				
Deduct: Beginning inventory	___	___	___	___
Units to be produced	___	___	___	___

9-2. Dodero Company's production budget for the next four months is given below:

	Production in Units
July	15,000
August	18,000
September	20,000
October	16,000

Five ounces of raw materials are used in the production of each unit of product. At the end of June, 11,250 ounces of material were on hand. The company wants to maintain an inventory of materials equal to 15 percent of the following month's production needs.

Complete the following materials purchases budget for the third quarter:

	July	August	Sept.	Third Quarter
Budgeted production in units				
Raw material needs per unit	_____	_____	_____	_____
Production needs in ounces				
Add: Desired ending inventory	_____	_____	_____	_____
Total needs in ounces				
Deduct: Beginning inventory	_____	_____	_____	_____
Raw materials to be purchased	_____	_____	_____	_____

9-3. Whitefish Company budgets its cash two months at a time. Budgeted cash disbursements for March and April, respectively, follow: for inventory purchases, $90,000 and $82,000; for selling and administrative expenses (includes $5,000 depreciation each month), $75,000 and $70,000; for equipment purchases, $15,000 and $6,000; and for dividend payments, $5,000 and $-0-. Budgeted cash collections from customers are $150,000 and $185,000 for March and April, respectively. The company will begin March with a $10,000 cash balance on hand. A minimum cash balance of $5,000 must be maintained. If needed, the company can borrow money at 12 percent per year. All borrowings are at the beginning of a month, and all repayments are at the end of a month. Interest is paid only when principal is being repaid.

Complete the following cash budget for March and April:

	March	April	Two Months
Cash balance, beginning			
Add: Collections from customers	_____	_____	_____
Total cash available	_____	_____	_____
Less disbursements:			
_____....................			
_____....................			
_____....................			
_____....................	_____	_____	_____
Total disbursements	_____	_____	_____
Excess (deficiency) of cash available over disbursements	_____	_____	_____
Financing:			
Borrowings (at beginning)			
Repayments (at ending)			
Interest (12% per year)	_____	_____	_____
Total financing	_____	_____	_____
Cash balance, ending	_____	_____	_____

9-4.   (Appendix E) Glidden Products produces a number of consumer items, including a microwave oven. A vital component part for the ovens is purchased from an outside supplier. In total, the company purchases 2,700 of the parts each year. It costs approximately $15 to place an order, and it costs approximately $.40 to carry one part in inventory for a year. The company works 50 weeks per year.

   a.   Compute the economic order quantity for the part, using the following formula:

$$E = \sqrt{\frac{2QP}{C}} \qquad \text{Where: } E = \text{economic order quantity}$$

$$E = \sqrt{\underline{\hspace{5cm}}}$$

$$E =$$

$$E =$$

   b.   It takes about three weeks to receive an order of parts from the supplier. The company normally uses 54 parts each week in production; usage can be as much as 75 parts per week, however.

   Compute the safety stock:

Maximum expected usage per week	_____ parts
Average usage per week	_____ parts
Excess	
Lead time	X _____
Safety stock	_____ parts

   c.   From the data in parts a and b, compute the reorder point:

Average weekly usage	_____ parts
Lead time	X _____
Normal usage	_____ parts
Safety stock	_____ parts
Reorder point	_____ parts

   In your own words, explain when and in what quantity orders will be made:

_____

_____

_____

_____

_____

_____

_____

_____

9-5. **Critical thought writing exercise:** "The most important reason a company prepares a cash budget is to see how much cash it will have in the bank at the end of the year." Explain why you do or do not agree with this statement.

_____

_____

_____

_____

_____

_____

_____

_____

Chapter 9
Answers to Questions and Exercises

True or False

1. F   Budget figures should be reflective of what is expected in the future—not just a restatement of what has happened in the past.

2. F   Budgeting is as valuable in smaller organizations as it is in large organizations.

3. T   A forecast of industry sales is needed as a basis for establishing a company's sales budget.

4. T   A sales forecast is a statement of expected sales in the entire industry; a sales budget represents a company's expected market share of these industry sales.

5. F   A self-imposed budget is one in which a manager prepares his or her own budget estimates.

6. F   Budgeting involves both planning and control. Once a budget is set, it then becomes a control device against which subsequent activities are compared.

7. T   This is a clear, straightforward statement of the purpose of responsibility accounting.

8. T   Depreciation does not involve a cash flow; hence, it is not included as part of a cash budget.

9. T   To be effective, responsibility accounting must be based on a system of well prepared budgets.

10. F   Operating budgets generally have planning horizons of one year or less.

11. T   Under a continuous or perpetual budget, a new month is added on the end as the current month is completed; thus, a constant 12-month planning horizon is maintained.

12. F   The reverse is generally true—budget data are prepared by middle and lower management and submitted upward through an organization.

13. F   Detailed budget figures are prepared by middle and lower management people. The budget committee is responsible for overall administration of the budget program.

14. T   This point is illustrated in Exhibit 9-2.

15. F   Ending inventories are carefully planned for if a company is following good budget procedures.

16. F   The primary purpose of the cash budget is to show how cash resources will be acquired and used over the budget period.

17. F   JIT purchasing is used by all types of organizations—retail, wholesale, distribution—as well as manufacturing.

18. F   The reverse is true—the costs of carrying inventories will increase.

19. T   This point is illustrated in Exhibit E-3.

20. T   The lead time is critical since there must be materials on hand during the lead time to support production. This point is illustrated in Exhibit E-3.

Multiple Choice

1. c This point is illustrated in Exhibit 9-1.

2. d This point is illustrated in Exhibit 9-2.

3. a The computations are:
$15,000 + $90,000 − $125,000 = $(20,000) cash deficiency. Since the company must maintain a minimum cash balance of $12,000, it must borrow $32,000.

4. b The computations are:

	April	May	June
Budgeted sales	30,000	40,000	60,000
Desired ending inventory	8,000	12,000	
Total needs	38,000	52,000	
Less beginning inventory	6,000	8,000	
Required production	32,000	44,000	

5. a The computations are:

Required production	32,000	44,000
Material X per unit	× 3 lbs.	× 3 lbs.
Production needs—lbs.	96,000	132,000
Desired ending inventory	33,000	
Total needs	129,000	
Less beginning inventory	24,000	
Required purchases	105,000	

6. a The computations are:

September sales, $60,000 × 30%	$18,000
August sales, $70,000 × 50%	35,000
July sales, $50,000 × 15%	7,500
Total cash receipts	$60,500

7. d Capital budgets have long planning horizons in order to have plant and equipment on line when needed.

8. b The minimization of these two classes of costs in computing the reorder point is discussed in the chapter.

9. e The lead time is used to compute only: (b) the reorder point, and (c) the safety stock.

10. c Ordering in amounts greater than the economic order quantity would result in larger inventories on hand than needed; therefore, inventory carrying costs would be greater.

Complete the Statements

1. planning, control
2. communicating
3. responsibility accounting
4. responsibility
5. self-imposed
6. budget commitee
7. sales forecast
8. cash
9. inventory
10. ordering, carrying, not carrying sufficient
11. minimize
12. safety stock

Exercises

9-1.

	April	May	June	Second Quarter
Budgeted sales	10,000	12,000	15,000	37,000
Add: Desired ending inventory	1,200	1,500	900	900
Total needs	11,200	13,500	15,900	37,900
Deduct: Beginning inventory	1,000	1,200	1,500	1,000
Units to be produced	10,200	12,300	14,400	36,900

9-2.

	July	August	Sept.	Third Quarter
Budgeted production in units	15,000	18,000	20,000	53,000
Raw material needs per unit	× 5 ozs.	× 5 ozs.	× 5 ozs.	× 5 ozs.
Production needs in ounces	75,000	90,000	100,000	265,000
Add: Desired ending inventory—ozs. ..	13,500	15,000	12,000*	12,000
Total needs in ounces	88,500	105,000	112,000	277,000
Deduct: Beginning inventory—ozs.	11,250	13,500	15,000	11,250
Raw materials to be purchased—ozs....	77,250	91,500	97,000	265,750

*16,000 units (for Oct.) × 5 ozs. = 80,000 ozs. × 15% = 12,000 ozs.

9-3.

	March	April	Two Months
Cash balance, beginning	$ 10,000	$ 5,000	$ 10,000
Add: Collections from customers	150,000	185,000	335,000
Total cash available	160,000	190,000	345,000
Less Disbursements:			
For inventory purchases	90,000	82,000	172,000
For selling and administrative expenses	70,000	65,000	135,000
For equipment purchases	15,000	6,000	21,000
For dividends	5,000	—	5,000
Total disbursements	180,000	153,000	333,000
Excess (deficiency) of cash available over cash disbursements	(20,000)	37,000	12,000
Financing:			
Borrowings (at beginning)	25,000	—	25,000
Repayments (at ending)	—	(25,000)	(25,000)
Interest (12% per year)	—	(500)*	(500)
Total financing	25,000	(25,500)	(500)
Cash balance, ending	$ 5,000	$ 11,500	$ 11,500

*$25,000 × 12% × 2/12 = $500.

9-4. a.
$$E = \sqrt{\frac{2QP}{C}} = \sqrt{\frac{2(2,700)(\$15)}{\$.40}} = \sqrt{202,500} = 450 \text{ parts}$$

b.

Maximum expected usage per week	75 parts
Average usage per week	54 parts
Excess	21 parts
Lead time	× 3 weeks
Safety stock	63 parts

c.

Average weekly usage	54 parts
Lead time	× 3 weeks
Normal usage	162 parts
Safety stock	63 parts
Reorder point	225 parts

Thus, an order for 450 parts will be placed when the stock on hand drops to 225 parts.

9-5. This is not the most important reason a company prepares a cash budget, although it is one reason. The most important reason is to see the inflows and outflows of cash and additional cash needs *during* the year. By knowing cash needs during the year, a company will be able to see periods in which borrowing will be required, periods in which borrowing can be repaid, and any problems that may be developing regarding the company's uses of cash. Thus, bank loans and other sources of financing can be anticipated and arranged well in advance of the actual time of need, and problems can be anticipated and perhaps avoided.

Standard Costs and JIT/FMS Performance Measures

The first part of the chapter deals with the setting of standard costs. This is important material, since it is easier to understand how standard costs are used if one first understands how they are derived. Exhibit 10-1 presents a *standard cost card*, which is the final product of the standard setting process. You will be using a standard cost card in the homework assignments in both this chapter and in Chapter 11 following, so be sure you understand what a standard cost card contains and how it is constructed.

The second part of the chapter deals with the use of standard costs in variance analysis. Exhibit 10-2 provides an overall perspective of variance analysis, and then Exhibits 10-3 through 10-6 give detailed examples of the analysis of materials, labor, and variable overhead. Notice that the figures used in the first part of the chapter to illustrate the setting of standards (see Exhibit 10-1) carry over into Exhibits 10-3, 10-4, and 10-5. As you study, follow the figures from Exhibit 10-1 into the following exhibits. This will help you tie the various parts of the chapter together into one integrated whole. Also, watch the terminology carefully; terms in this chapter are particularly important.

The third part of the chapter discusses performance measures in an automated environment. These performance measures are summarized in Exhibit 10-9, which is the key exhibit in this section. Spend the bulk of your study time on the delivery performance measures, which include computations of delivery cycle time, throughput, and manufacturing cycle efficiency.

The chapter concludes with a review problem which you should follow through step by step before attempting the homework material.

CHAPTER HIGHLIGHTS AND STUDY GUIDE

A.   A standard can be defined as a benchmark or "norm" for evaluating performance. Standards are found in many facets of day-to-day life.

1. Fast food outlets set quantity standards on the amount of meat going into a sandwich, and auto service centers set time standards on routine service work.

2. The broadest application of the standard idea is found in manufacturing firms, where exacting standards relating to materials, labor, and overhead are developed for each separate product line.

a. These standards are set for both the quantity and the cost of inputs going into manufactured goods.

b. The standards are organized onto a standard cost card, which tells the manager what the final manufactured cost should be for a single unit of product.

c. Actual quantities and costs of inputs are compared against the standards shown on the standard cost card, with any differences brought to the attention of management. This is called *management by exception.*

B.   The initial setting of quantity and cost standards is a vital step in the control process. Standards must be set carefully and accurately if they are to be of maximum use to the manager in cost control.

1. Many persons are involved in the setting of standards, including the accountant, the purchasing agent, the industrial engineer, production supervisors, and line managers.

2. Standards tend to fall into two categories—either ideal or practical.

a. Ideal standards are those that can be attained only by working at top efficiency 100 percent of the time. They allow for no machine breakdowns or lost time.

b. Practical standards, by contrast, allow for breakdowns and normal lost time (such as for coffee breaks). Practical standards are standards which are "tight, but attainable."

c. Most managers feel that practical standards have better motivational characteristics than ideal standards.

3. Direct material standards are set for both the price and quantity of inputs into units of product.

a. Price standards should reflect the final, delivered cost of materials. This price should include freight, handling, and other costs necessary to get the material into a condition ready to use. It should also reflect any cash discounts allowed.

b. Quantity standards should reflect the amount of material going into each finished product, as well as allowances for unavoidable waste, spoilage, and other normal inefficiencies.

4. Direct labor price and quantity standards are usually expressed in terms of labor rate and labor hours.

a. The standard direct labor rate per hour would include not only wages earned but also an allowance for fringe benefits, employment taxes, and other labor-related costs.

b. The standard labor hours per unit should include allowances for coffee breaks, personal needs of employees, clean-up, and machine down time.

5. As with direct labor, the price and quantity standards for variable overhead are generally expressed in terms of rate and hours. The rate represents the variable portion of the predetermined overhead rate.

6. The price and quantity standards for materials, labor, and overhead are summarized on a standard cost card.

a. Study the standard cost card in Exhibit 10-1 with care, and trace the figures in it back through the examples on the preceding pages.

b. Essentially, a standard cost card represents the budgeted cost for a single unit of product.

C.   A number of advantages and disadvantages can be associated with the use of standard costs.

1. Perhaps the most important advantage is that standard costs facilitate the use of "management by exception." Other advantages are cited in the text, and should be reviewed before going on.

2. Perhaps the most important disadvantage is that the use of standard costs can cause a number of behavioral problems in an organization. The nature of these problems is cited in the text, along with other disadvantages, and should be reviewed before going on.

D. A *variance* is the difference between standard prices and quantities and actual prices and quantities. A general model exists which is very helpful in variance analysis. This model is presented in Exhibit 10-2 in the text.

1. Notice from the model that a price variance and a quantity variance can be computed for all three variable cost inputs—materials, labor, and overhead.

2. Also notice from the model that variance analysis is a matter of input/output analysis.

a. The inputs represent the actual cost or quantity of materials, labor, and overhead used in production; the output represents the good production of the period.

b. The *standard quantity allowed* represents the amount of inputs that *should have been used* in completing the output of the period. This is a key term in the chapter!

3. Exhibit 10-3 shows the variance analysis of direct materials. As you study the exhibit, notice that the center column (Actual Quantity of Inputs, at Standard Price) plays a part in the computation of both the price and quantity variances. This is a key point in variance analysis.

a. The materials price variance can be expressed in formula form as:

$$(AQ \times AP) - (AQ \times SP) = \text{Price variance}$$
$$\text{or}$$
$$AQ(AP - SP) = \text{Price variance}$$

b. Causes of the materials price variance would include excessive freight costs, loss of quantity discounts, improper grade of materials purchased, and rush orders.

c. The materials quantity variance can be expressed in formula form as:

$$(AQ \times SP) - (SQ \times SP) = \text{Quantity variance}$$
$$\text{or}$$
$$SP(AQ - SQ) = \text{Quantity variance}$$

d. Causes of the materials quantity variance would include untrained workers, faulty machines, and improper grade of materials used in production.

e. The materials price variance is generally isolated at the time materials are purchased, whereas the quantity variance is isolated at the time materials are placed into production.

4. Exhibit 10-5 shows the variance analysis of direct labor. Notice that the format is the same as for direct materials, but that in place of the terms "price" and "quantity" the terms "rate" and "hours" are used.

a. The price variance for labor is called a "rate" variance. The formula is:

$$(AH \times AR) - (AH \times SR) = \text{Rate variance}$$
$$\text{or}$$
$$AH(AR - SR) = \text{Rate variance}$$

b. Causes of the rate variance would include misallocation of workers, unplanned overtime, and pay increases.

c. The quantity variance for labor is called an "efficiency" variance. The formula is:

$$(AH \times SR) - (SH \times SR) = \text{Efficiency variance}$$
$$\text{or}$$
$$SR(AH - SH) = \text{Efficiency variance}$$

d. Causes of the efficiency variance would include poorly trained workers, poor quality materials, faulty equipment, and poor supervision.

5. Exhibit 10-6 shows the variance analysis of variable overhead. Notice that the variances are termed "spending" variance and "efficiency" variance. The formulas for these variances are the same as for direct labor.

E. Performance in a standard cost system is communicated to management through a pyramiding system of reports.

1. Performance reports build upward, with each manager receiving information on his or her own performance, as well as on the performance of each manager under him or her in the chain of responsibility.

2. Each manager is charged *only* with those costs over which he or she has control. Exhibit 10-7 shows how reports are structured in a standard costing system.

3. Through a system of performance reports such as shown in Exhibit 10-7, managers at each level of responsibility can see where their time and their subordinates' time can best be spent in order to control costs and achieve the company's goals.

F. Not all differences between standard costs and quantities and actual costs and quantities can be termed "exceptions." The manager is interested only in those differences that are significant.

1. Statistical analysis is often used to determine whether variances are significant and therefore can be termed "exceptions." This is done through use of a statistical control chart, such as is illustrated in Exhibit 10-8.

G. In an automated environment, the traditional standards discussed above are often deemed to be inappropriate for management's use. There are several reasons why this is so.

1. In an automated environment labor is less significant and tends to be more fixed. Thus, the traditional labor variances are of little use to management, and a focus on items such as the labor efficiency variance may even result in overproduction.

2. A key objective in the new manufacturing environment is to increase quality rather than to just minimize cost. A preoccupation with items such as the materials price variance often results in the purchase of low quality materials or the stockpiling of materials to take advantage of quantity discounts.

3. The manufacturing process is more reliable in an automated environment, and as a result the traditional variances are either minimal or cease to exist.

H. The performance measures used in an automated environment can be classified into five general groupings, as shown in Exhibit 10-9. The computation and use of these performance measures differs in several ways from standard costs.

1. First, they are generally computed on an *on-line* basis so that management is able to monitor activities continually. On-line access to data allows problems to be identified and corrected "on the factory floor."

2. Second, in an automated plant the performance measures are computed at the plant level, rather than at a department level.

3. Third, in using the new performance measures, managers focus more directly on trends over time than on any particular change during the current period. The key objectives are progress and improvement, rather than meeting any specific standards.

I. Perhaps the most important measures in an automated environment are those relating to delivery performance. Several key definitions relate to delivery performance in a company.

1. The delivery cycle time represents the amount of time required from receipt of an order from a customer to shipment of the completed goods. It consists of wait time plus throughput time, as shown in Exhibit 10-10.

2. Throughput time measures the amount of time required to turn raw materials into completed products. It is also known as the manufacturing cycle time.

3. The manufacturing cycle efficiency (MCE) is a measure of the efficiency of the production process. It is computed by the following formula:

$$MCE = \frac{\text{Value-Added Time}}{\text{Throughput (manufacturing cycle) time}}$$

a. If the MCE is less than 1, then it means that non-value-added time is present in the production process. An MCE of 0.25 for example, would mean that 75% of the total production time consisted of non-value-added activities.

b. By monitoring the MCE, companies are able to pare away non-value-added activities and thus get products into the hands of customers more quickly.

c. Non-value-added time consists of inspection time, move time, and queue time.

J. With the introduction of new performance measures, important changes have taken place in the way standard costs are used in companies that employ JIT/FMS concepts. In these companies:

1. Standard costs are generally not used to measure performance. Their use shifts more toward the financial purposes of valuing inventory and determining cost of goods sold.

2. Engineered standard are often replaced either by a rolling average of actual costs or by target costs.

3. Variances are computed on a more frequent basis, and the focus is on the *trend* of the variances rather on their *magnitude*.

4. Standard costs are generally used only for materials and overhead, since labor often is not accounted for as a separate element of cost.

Appendix F: General Ledger Entries to Record Variances

A. Most companies prefer to make general ledger entries to record variances in the books of account. There are three reasons why this is so:

1. Entry into the accounting records encourages early recognition of variances, thereby facilitating cost control.

2. Entry into the accounting records gives variances a greater emphasis than is possible through informal, out-of-records computations.

3. Entry into the accounting records simplifies the bookkeeping process, by allowing companies to carry inventories at standard cost.

B. Favorable variances are recorded by credits, and unfavorable variances are recorded by debits in the accounting records.

1. A sample entry to record an unfavorable material price variance would be:

Raw Materials	XX	
Materials Price Variance		
(unfavorable)	X	
Accounts Payable		XXX

2. A sample entry to record a favorable material quantity variance would be:

Work in Process	XXX	
Materials Quantity Variance		
(favorable)		X
Raw Materials		XX

3. A sample entry to record direct labor variances would be:

Work in Process	XXX	
Labor Efficiency Variance		
(unfavorable)	XX	
Labor Rate Variance		
(favorable)		XX
Wages Payable		XXX

4. Variable overhead variances generally aren't recorded in the accounts separately; rather, they are determined as part of the general analysis of overhead. Overhead analysis is illustrated in Chapter 11.

REVIEW AND SELF TEST
Questions and Exercises

True or False

For each of the following statements, enter a T or an F in the blank to indicate whether the statement is true or false.

_____ 1. Standards play an important part in many aspects of day-to-day life.

_____ 2. The standard cost card tells the manager what the final manufactured cost should be for a single unit of product.

_____ 3. Standard costs are generally determined by analyzing actual costs of prior periods.

_____ 4. Practical standards are generally viewed as having better motivational characteristics than ideal standards.

_____ 5. Ideal standards allow for machine breakdown time and other normal inefficiencies.

_____ 6. In determining a material price standard, the invoice cost should be included, but any freight or handling costs should be excluded.

_____ 7. The material used in rejected or spoiled units of product should be added to good units in computing the standard quantity of material allowed per unit.

_____ 8. The standard rate for variable overhead consists of the variable portion of the predetermined overhead rate.

_____ 9. The difference between a standard and a budget is that a standard is a unit concept, whereas a budget is a total concept.

_____ 10. Raw materials price variances are best isolated when materials are placed into production.

_____ 11. Price- and quantity-type variances can be computed for materials, labor, and overhead.

_____ 12. Waste on the production line will result in a materials price variance.

_____ 13. If the actual price or quantity exceeds the standard price or quantity, the variance is unfavorable.

_____ 14. Raw materials are generally carried in inventory at standard cost.

_____ 15. Labor rate variances are largely out of the control of management.

_____ 16. All differences (variances) between standard cost and actual cost should be given attention by management.

_____ 17. One reason standard costs are not appropriate in an automated environment is that a focus on the labor efficiency variance may cause companies to overproduce and create needless inventories.

_____ 18. One weakness of performance measures in an automated environment is that feedback (reports) to management generally take longer to prepare than the variance reports under traditional standard costing.

_____ 19. The performance measures in an automated environment focus more on trends over time than on meeting any specific standards.

_____ 20. In measuring performance in an automated environment, a decreasing turnover of inventory would be a positive sign.

_____ 21. In an automated environment, the goal is to keep all machines in use 100% of the time.

_____ 22. If the MCE is less than 1, then non-value-added time is present in the production process.

_____ 23. (Appendix F) The use of standard costs simplifies the bookkeeping process.

_____ 24. (Appendix F) An unfavorable variance would be recorded as a debit in the books of account.

Multiple Choice

Choose the best answer or response by placing the identifying letter in the space provided.

_____ 1. Studies show that the use of standard costs: a) is increasing; b) has stopped completely in automated companies; c) has not changed for many years.

_____ 2. It is best to recognize the price variance for raw materials when: a) the materials are placed into production; b) goods are completed and transferred to finished goods; c) the materials are purchased; d) none of these.

_____ 3. The labor rate variance is determined by multiplying the difference between the actual labor rate and the standard labor rate by: a) the standard hours allowed; b) the actual hours worked; c) the budgeted hours allowed; d) none of these.

_____ 4. If inferior-grade materials are purchased, the result may be: a) an unfavorable materials price variance; b) a favorable materials price variance; c) an unfavorable labor efficiency variance; d) a favorable labor efficiency variance; e) responses *b* and *c* are both correct; f) responses *a* and *d* are both correct.

_____ 5. During June, Bradley Company produced 4,000 units of product. The standard cost card indicates the following for labor costs (per unit): 3.5 hours @ $6 = $21. During the month, the company worked 15,000 hours. The standard hours allowed for the month were: a) 14,000 hours; b) 15,000 hours; c) 24,000 hours; d) none of these.

_____ 6. The "price" variance for variable overhead is called a: a) rate variance; b) spending variance; c) budget variance; d) none of these.

_____ 7. The delivery cycle time consists of: a) the time required to get a product to a customer after production is complete; b) the time required to get delivery of raw materials; c) the velocity of production plus the throughput time; d) the time required from receipt of an order from a customer to shipment of the completed goods.

____ 8. Given the following data:

Wait time to start production .... 15.0 days
Inspection time .... 0.6 days
Process time .... 3.0 days
Move time .... 1.4 days
Queue time .... 7.0 days

The throughput time would be: a) 12.0 days; b) 7.0 days; c) 5.0 days; d) 20.0 days.

____ 9. Refer to the data in question 8 above. The MCE would be: a) 75%; b) 30%; c) 25%; d) 42%.

____ 10. Refer again to the data in question 8 above. What percentage of the production time is spent in non-value-added activities: a) 25%; b) 70%; c) 75%; d) 58%.

Complete the Statements

Fill in the necessary words to complete the following statements.

1. In a manufacturing setting, standards are set for both the _____ and _____ of inputs that should go into a unit of product.

2. Standard costs for material, labor, and overhead are summarized on a _____ _____ _____, which tells the manager what the final, manufactured cost should be for a single unit of product.

3. Standards that do not allow for lost time, work interruptions, spoiled units, or machine breakdowns are called _____ standards.

4. _____ standards can be defined as standards that are "tight, but attainable."

5. A standard can be defined as the _____ for a single unit of product.

6. The difference between actual cost and standard cost is called a _____.

7. Variance analysis is actually a matter of _____/ _____ analysis. The _____ represents the actual quantity of materials, labor, and overhead used in production, and the _____ represents the good production of the period.

8. The amount of material that *should have been used* to complete the output of the period is called the _____ _____ _____.

9. The "price" and "quantity" variances for labor are called the labor _____ variance and the labor _____ variance.

10. Variance analysis through the use of standard costs is one means of implementing the concept of management by _____.

11. The _____ time measures the amount of time required to turn raw materials into completed products.

12. The _____ _____ _____ is computed by dividing the value-added time by the throughput time.

13. Non-value-added time consists of _____ time, _____ time, and _____ time.

14. The goal of companies is to get the velocity of production to (increase/decrease) _____ over time.

Exercises

10-1. Selected information relating to Miller Company's operations for April, 19x2 is given below:

Number of units produced	500 units
Number of actual direct labor hours worked	1,400 hours
Total actual direct labor cost	$10,850

The standard cost card indicates that 2.5 hours of direct labor time is allowed per unit, at a rate of $8 per hour.

a. Complete the following analysis of direct labor cost for the month:

Actual Hours of Input, at the Actual Rate (AH x AR)	*Actual Hours of Input, at the Standard Rate (AH x SR)*	*Standard Hours Allowed for Output, at the Standard Rate (SH x SR)*

b. Redo the analysis of direct labor cost for the month, using the following "short-cut" formulas:

$$AH \, (AR - SR) = \text{Rate variance}$$

$$SR \, (AH - SH) = \text{Efficiency variance}$$

10-2. The following activity took place in Solo Company during May 19x6:

Number of units produced	450 units
Material purchased	1,500 feet
Material used in production	720 feet
Cost per foot for material purchased	$3

The standard cost card indicates that 1.5 feet of materials are allowed for each unit of product. The standard cost of the materials is $4 per foot.

a.   Complete the following analysis of direct materials cost for the month:

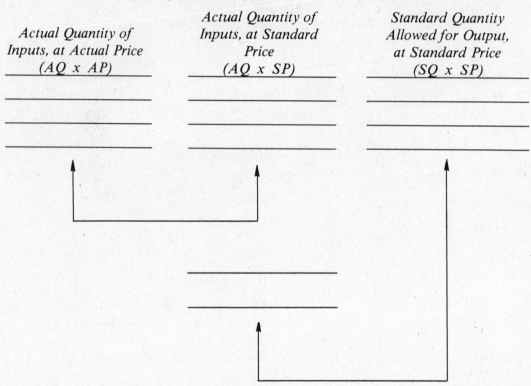

Actual Quantity of Inputs, at Actual Price (AQ x AP)	Actual Quantity of Inputs, at Standard Price (AQ x SP)	Standard Quantity Allowed for Output, at Standard Price (SQ x SP)

(A total variance can't be computed in this situation, since the amount of materials purchased differs from the amount of materials used in production.)

b.   Redo the analysis of direct materials cost for the month, using the following "short-cut" formulas:

$$AQ(AP - SP) = \text{Price variance}$$

$$SP(AQ - SQ) = \text{Quantity variance}$$

10-3. (Appendix F) Refer to the data for Solo Company in exercise 10-2 on the previous page. Prepare journal entries to record all activity relating to direct materials for the month:

	Debit	Credit

10-4.   During the last quarter, Scott Company recorded the following average times for each order received and processed:

Wait time to start production . . . . 9.0 days
Inspection time . . . . .0.8 days
Process time . . . . .3.0 days
Move time . . . . .0.2 days
Queue time . . . . 6.0 days

Goods are shipped as soon as production is completed.

a. Compute the throughput time.

Throughput time = Process time + Inspection time + Move time + Queue time

Throughput time =

Throughput time =

b. Compute the manufacturing cycle efficiency (MCE).

$$MCE = \frac{Value\text{-}Added\text{-}Time}{Throughput\ Time}$$

MCE   =

c. What percentage of the production time is spent in non-value-added activities?

d. Compute the delivery cycle time.

Delivery Cycle Time = Wait time + Throughput time

Delivery Cycle Time =

10-5. Critical thought writing exercise: What relationship(s) do or can exist between the material price and quantity variances and the direct labor rate and efficiency variances?

_____

_____

_____

_____

_____

_____

_____

_____

Chapter 10
Answers to Questions and Exercises

True or False

1. T   Standards are used in many situations that people encounter in day-to-day life, including in fast food outlets, hospitals, auto service centers, and so forth.

2. T   This is the purpose of the standard cost card.

3. F   Standard costs are determined by deciding what costs *should be*—not what they have been.

4. T   Practical standards have better motivational characteristics because they are attainable by workers.

5. F   Ideal standards do not allow for either machine breakdown time or other normal inefficiencies.

6. F   Freight and handling costs should be included in the material price standard, along with the invoice cost of the material.

7. T   By including the material used in rejected or spoiled units, the standard becomes a practical standard that is usable to control abnormal variances.

8. T   This statement is true by definition.

9. T   This statement is true by definition.

10. F   Raw materials price variances are best isolated when materials are purchased.

11. T   This point is illustrated in Exhibit 10-2.

12. F   Waste will result in a materials quantity variance.

13. T   This statement is true by definition.

14. T   The reason is that any variance is broken out at time of purchase.

15. F   Labor rate variances can arise from how labor is used, and the use of labor is within the control of management.

16. F   Only those variances that are deemed to be significant in amount are given attention by management.

17. T   In an automated environment, production is geared to sales.

18. F   In an automated environment, feedback is provided on an "on line" basis. This means that feedback is communicated to managers on the factory floor as problems arise.

19. T   The goals in an automated environment are defined in terms of progress and improvement rather than in terms of meeting specific standards.

20. F   Since companies want to reduce inventories in an automated environment, an *increasing* turnover of inventories would be a positive sign.

21. F   Only machines in bottleneck operations should be in use 100% of the time.

22. T   Since the MCE is measured by value-added time divided by throughput time, an MCE of less than 1 means that the throughput time contains some amount of non-value-added time.

23. T   The use of standard costs simplifies the bookkeeping process since standards permit costs for all units to be carried at the same price.

24. T   This statement is true by definition.

Multiple Choice

1. a   The use of standard costs is increasing because companies are applying them to smaller units and computing them more frequently.

2. c   Recognizing the price variance when materials are purchased allows for early control of any problems that may be developing, such as with quality purchased, quantity purchased, method of freight, and so forth.

3. b   This point is illustrated in Exhibit 10-5.

4. e   The materials price variance will probably be favorable, since the inferior grade materials probably will cost less; the labor efficiency variance probably will be unfavorable, since the inferior grade materials probably will require more work time on the assembly line.

5. a   The computation is: 4,000 units $\times$ 3.5 hours = 14,000 standard hours.

6. b   This point is illustrated in Exhibit 10-2.

7. d   This point is illustrated in Exhibit 10-10.

8. a   Throughput time = Process time + Inspection time + Move time + Queue time

Throughput time = 3.0 days + 0.6 days + 1.4 days + 7.0 days

Throughput time = 12.0 days

9. c $$MCE = \frac{\text{Value-added time}}{\text{Throughput time}}$$

$$= \frac{3.0 \text{ days}}{12.0 \text{ days}} = 25\%$$

10. c   If the MCE is less than one, then it means that non-value-added time is present in the production process. In this case, since the MCE is 25%, 75% of the time is spent in non-value-added activities (1.00 − 0.25 = 0.75 or 75%).

Complete the Statements

1. cost, quantity
2. standard cost card
3. ideal
4. Practical
5. budget

6. variance
7. input/output, input, output
8. standard quantity allowed
9. rate, efficiency
10. exception

11. throughput
12. manufacturing cycle efficiency
13. inspection, move, queue
14. increase

Exercises

10-1. a.

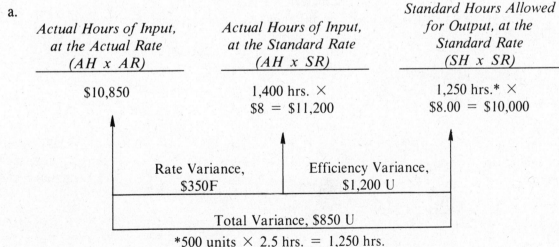

Actual Hours of Input, at the Actual Rate (AH x AR)	*Actual Hours of Input, at the Standard Rate (AH x SR)*	*Standard Hours Allowed for Output, at the Standard Rate (SH x SR)*
$10,850	1,400 hrs. $\times$ $8 = $11,200	1,250 hrs.* $\times$ $8.00 = $10,000

Rate Variance, $350F   Efficiency Variance, $1,200 U

Total Variance, $850 U

*500 units $\times$ 2.5 hrs. = 1,250 hrs.

b. AH (AR − SR) = Labor Rate Variance
1,400 hrs. ($7.75* − $8.00) = $350F
*$10,850 ÷ 1,400 hrs. = $7.75/hr.

SR (AH − SH) = Labor Efficiency Variance
$8.00 (1,400 hrs. − 1,250 hrs.) = $1,200 U

10-2. a.

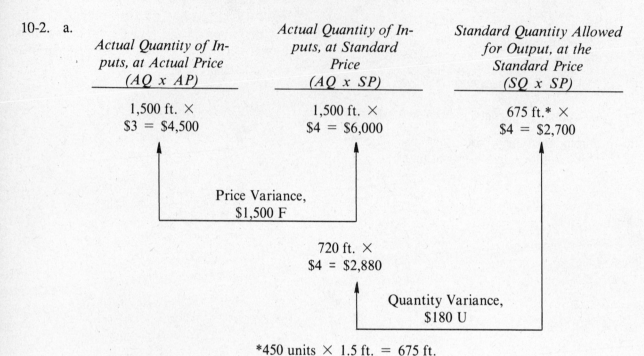

Actual Quantity of In-puts, at Actual Price (AQ x AP)	Actual Quantity of In-puts, at Standard Price (AQ x SP)	Standard Quantity Allowed for Output, at the Standard Price (SQ x SP)
1,500 ft. × $3 = $4,500	1,500 ft. × $4 = $6,000	675 ft.* × $4 = $2,700

Price Variance, $1,500 F

720 ft. × $4 = $2,880

Quantity Variance, $180 U

*450 units × 1.5 ft. = 675 ft.

b. AQ (AP − SP) = Materials Price Variance
1,500 ft. ($3 − $4) = $1,500 F

SP (AQ − SQ) = Materials Quantity Variance
$4 (720 ft. − 675 ft.) = $180 U

Notice that a different quantity of materials was purchased (1,500 ft.) than was used in production for the period (720 ft.). This is why a different "AQ" figure is used in the price variance computation than is used in the quantity variance computation.

10-3. Raw Materials	6,000	
Materials Price Variance		1,500
Accounts Payable		4,500
Work in Process	2,700	
Materials Quantity Variance	180	
Raw Materials		2,880

10-4.   a. Throughput time = Process time + Inspection time + Move time + Queue time
$$= 3.0 \text{ days} + 0.8 \text{ days} + 0.2 \text{ days} + 6.0 \text{ days}$$
$$= 10.0 \text{ days}$$

  b. MCE $= \dfrac{\text{Value-added time}}{\text{Throughput time}} \quad \dfrac{3.0 \text{ days}}{10.0 \text{ days}} = 30\%$

   Notice that value-added time does not include inspection time, move time, or queue time

  c. Since the MCE is 30%, the complement of this figure, or 70% of the total production time, is spent in non-value-added activities.

  d. Delivery cycle time = Wait time + Throughput time
$$= 9.0 \text{ days} + 10.0 \text{ days}$$
$$= 19.0 \text{ days}$$

10-5.   Several relationships do or can exist. First, both sets of variances are computed in the same way, as shown in Exhibit 10-2. Second, a purchase of poor quality materials can result in an unfavorable materials quantity variance, which in turn can cause an unfavorable labor efficiency variance due to excessive labor time needed to work the materials. And third, poorly trained labor can result in an unfavorable labor efficiency variance, which in turn can cause an unfavorable materials quantity variance due to excessive waste.

Chapter 11

Flexible Budgets and Overhead Analysis

Chapter Study Suggestions

The chapter is divided into three parts. The first part covers flexible budgets, with Exhibit 11-8 providing a comprehensive example of how a flexible budget is prepared. As you study the material in this part, pay close attention to the differences that are drawn between a flexible budget and a static budget. These differences are subtle but important.

The middle part of the chapter expands on the variance analysis of variable overhead, by showing how the variable overhead spending and efficiency variances can be organized on a performance report. Exhibits 11-5, 11-6, and 11-7 are the key exhibits here. Notice particularly how the flexible budget data from Exhibit 11-5 ties into the performance reports in Exhibits 11-6 and 11-7.

The last part of the chapter covers fixed overhead analysis. Three things in this part deserve special attention in your study. First, be sure you understand fully what the "denominator activity" is, and how it is used. Second, be sure you understand the difference between a "normal-cost system" and a "standard-cost system," as illustrated in Exhibit 10-10. Third, be sure you understand the variance analysis of fixed overhead illustrated in Exhibit 11-11.

The chapter concludes with a detailed example of flexible budgets and fixed overhead analysis. Follow the example through step by step before attempting the homework material.

CHAPTER HIGHLIGHTS AND STUDY GUIDE

A. The sales budgets, production budgets, and cash budgets which we studied in Chapter 8 are *static* budgets. They are static in the sense that they are geared toward a single level of activity.

1. The main deficiency of a static budget is that it fails to distinguish between the production control and cost control dimensions of a manager's responsibilities.

a. Production control means seeing that production goals in terms of output are met.

b. Cost control means seeing that the output of a period is produced at the least possible cost, consistent with quality standards.

2. Of these two responsibilities, the static budget does a good job of measuring only how well production goals are being met. The static budget can't be used to measure cost control, since actual activity will rarely coincide with the original static budget level.

B. A flexible budget is geared to a *range* of activity, rather than to a single level. This can be seen from the flexible budget presented in Exhibit 11-3. Notice especially how a "cost formula" is used in the flexible budget.

1. There are four basic steps involved in preparing a flexible budget:

a. Determine the relevant range of activity.

b. Separate costs by their cost behavior patterns (variable, fixed, mixed).

c. Analyze the mixed costs, as discussed in Chapter 6, by determining their fixed and variable elements.

d. Using the cost formulas developed in "b" and "c" above, prepare a budget showing what costs will be incurred at various points throughout the relevant range.

2. The flexible budget is a dynamic tool, in that budgeted costs can be developed to correspond to any actual level of activity within the relevant range.

3. The activity base underlying the flexible budget must be carefully chosen. Generally, this will be the same base as used in computing predetermined overhead rates (direct labor hours, machine hours, etc.).

4. Although the term "flexible budget" implies only variable costs, fixed costs are often included as well. This concept is illustrated in Exhibit 11-8 in the text.

a. One reason for including fixed costs is that the manager may have control over the fixed costs; if so, they should be used in the evaluation of his or her performance.

b. A second reason for including fixed costs is that the flexible budget is often used as a basis for computing predetermined overhead rates.

C. A performance report for variable overhead can be constructed to show just a spending variance or both a spending and an efficiency variance.

1. Just a spending variance will be shown on the performance report if budget allowances are based on the actual number of hours worked during the period.

a. In preparing a performance report, the cost formulas in the flexible budget are applied to the actual number of hours worked for the period.

b. The budget allowances computed in "a" above are then compared against actual costs of the period and a spending variance results. This concept is illustrated in Exhibit 11-11 in the text.

2. The overhead spending variance consists of two things: price variations and waste or excessive usage of overhead items.

a. Thus, the overhead spending variance contains both price and quantity (waste) elements. This makes it different from the price variance for materials and the rate variance for labor.

3. Both a spending and an efficiency variance will be shown on the performance report if budget allowances are based on both the actual number of hours worked and the standard hours allowed for the output of the period.

a. A performance report showing both variances is illustrated in Exhibit 11-7. Study the column headings in this exhibit carefully.

b. The term "overhead efficiency variance" is a misnomer. The inefficiency is really in the *base* underlying the application of overhead.

D. Flexible budgeting enhances a company's ability to construct and operate an activity-based costing system.

1. The key difference between a company that uses activity-based costing and one that uses a more traditional costing system lies in the *number* of flexible budgets that are used.

2. Under activity-based costing, a flexible budget is prepared for each activity center. Thus, if a company has five activity centers, it will have five flexible budgets.

E. The flexible budget often serves as the basis for computing predetermined overhead rates for product costing purposes.

1. The predetermined overhead rate formula is:

$$\frac{\text{Estimated manufacturing overhead costs}}{\substack{\text{Estimated direct labor} \\ \text{hours, etc.} \\ \text{(denominator activity)}}} = \substack{\text{Predetermined} \\ \text{overhead} \\ \text{rate}}$$

2. Notice that the estimated activity part of the formula is termed the "denominator activity."

3. Exhibit 11-10 is an extremely important exhibit in Chapter 11. It shows that overhead is applied to work in process differently under a standard-cost system than it is under a normal-cost system.

a. We studied normal-cost systems in Chapter 3. There we learned that overhead is applied by multiplying the predetermined overhead rate by the actual hours of activity for a period.

b. By contrast, under a standard-cost system overhead is applied to work in process by multiplying the predetermined overhead rate by the standard hours allowed for the output of the period.

F. Two variances can be computed for fixed overhead—a budget variance and a volume variance.

1. The budget variance represents the difference between actual fixed overhead costs and budgeted fixed overhead costs. The variance can be shown in the following format:

Actual fixed overhead costs .... $XXX
Budgeted fixed overhead costs
  (from the flexible budget) XXX
Budget variance .... $XXX

a. The fixed overhead budget variance is similar to the variable overhead spending variance.

b. However, one must keep in mind that fixed costs are often beyond immediate managerial control. When this is true, the budget variance will be largely informational in nature rather than a measure of managerial performance.

2. The volume variance is a measure of utilization of plant facilities. The formula is:

$$\substack{\text{Fixed portion} \\ \text{of the prede-} \\ \text{termined over-} \\ \text{head rate}} \times \left(\substack{\text{Denom-} \\ \text{inator} \\ \text{hours}} - \substack{\text{Stan-} \\ \text{dard} \\ \text{hours}} \right) = \substack{\text{Volume} \\ \text{variance}}$$

a. The volume variance does not measure over- or underspending. It is a measure only of plant utilization.

b. If the denominator activity and the standard hours allowed for the output of the period are the same, then there is no volume variance.

c. If the denominator activity is greater than the standard hours allowed for the output of the period, then the volume variance is unfavorable.

d. If the denominator activity is less than the standard hours allowed for the output of the period, then the volume variance is favorable.

REVIEW AND SELF TEST

Questions and Exercises

True or False

For each of the following statements, enter a T or an F in the blank to indicate whether the statement is true or false.

____ 1. A budget prepared for a single level of activity is called a static budget.

____ 2. The only difference between a flexible budget and a static budget is that a flexible budget never contains fixed costs.

____ 3. Although a static budget is effective in measuring production control, it is not effective in measuring cost control.

____ 4. A flexible budget is geared toward a range of activity rather than toward a single level of activity.

____ 5. Direct labor cost would generally be a better base to use in preparing a flexible budget than direct labor hours.

____ 6. A variable overhead spending variance is affected by waste and excessive usage as well as price differentials.

____ 7. In variable overhead analysis, the spending variance is generally viewed as being less useful to the manager than the efficiency variance.

____ 8. The term "overhead efficiency variance" is really a misnomer since this variance has nothing to do with efficiency in the use of overhead.

____ 9. If overhead is applied to production on a basis of direct labor hours, there will be a close relationship between the labor efficiency variance and the overhead efficiency variance.

____ 10. Fixed costs should never be included in the flexible budget.

____ 11. The flexible budget is often used as a basis for preparing the predetermined overhead rate.

____ 12. The estimated activity figure in the predetermined overhead rate formula is known as the denominator activity.

____ 13. The denominator activity figure should be changed from month to month as the level of actual activity rises and falls.

____ 14. Fixed overhead costs should never be included on the standard cost card.

____ 15. The fixed overhead budget variance is largely beyond the immediate control of management.

____ 16. The fixed overhead volume variance is a key measure of over- or underspending in an organization.

____ 17. If the denominator activity figure exceeds the standard hours allowed for the output of a period, one would expect the volume variance to be favorable.

____ 18. The volume variance is associated with fixed overhead rather than with variable overhead.

Multiple Choice

Choose the best answer or response by placing the identifying letter in the space provided.

____ 1. In a standard-cost system, overhead is applied to production on a basis of: a) the actual hours required to complete the output of the period; b) the standard hours allowed to complete the output of the period; c) the denominator hours chosen for the period; d) none of these.

____ 2. A flexible budget: a) is geared to a range of activity; b) excludes fixed costs; c) is conceptually inferior to a static budget; d) none of these.

____ 3. If the standard hours allowed for the output of a period exceed the denominator hours used in setting overhead rates, there will be: a) a favorable budget variance; b) an unfavorable budget variance; c) a favorable volume variance; d) an unfavorable volume variance; e) none of these.

____ 4. If a company has a large unfavorable volume variance, one would expect the Manufacturing Overhead account to show: a) underapplied overhead; b) overapplied overhead; c) the volume variance would have no effect on the manufacturing overhead account; d) none of these.

___ 5. The volume variance is a measure of: a) over- or underspending; b) the difference between actual fixed overhead costs and budgeted fixed overhead costs; c) plant utilization; d) responses *a, b,* and *c* are all correct; e) none of these.

___ 6. Herd Company reported the following data for 19x2: actual hours, 40,000; denominator hours, 50,000; standard hours allowed for output, 42,000. The predetermined overhead rate was $9 per hour, of which $3 was variable and $6 was fixed. Given these data, the company's volume variance for the year was: a) $12,000 U; b) $48,000 U; c) $72,000 F; d) $60,000 U.

Complete the Statements

Fill in the necessary words to complete the following statements.

1. A production manager has two prime responsibilities to discharge in the performance of his duties—_____ control and _____ control.

2. A budget which is geared to a single level of activity is called a _____ budget.

3. The overhead spending variance is affected as much by _____ as it is by price changes. This is why it is called a "spending" variance.

4. The term "overhead _____ variance" is a misnomer, since it has nothing to do with the _____ of overhead.

5. The expected activity portion of the predetermined overhead rate formula is often called the _____ _____.

6. The _____ _____ _____ is often used as a basis for preparing predetermined overhead rates.

7. In a _____-cost system, overhead is applied to work in process on a basis of the standard hours allowed for the output of the period.

8. Two variances can be computed for fixed overhead, a _____ variance and a _____ variance.

9. If the denominator activity is less than the standard hours allowed for the output of the period, then the _____ variance will be _____.

10. There can be no volume variance for _____ overhead.

Exercises

11-1. Given the following cost formulas for overhead:

Item	Cost Formula
Utilities	$ 6,000 per year, plus $.30 per machine hour
Supplies	$10,000 per year, plus $.80 per machine hour
Depreciation	$25,000 per year
Indirect labor	$21,000 per year, plus $.40 per machine hour
Insurance	$ 8,000 per year

Complete the following flexible budget:

Overhead Costs	Cost Formula	Machine Hours 8,000	10,000	12,000
Variable overhead costs:				
Total variable costs				
Fixed overhead costs:				
Total fixed costs				
Total Overhead Costs				

11-2. Refer to the flexible budget data in Exercise 11-1. The standard time to complete one unit of product is 1.6 machine hours. For the year 19x2 the company budgeted to operate at a 10,000 machine-hour level of activity. During the year the following actual activity took place:

Number of units produced	5,000	units
Actual machine hours worked	8,500	hours
Overhead costs:		
Utilities ($6,000 fixed)	$ 8,500	
Supplies ($10,000 fixed)	17,000	
Indirect labor ($21,000 fixed)	25,000	
Depreciation	25,000	
Insurance	8,000	

Prepare a performance report for 19x2. Show only a spending variance on the report.

Performance Report
For the Year 19x2

Budgeted machine hours ....
Actual machine hours ....
Standard machine hours ....

	Cost Formula	Actual Costs Incurred 8,500 Hrs.	Budget Based on Hrs.	Spending Variance
Variable overhead costs:				
Fixed overhead costs:				
Total Overhead Costs				

11-3. The flexible budget for Marina Company is given below:

MARINA COMPANY
Flexible Budget

Overhead Costs	Formula	Direct Labor Hours 10,000	12,000	14,000
Variable costs:				
Electricity	$.15/DLH	$ 1,500	$ 1,800	$ 2,100
Indirect materials.........	.50/DLH	5,000	6,000	7,000
Indirect labor	.25/DLH	2,500	3,000	3,500
Total variable costs	$.90/DLH	9,000	10,800	12,600
Fixed costs:				
Depreciation		11,500	11,500	11,500
Property taxes.........................		8,500	8,500	8,500
Insurance		4,000	4,000	4,000
Total fixed costs		24,000	24,000	24,000
Total Overhead Costs		$33,000	$34,800	$36,600

A denominator activity level of 12,000 direct labor hours is used in setting predetermined overhead rates. The standard time to complete one unit of product is 1.5 direct labor hours.

For the company's most recent year, the following actual operating data are available:

Units produced	9,000 units
Actual direct labor hours worked	14,000 hours
Actual fixed overhead cost	$23,750

a. Compute the predetermined overhead rate that would be used by the company, and break it down into variable and fixed cost elements:

Predetermined overhead rate ....$_____
Variable cost element ....$_____
Fixed cost element ....$_____

b. How much overhead would have been applied to work
in process during the most recent year? ....$_____
How much of the overhead applied was variable? .....$_____
How much of the overhead applied was fixed? ....$_____

c. Complete the following analysis of fixed overhead cost for the company's most recent year:

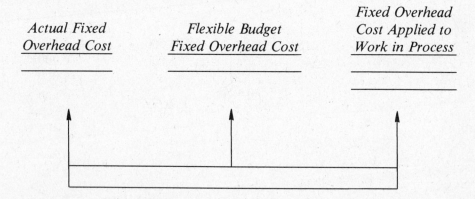

Actual Fixed Overhead Cost	*Flexible Budget Fixed Overhead Cost*	*Fixed Overhead Cost Applied to Work in Process*

d. Redo the variance analysis of fixed overhead, using the following alternate formats:

Actual fixed overhead cost .... $
Budgeted fixed overhead cost .... _____
Budget variance .... $_____

Fixed Portion of the Predetermined Overhead Rate $\times$ (Denominator Hours $-$ Standard Hours Allowed) $=$ Volume Variance

11-4. **Critical thought writing exercise:** Taylor Company's manufacturing overhead cost was overapplied for 19x3. Would you expect the total of the company's overhead variances for the year to be favorable or unfavorable? Why?

_____

_____

_____

_____

_____

_____

_____

_____

Chapter 11
Answers to Questions and Exercises

True or False

1. T   This statement is true by definition.

2. F   The difference between a flexible budget and a static budget is that a flexible budget is geared to a range of activity whereas a static budget is geared toward only a single level of activity.

3. T   The major problem with the static budget approach is that it is not effective in measuring cost control.

4. T   This statement is true by definition.

5. F   Direct labor cost is influenced by many variables, such as wage rate changes, that make it difficult to use as a base in preparing a flexible budget.

6. T   The inclusion of waste elements in the spending variance is what makes it different from the materials price variance and the labor rate variance.

7. F   The reverse is true—the spending variance is generally viewed as being more useful than the efficiency variance.

8. T   The overhead efficiency variance really measures efficiency in the *base* underlying the application of overhead.

9. T   The reason for the close relationship is that both variances will be computed using the same hours figures.

10. F   Fixed costs should always be included in the flexible budget (1) if the manager has control over the costs or (2) if the flexible budget is to be used as a basis for preparing predetermined overhead rates.

11. T   The flexible budget is the source of both the estimated cost and the estimated activity figures needed for computing the predetermined overhead rate.

12. T   This statement is true by definition.

13. F   The denominator activity figure is typically selected before the year begins, and it is left unchanged throughout the year.

14. F   Fixed overhead cost must be included on the standard cost card to show the full cost of a unit of product.

15. T   The fixed overhead budget variance is typically a result of changes in property tax rates, insurance rates, and so forth, which are beyond the immediate control of management.

16. F   The fixed overhead volume variance is a measure of capacity utilization—not a measure of spending.

17. F   The reverse is true—one would expect the volume variance to be unfavorable.

18. T   There can be no volume variance with variable overhead.

Multiple Choice

1. b   This point is illustrated in Exhibit 11-10.

2. a   A flexible budget is geared to all levels of activity within the relevant range.

3. c   The volume variance will be favorable because more hours will have been worked (at standard) than was planned for during the period; this is viewed as being a favorable situation since the company's facilities will have been utilized to a greater extent than was anticipated when the period began.

4. a   An unfavorable volume variance would mean that less overhead cost was applied to production than planned; therefore, the Manufacturing Overhead account would show underapplied overhead cost for the period.

5. c   The volume variance measures how much the company's plant has been utilized in comparison to the level planned for the period.

6. b   The computations are:

$$\begin{pmatrix} \text{Fixed portion} \\ \text{of the prede-} \\ \text{termined over-} \\ \text{head rate} \end{pmatrix} \times \begin{pmatrix} \text{Denom-} \\ \text{inator} \\ \text{hours} \end{pmatrix} - \begin{pmatrix} \text{Stan-} \\ \text{dard} \\ \text{hours} \end{pmatrix} = \begin{pmatrix} \text{Volume} \\ \text{variance} \end{pmatrix}$$

$6(50,000 \text{ hours} - 42,000 \text{ hours}) = \$48,000 \text{ U}$

Complete the Statements

1. activity, cost
2. static
3. waste
4. efficiency, efficiency
5. denominator activity
6. overhead flexible budget
7. standard
8. budget, volume
9. volume, favorable
10. variable

Exercises

11-1.

Overhead Costs	Cost Formula	Machine Hours		
		8,000	10,000	12,000
Variable overhead costs:				
Utilities......................	$ .30/MH	$ 2,400	$ 3,000	$ 3,600
Supplies	.80/MH	6,400	8,000	9,600
Indirect labor..................	.40/MH	3,200	4,000	4,800
Total variable costs............	$1.50/MH	12,000	15,000	18,000
Fixed overhead costs:				
Utilities		6,000	6,000	6,000
Supplies.......................		10,000	10,000	10,000
Depreciation...................		25,000	25,000	25,000
Indirect labor		21,000	21,000	21,000
Insurance		8,000	8,000	8,000
Total fixed costs...............		70,000	70,000	70,000
Total Overhead Costs		$82,000	$85,000	$88,000

11-2.

Performance Report
For the Year 19x2

Budgeted machine hours	10,000
Actual machine hours	8,500
Standard machine hours	8,000

	Cost Formula	Actual Costs Incurred 8,500 Hrs.	Budget Based on 8,500 Hrs.	Spending Variance
Variable overhead costs:				
Utilities........................	$ .30/MH	$ 2,500*	$ 2,550	$ (50)
Supplies	.80/MH	7,000	6,800	200
Indirect labor...................	.40/MH	4,000	3,400	600
Total variable costs.............	$1.50/MH	13,500	12,750	750
Fixed overhead costs:				
Utilities		6,000	6,000	—
Supplies........................		10,000	10,000	—
Depreciation....................		25,000	25,000	—
Indirect labor		21,000	21,000	—
Insurance		8,000	8,000	—
Total fixed costs................		70,000	70,000	—
Total Overhead Costs		$83,500	$82,750	$750

*$8,500 − $6,000 = $2,500.

11-3. a. Predetermined overhead rate: $34,800 ÷ 12,000 DLH = $2.90/DLH

> Variable element: $10,800 ÷ 12,000 DLH = $.90/DLH
> Fixed element: $24,000 ÷ 12,000 DLH = $2.00/DLH

b. Overhead applied:

> 9,000 units × 1.5 hrs./unit = 13,500 standard hours allowed
> 13,500 standard hours × $2.90 = $39,150 overhead applied

> Variable element: 13,500 standard hours × $.90 = $12,150
> Fixed element: 13,500 standard hours × $2.00 = $27,000

c.

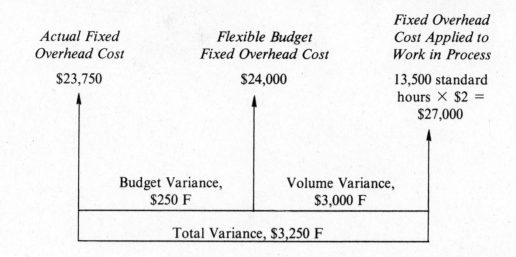

Actual Fixed Overhead Cost	Flexible Budget Fixed Overhead Cost	Fixed Overhead Cost Applied to Work in Process
$23,750	$24,000	13,500 standard hours × $2 = $27,000

Budget Variance, $250 F   Volume Variance, $3,000 F

Total Variance, $3,250 F

d. Actual fixed overhead cost $23,750
Budgeted fixed overhead cost 24,000
Budget Variance, Favorable .... $ (250)

$2.00 (12,000 hrs. − 13,500 hrs.) = $3,000 F

11-4. The total overhead variances would be favorable. If manufacturing overhead cost is overapplied for the year, then a credit balance exists in the account. As we learned in the prior chapter, favorable variances appear as credit balances in the accounts. Thus, overapplied overhead cost, which appears as a credit balance, would consist of a net amount of favorable variances.

Segment Reporting, Profitability Analysis, and Decentralization

Chapter Study Suggestions

This chapter is divided into three parts. The first part covers segment reporting. Before you start reading this part of the chapter, study Exhibits 12-2, 12-3, and 12-4. These exhibits illustrate what is meant by the term *segment reporting*. Notice particularly that on a segmented report the total company is divided into smaller parts, so that the manager can look at various pieces of the company rather than just at the whole. In studying the text material, spend the time necessary to fully understand the difference between direct and common costs, and the difference between segment margin and contribution margin.

The second part of the chapter covers responsibility accounting, along with return on investment (ROI) and residual income computations. The formulas for ROI and residual income should be committed to memory, since they are used extensively in the homework material.

The third part of the chapter deals with transfer pricing. A general formula is given for computing a transfer price, which you should learn immediately. In your study, you should spend the bulk of your time on the sections dealing with transfers at market price and at negotiated price. These are the key sections in this part of the chapter.

CHAPTER HIGHLIGHTS AND STUDY GUIDE

A. Three business practices are in use that greatly hinder proper cost assignment to segments of a company. These three practices are discussed below.

1. Some costs are omitted in the assignment process. Companies assign the manufacturing costs, but frequently do not assign the selling, general, and administrative costs to products. All costs along the *value chain* should be assigned in order to determine product profitability.

2. Companies often fail to trace costs directly to segments. Rather, they often use a base such as sales dollars to assign costs. This practice results in a cross-subsidization of costs between segments.

3. Companies sometimes try to allocate common costs to segments.

B. To operate effectively, the manager needs much more information than that provided by a single income statement. He or she needs information that focuses on the *segments* of the organization.

1. A segment can be defined as any part or activity of an organization about which the manager seeks cost data. Examples of segments would include sales territories, manufacturing divisions, producing departments and/or operations, and groups or lines of products.

2. Internally, segmented reports are prepared in the contribution format with which you are already familiar.

3. Exhibit 12-2 contains an illustration of one way that a series of segmented reports can be prepared. Notice that as we go from one segmented report to another in the exhibit, we are looking at smaller and smaller pieces of the company.

4. By preparing segmented reports such as those illustrated in Exhibit 12-2, the manager may uncover problems that otherwise would have remained hidden from view. For example, some product lines may be unprofitable; some sales territories may have a poor sales mix; other sales territories may be using ineffective promotional strategies, etc. Problems such as these can be highlighted by the use of segmented reports.

C. Two general guidelines are used in allocating costs to the various segments when the contribution approach is used.

1. First, costs are allocated according to cost behavior patterns; that is, according to whether they are variable or fixed.

2. Second, costs are allocated according to whether they are *traceable* or *common* to the various segments.

a. Only traceable costs are charged directly to the segments.

b. Common costs are not charged to the segments; rather, common costs are kept separate from the segments and charged only against the company as a whole.

D. A key concept in the chapter is the distinction between traceable and common fixed costs.

1. The placement of traceable and common fixed costs on a segmented income statement is as follows:

	Total	Segment A	Segment B
Sales	$XXXX	$XX	$XX
Less variable expenses .	XXX	X	X
Contribution margin . .	XXX	X	X
Less traceable fixed expenses	XX	X	X
Segment margin	XX	$ X	$ X
Less common fixed expenses	X		
Net Income	$ X		

2. Classifications between traceable and common fixed costs are not static. As an organization is segmented into smaller and smaller pieces, some costs which were previously traceable will become common. This is because there are limits to how finely a cost can be divided.

3. The segment margin is a highly useful piece of data, showing the manager the long-run profitability of a segment after it has covered all of the costs which can be traced directly to it.

a. The segment margin is used by the manager in decision situations relating to long-run needs and performance, such as capacity changes, long-run pricing policy, and segment return on investment.

b. By contrast, the contribution margin is most useful in those situations involving short-run decisions, such as pricing of special orders and special promotional campaigns.

4. Common costs are not allocated to segments, since such an allocation would destroy the usefulness of the segment margin as a tool for assessing segment performance.

a. In addition, allocating common costs may create a bias for or against a particular segment, since such allocations are always arbitrary in nature.

E. A responsibility accounting system functions best in an organization that is *decentralized*. A decentralized organization is one in which decision making is spread throughout the organization, with managers at all levels making decisions relating to their sphere of responsibility.

F. In a decentralized organization, the responsibility accounting system is structured around a number of centers. These consist of cost centers, profit centers, and investment centers, each of which defines an area of responsibility in the organization.

1. A cost center is any responsibility center that has control over the incurrence of cost. A cost center has no control over revenues.

2. A profit center has control over both cost and revenue.

3. An investment center has control over cost and revenue, and also has control over the use of investment funds. "Investment" represents the investment in plant and equipment, receivables, inventory, and other assets.

G. The concepts of responsibility accounting are very important, since they assist in defining a manager's sphere of responsibility and also in determining how performance will be evaluated, as shown below:

Type of Center	*Measure of Performance*	*Manager Goal*
Cost Center	Cost standards or budgets	Minimizing costs in achieving objectives.
Profit Center	Income statement	Maximize net income by meeting sales and cost objectives.
Investment Center	Return on investment	Maximize net income by meeting sales and cost objectives, and do so by fully utilizing investment funds. In other words, maximize ROI.

H. As stated above, performance in an investment center is measured by the return on investment (ROI) formula. The ROI formula is: Margin x Turnover = Return on investment (ROI), where:

$$\text{Margin} = \frac{\text{Net operating income}}{\text{Sales}}$$

$$\text{Turnover} = \frac{\text{Sales}}{\text{Operating assets}}$$

Therefore, the ROI formula becomes:

$$\frac{\text{Net operating income}}{\text{Sales}} \times \frac{\text{Sales}}{\text{Operating assets}} = \text{ROI}$$

The formula can be factored into simpler form as:

$$\frac{\text{Net operating income}}{\text{Operating assets}} = \text{ROI}$$

1. Net operating income is income before interest and taxes. It is also known as EBIT (earnings before interest and taxes).

2. Operating assets would include cash, accounts receivable, inventory, and all other assets held for productive use in an organization. Assets common to all divisions (such as assets associated with corporate headquarters) should not be allocated to the divisions in making ROI computations.

I. A company's return on investment can be improved if the manager can either (1) increase sales, (2) reduce expenses, or (3) reduce assets.

J. Another approach to measuring performance in an investment center is known as *residual income*. Residual income is the net operating income which an investment center is able to earn *above* some minimum rate of return on operating assets.

1. When residual income is used to measure performance, the purpose is to maximize the total amount of residual income, not to maximize the overall ROI figure.

2. Residual income is computed as follows:

Average operating assets	$100,000
Net operating income	$ 25,000
Minimum required rate of return is assumed to be 20%.	
20% × $100,000	20,000
Residual income	$ 5,000

3. Residual income is viewed by some to be a better measure of performance than ROI since it encourages investment in projects that would be rejected under ROI.

4. A major disadvantage of the residual income approach is that it can't be used to compare divisions of different sizes. The reason is that it can create a bias in favor of the larger divisions, due to the larger numbers involved.

K. A transfer price is the price charged by one segment of an organization for a good or service which it provides to another segment of the organization. Three general approaches are used in setting transfer prices: (1) set transfer prices at cost, (2) set transfer prices at market price, and (3) set transfer prices at a negotiated price.

L. Many firms base transfer prices on cost. This can consist either of the variable costs of the goods being transferred, or fixed costs may also be included, with the transfer price thus based on full (absorption) costs.

1. Although cost-based transfer prices are widely used, they have a number of disadvantages.

a. They can lead to dysfunctional decisions in a company, because they have no built-in mechanism for telling the manager when transfers should or should not be made between divisions.

b. The only division that will show any profits is the one that makes a final sale to an outside party. Other divisions will show no profits for their efforts, and therefore evaluation by the ROI formula, or by the residual income approach, will not be possible.

c. There is no incentive for the control of costs, since one division simply passes its costs on to the next division.

2. As a partial offset to these shortcomings, advocates of cost-based transfer prices argue that they are easily understood and highly convenient to use.

3. If cost-based transfer prices are used, then they should be standard costs, rather than actual costs. This will avoid the passing on of inefficiency from one division to another.

M. Some form of competitive market price is generally regarded as the best approach to the transfer pricing problem.

1. The general formula for computing a market-based transfer price is:

$$\text{Transfer price} = \text{Variable costs per unit} + \text{Lost contribution margin per unit on outside sales}$$

2. Use of market price as a transfer price overcomes the disadvantages listed above in connection with cost-based transfer prices.

3. In addition to the formula given above, there are certain guidelines that should be followed when using market prices to control transfers between divisions. These guidelines are:

a. The buying division must purchase internally so long as the selling division meets all bona fide outside prices.

b. If the selling division does not meet all bona fide outside prices, then the buying division is free to purchase outside.

c. The selling division must be free to reject internal business if it prefers to sell outside.

d. An impartial board must be established to arbitrate all disputes over prices.

4. One reason for using market price in transfer pricing is to guard against setting transfer prices below the selling division's opportunity costs. (Opportunity cost can be defined as the potential benefit that is lost or sacrificed when the choice of one course of action makes it necessary to give up a competing course of action.)

a. If the selling division is selling all that it can produce to outside customers, then its opportunity cost is the contribution margin that will be lost as a result of giving up any of these outside sales.

b. The transfer price charged internally must be set high enough to cover this opportunity cost, along with the variable costs associated with the sale, or both the selling division and the company as a whole will suffer a loss of profits.

5. If the selling division has idle capacity, then so long as the transfer price it receives is greater than its variable costs, all parties will benefit by having the buying division purchase inside rather than going outside.

a. If the selling division has idle capacity, and the buying division purchases outside, then suboptimization will result, which means that overall company profitability will be less than it could have been.

b. Where idle capacity exists, the buying and selling divisions will often negotiate a transfer price somewhere between the selling division's variable costs and the current market price.

N. Sometimes transfer prices are based on a negotiated price. A negotiated price is a price agreed upon between the buying and selling divisions that reflects unusual or mitigating circumstances.

1. Possibly the widest use of negotiated prices is in those situations where no intermediate market price exists. For example, the selling division may produce an item that is not available anywhere else.

2. Negotiated prices are also used when the selling division has idle capacity, as mentioned above, and when the buying division purchases in large enough quantities to justify a quantity discount.

O. There is a difficult balance between respecting divisional autonomy in a company and still optimizing profits. The overwhelming experience of multidivisional companies is that divisional autonomy and independent profit responsibility lead to much greater success and profitability than closely-controlled, centrally administered operations.

REVIEW AND SELF TEST
Questions and Exercises

True or False

For each of the following statements, enter a T or an F in the blank to indicate whether the statement is true or false.

_____ 1. Common costs should be allocated to product line segments on a basis of sales dollars.

_____ 2. A series of segmented reports focuses on progressively smaller pieces of an organization.

_____ 3. Contribution margin is basically a short-run planning tool and is especially valuable in decisions relating to temporary uses of capacity, special orders, and short-run promotional strategy.

_____ 4. A key idea relating to the contribution approach to costing is that fixed costs are relatively unimportant in most organizations.

_____ 5. The terms "traceable cost" and "variable cost" are synonymous.

_____ 6. As an organization is broken down into smaller segments, costs that were traceable to the larger segments may become common to the smaller segments.

_____ 7. The segment margin is viewed as being the best gauge of the long-run profitability of a segment.

_____ 8. A decentralized organization is one in which decision making is confined to top management.

_____ 9. Residual income is equal to the difference between total revenues and operating expenses.

_____ 10. Use of the ROI formula may cause rejection of investment opportunities that would be beneficial to the company as a whole.

_____ 11. A profit center is responsible for generating revenue, but it is not responsible for controlling costs.

_____ 12. When a division is operating at capacity, the transfer price to other divisions includes an element of opportunity cost.

_____ 13. Transfer prices based on cost are superior in that they provide incentive for the control of costs between transferring divisions.

_____ 14. A reduction in operating assets will increase a division's ROI even if sales and expenses remain unchanged.

_____ 15. One way for a manager to improve his or her division's ROI is to increase the operating assets.

_____ 16. In computing the residual income, expenses incurred in operating corporate headquarters should be allocated to the separate divisions on the basis of sales dollars.

_____ 17. Under the residual income approach, the manager seeks to maximize the rate of return on operating assets.

_____ 18. Using "cost" as a transfer price can lead to reduced profits in a company.

_____ 19. The residual income approach is superior to ROI as a method of measuring performance in divisions that differ substantially in size.

_____ 20. In a decentralized organization, decision making takes place at many levels of management.

_____ 21. An increase in total sales would typically increase the turnover of assets but it would have no effect on the margin.

_____ 22. The transfer price established by the transfer pricing formula represents a lower limit for a transfer price, but frequently the transfer price can be higher.

_____ 23. Any transfer price different from the one set by the transfer pricing formula will result in lower profits for the company as a whole.

Multiple Choice

Choose the best answer or response by placing the identifying letter in the space provided.

_____ 1. If the level of inventory in a company is reduced, and if sales and expenses remain unchanged, one would expect the company's ROI to: a) increase; b) decrease; c) remain unchanged; d) it is impossible to tell what would happen to ROI; e) none of these.

_____ 2. Given the following data:

Total liabilities	$ 30,000
Average operating assets	45,000
Sales	180,000
Contribution margin	21,600
Net operating income	9,000

The company's ROI would be: a) 48%; b) 12%; c) 20% d) 30%; e) none of these.

_____ 3. The purpose of the residual income approach is to: a) maximize a segment's overall rate of return; b) maximize the ROI which a segment is able to get on its operating assets; c) maximize the total amount of the residual income; d) none of these.

_____ 4. Given the following data for Division A:

Selling price to outside customers $	60
Variable cost per unit	40
Total fixed cost	100,000
Capacity in units	20,000

Division B now purchases 5,000 units from an outside supplier at a price of $58 per unit. If Division B wants to purchase these 5,000 units from Division A, and Division A has no idle capacity, the transfer price should be: a) $60; b) $58; c) $40; d) $45; e) none of these.

_____ 5. Refer to the data in question (4) above. If Division A has idle capacity, the transfer price should be: a) $60; b) $40; c) between $45 and $58; d) between $40 and $58; e) none of these.

_____ 6. A manager can *always* increase a division's ROI by: a) expanding the operating assets while holding sales and expenses constant; b) increasing the division's residual income; c) increasing sales while holding expenses and operating assets constant; d) responses (a), (b), and (c) are all correct.

_____ 7. The market price approach to transfer pricing is designed for use in: a) highly centralized organizations; b) organizations in which little or no autonomy is given to divisional managers; c) organizations which cannot use the return on investment formula; d) none of these.

_____ 8. A negotiated market price should be used when: a) the selling division is operating at full capacity, selling all that it can produce in an intermediate market; b) the residual income approach is used to measure divisional performance; c) the selling division is the only supplier of the goods being transferred; d) none of these.

_____ 9. Armco, Inc., produces and sells five product lines. Which of the following costs would typically be a traceable fixed cost of one product line: a) advertising costs of the product lines; b) the salary of the company's president; c) depreciation of facilities used jointly to produce several product lines; d) responses a, b, and c, are all correct.

_____ 10. If a segment has a negative segment margin: a) the segment should be dropped; b) the segment should be retained only if it has a positive contribution margin; c) the segment is not covering its own traceable costs, but it still may be of benefit to the company; d) none of these.

Complete the Statements

Fill in the necessary words to complete the following statements.

1. _____ _____ is a reporting system in which costs are accumulated and reported by levels of responsibility in an organization.

2. A responsibility accounting system functions most effectively in an organization that is highly _____.

3. By contrast to a cost center, a _____ center has control over both cost and revenue.

4. The return on investment formula is used to measure performance in a/an _____ center.

5. When being measured by the ROI formula, a manager can improve his or her division's performance by increasing _____, by reducing _____, or by reducing _____.

6. It is argued that the _____ _____ approach to performance evaluation encourages managers to make profitable investments that would be rejected by managers being measured by the _____ approach.

7. The transfer pricing formula states that the transfer price should be equal to the unit _____ _____ of the good being transferred, plus the _____ _____ per unit which is lost to the selling division as a result of giving up outside sales.

8. Some form of competitive _____ _____ is generally regarded as the best approach to the transfer pricing problem.

9. If the selling division has _____ _____, then any price which it receives above its variable costs will improve profits for both it and the company as a whole.

10. _____ is computed by dividing sales by the operating assets.

11. To uncover problems such as unprofitable product lines and a poor sales mix, the manager needs income statement data that focus on the _____ of a company.

12. Costs that are shared jointly by several segments of a company are called _____ costs.

13. The manager should treat as _____ costs of a segment only those costs that are added as a result of adding the segment.

14. The _____ margin is viewed as being the best gauge of the long-run profitability of a segment.

Exercises

12-1. Fill in the missing information:

	Company		
	1	2	3
Sales	$750,000	$600,000	$ _____
Net operating income	60,000	_____	27,000
Average operating assets	300,000	200,000	_____
Margin	_____	7.5%	_____
Turnover	_____	_____	1.8
Return on investment (ROI)	_____	_____	27%

12-2. Frankel Company uses the residual income approach to measure performance in its divisions. For the year 19x5, Division A reported the following data: sales, $2,000,000; net operating income, $160,000; average operating assets, $800,000. The company feels that the divisions should earn a minimum return of 16 percent on their assets. Compute Division A's residual income for 19x5:

Net operating income .... $

Minimum required net operating
income (   ) ....   _____

Residual income .... $ _____

12-3. Perchon Company's Division A produces a small valve that is used by many outside manufacturers as a key part in their products. Cost and sales data relating to the valve are given below:

Selling price per unit $50
Variable costs per unit   30
Fixed costs per unit   12*

*Based on Division A's capacity of 40,000 valves per year.

Perchon Company's Division B is introducing a new product that will use a valve such as the one produced in Division A. An outside supplier has quoted Division B a price of $48 per valve. This represents the normal $50 price, less a quantity discount due to the large number of valves which Division B will be purchasing. Division B would like to purchase the valves from Division A, if an acceptable transfer price can be worked out.

a.   Assume that Division A is presently selling all of the valves it can produce to outside customers. Use the transfer pricing formula to determine the transfer price it should quote to Division B:

Transfer price = Variable costs per unit + Lost contribution margin per unit on outside sales

b.   Should Division B purchase the valves from Division A or from the outside supplier? Explain.

_____

_____

_____

_____

c.   Assume Division B needs 15,000 valves per year. If it purchases the valves from Division A at the price you have computed above, what will be the effect on overall company profits?

_____

_____

_____

_____

d.   Refer to the original data. Assume that Division A has ample idle capacity to handle all of Division B's needs. Use the transfer pricing formula to determine the minimum acceptable transfer price between the two divisions.

e.   Under the conditions given in "d" above, what is the *maximum* acceptable transfer price between the two divisions? Explain.

_____

_____

_____

_____

12-4. From the following data, prepare a segmented income statement for the Bylund Company for July 19X8

	Total	Product X	Product Y
Number of units sold	—	10,000	12,000
Selling price per unit	—	$20.00	$25.00
Variable cost per unit:			
Production	—	9.00	10.00
Selling and administrative	—	3.00	3.75
Fixed costs:			
Production	$155,000		
Selling and administrative	20,000		

Some $50,000 of the fixed production costs are traceable directly to the production of Product X and $75,000 are traceable directly to the production of Product Y.

BYLUND COMPANY
Income Statement
For the Month Ended July 31, 19x8

	Total		Product X		Product Y	
	Amount	%	Amount	%	Amount	%
Sales	$_____	__	$_____	__	$_____	__
Less variable expenses:						
Total variable expenses	_____	__	_____	__	_____	__
Contribution margin						
Less traceable fixed expenses	_____		_____	__	_____	__
Product line segment margin	_____		_____	__	_____	__
Less common fixed expenses:						
Total fixed expenses	_____					
Net Income	$_____					

12-5. **Critical thought writing exercise:** One criticism of ROI is that it can lead to dysfunctional decisions in a company. In what way can it lead to dysfunctional decisions, and how can the problem be avoided?

_____

_____

_____

_____

_____

_____

_____

_____

Chapter 12
Answers to Questions and Exercises

True or False

1. F Common costs should never be allocated to segments since such allocations are arbitrary and could prove to be misleading to managers.

2. T This point is illustrated in Exhibit 12-2.

3. T Contribution margin is a short-run planning tool because the elements involved—selling price, variable expense, and volume—can be adjusted as needed in the short run to achieve desired results.

4. F Fixed costs are very important in any organization. They are separated from the variable costs under the contribution approach because they behave differently and therefore must be controlled differently.

5. F A traceable cost can be either variable or fixed.

6. T The reason that more costs become common as an organization is divided into smaller and smaller segments is that there are limits to how finely a cost can be divided.

7. T The segment margin is the best gauge of the long-run profitability of a segment because in the long run a segment must cover all of its costs—both variable and fixed.

8. F In a decentralized organization, decision making is spread through all levels of management.

9. F Residual income is the difference between net operating income and the minimum return that must be generated on operating assets.

10. T This is a major criticism of the ROI method.

11. F A profit center is responsible for controlling costs as well as generating revenues. Typically, the costs would be those that appear on the profit center's income statement.

12. T The opportunity cost is the contribution margin lost from giving up outside sales.

13. F The opposite is true—studies show that when cost is used as a transfer price, there is little or no incentive to control costs since whatever amount is incurred can simply be transferred on to the next division.

14. T A reduction in assets will result in an increase in the turnover figure, and an increase in the ROI.

15. F A reverse is true, for the reason stated in the answer to question 14 above.

16. F Common expenses, such as those associated with operating corporate headquarters, should not be allocated to segments when making either residual income or ROI computations.

17. F Under the residual income approach, the manager seeks to maximize the residual income figure.

18. T The use of "cost" as a transfer price provides no signal to the manager as to when transfers should not be made; thus, a transfer can be made that will reduce the company's profits.

19. F The reverse is true, since residual income can't be used to measure performance in divisions that differ substantially in size.

20. T This statement is true by definition.

21. F The margin would also increase, since the net operating income would generally increase more rapidly than sales (due to the effects of operating leverage).

22. T The transfer price can be higher, for example, when the selling division has idle capacity or when costs can be avoided on intracompany sales.

23. F   The transfer price can be higher in some situations, as explained in the answer to question (22) above. However, the transfer price can never be lower than the one set by the transfer pricing formula.

Multiple Choice

1. a   If the level of inventory is reduced, then operating assets will also be reduced. The result will be a higher turnover figure and an increase in the ROI.

2. c   The computations are:

$$\frac{\$9,000}{\$180,000} \times \frac{\$180,000}{\$45,000} = ROI$$

$$5\% \times 4 = 20\%$$

3. c   Residual income has nothing to do with ROI; moreover, as residual income increases ROI frequency decreases (as shown in examples in the chapter). The only purpose of residual income is to maximize the total amount of residual income generated by a segment.

4. a   The computations are:

Transfer price = Variable costs + Lost contribution margin
Transfer price = $40 + ($60 − $40 = $20)
Transfer price = $60

5. d   The computations are:

Transfer price = Variable costs + Lost contribution margin
Transfer price = $40 + $ -0-
Transfer price = $40

But $40 represents a lower limit for a transfer price; the price can be as high as the $58 that Division B is presently paying to the outside supplier. Thus, the transfer price should be within the range of $40 to $58 per unit.

6. c   Response (a) is not correct, since expanding the operating assets will result in a reduced turnover and a lower ROI; response (b) is not correct, since increasing the residual income will not *always* increase the ROI (as illustrated in the examples in the chapter). Response (c) is correct, since an increase in sales will increase both the margin and the turnover, and thus increase the ROI.

7. d   The market price approach is designed for use in highly decentralized organizations in which a large amount of autonomy is given to divisional managers.

8. c   If the selling division is the only supplier of the goods being transferred, then no market price exists and one must be negotiated between the buying and selling divisions.

9. a   Since advertising costs would arise because of the existence of the various product lines and tailored to the needs of these lines, the advertising costs would be traceable fixed costs on a segmented statement.

10. c   A negative segment margin means that a segment is not covering its own traceable costs. However, the segment may still be of value to the company if it is necessary to the sale of other product.

Complete the Statements

1. Responsibility accounting
2. decentralized
3. profit
4. investment
5. sales; expenses; assets
6. residual income; ROI
7. variable costs; contribution margin
8. market price
9. idle capacity
10. Turnover
11. segments
12. common
13. traceable
14. segment

Exercises

12-1.

	Company		
	1	*2*	*3*
Sales	$750,000*	$600,000*	$180,000
Net operating income	60,000*	45,000	27,000*
Average operating assets	300,000*	200,000*	100,000
Margin	8%	7.5% *	15%
Turnover	2.5	3	1.8*
Return on investment (ROI)	20%	22.5%	27%*

*Given

12-2.

Net operating income	$160,000
Minimum required net operating income (16% × $800,000)	128,000
Residual income	$ 32,000

12-3.

a. Transfer Price = $30 + $20 ($50 − $30 = $20)
    Transfer Price = $50

b. Division B should purchase the valves from an outside supplier, since the price will be only $48 per valve, as compared to a price of $50 internally. Division A can't accept less than $50 per valve, since it is presently receiving this amount from outside customers. Thus, the $50 represents Division A's opportunity cost per valve.

c. Overall company profits will be reduced by $30,000 per year. Division B will be paying $2 per valve more than it should be paying, thus reducing the company's profits by a total of $30,000 per year: $2 × 15,000 valves = $30,000.

d. Transfer Price = $30 + $-0- (No lost contribution margin, since Division A has idle capacity.)
    Transfer Price = $30

e. The maximum acceptable transfer price is $48 per valve. This is the price that Division B would have to pay to the outside supplier. The $50 normal price can't be justified, since Division A has idle capacity.

12-4.

BYLUND COMPANY
Income Statement
For the Month Ended July 31, 19x8

	Total Amount	%	Product X Amount	%	Product Y Amount	%
Sales	$500,000	100	$200,000	100	$300,000	100
Less variable expenses:						
Production	210,000	42	90,000	45	120,000	40
Selling and administrative	75,000	15	30,000	15	45,000	15
Total variable expenses	285,000	57	120,000	60	165,000	55
Contribution margin	215,000	43	80,000	40	135,000	45
Less traceable fixed expenses	125,000	25	50,000	25	75,000	25
Product line segment margin	90,000	18	$ 30,000	15	$ 60,000	20
Less common fixed expenses:						
Production	30,000					
Selling and administrative	20,000					
Total fixed expenses	50,000					
Net Income	$ 40,000					

12-5. ROI can lead to dysfunctional decisions in that an investment center manager may reject an otherwise profitable investment opportunity simply because the return from the investment would reduce the investment center's overall ROI. That is, the return from the investment might be greater than the ROI being earned in the company as a whole, but less than the ROI being earned in the investment center itself. Thus, accepting the investment would benefit the company as a whole, but reduce the overall return to the investment center. This problem can be overcome by using residual income, rather than ROI, in evaluating performance in an investment center.

Chapter 13

Relevant Costs for Decision Making

Chapter Study Suggestions

In the first few pages of the chapter, guidelines are given for identifying relevant costs. Study these pages carefully, since these guidelines are used many times in the remaining pages of the chapter to show how relevant costs can be identified in various decision-making situations.

Three decision-making situations identified in the chapter are of particular importance. These are (1) adding and dropping product lines, (2) make or buy, and (3) sell or process further. Concentrate your study on Exhibits 13-3, 13-5, and 13-7, which deal with these three topics. You must have a thorough understanding of the analytical procedure followed in each of these exhibits in order to be able to do the homework material.

CHAPTER HIGHLIGHTS AND STUDY GUIDE

A. A relevant cost can be defined as a cost which is applicable to a particular decision in the sense that it will have a bearing on which alternative the manager selects.

1. All costs are relevant in decision making except costs which are not avoidable. Costs which are not avoidable fall into two categories: (a) sunk costs, and (b) future costs which do not differ between alternatives.

2. The relevant costs in a decision can also be identified as those costs (and revenues) which are differential between the alternatives being considered.

3. To identify those costs which are differential and therefore relevant, the manager should take the following steps:

a. Assemble *all* costs associated with *each* alternative being considered.

b. Eliminate those costs which are sunk.

c. Eliminate those costs which do not differ between alternatives.

d. Make a decision based on the remaining cost data. These will be the differential or avoidable costs, and hence the costs relevant to the decision to be made.

4. Costs which are relevant in one situation may not be relevant in another situation. Simply put, this means that the manager needs different costs for different purposes.

B. Sunk costs are never relevant in decision making since they are not avoidable.

1. The book value of (and depreciation on) old equipment represents a sunk cost. Hence, it is not relevant in decision making.

2. However, we must note that depreciation is a sunk cost *only* if it relates to old equipment (e.g., equipment which has already been purchased). Thus, depreciation on *new* equipment would be a relevant cost in decision making.

C. Future costs that do not differ between alternatives are not relevant costs.

1. For example, Hewlett Company is considering the purchase of Machine A or Machine B. Main-tenance costs will be the same regardless of which machine is purchased. Thus, maintenance costs are irrelevant to the choice between the machines, since they will be of no help in determining which machine should be purchased.

2. Relevant costs should be isolated in cost analysis for two reasons:

a. Only rarely will enough information be available to prepare a detailed income statement such as those illustrated in the chapter. Typically, only limited data are available; therefore, the decision maker *must* know how to recognize which costs are relevant and which are not.

b. The use of irrelevant costs intermingled with relevant costs may draw the decision maker's attention away from the matters that are really critical to the problem being studied.

D. Adding or dropping product lines is a difficult problem with which management is confronted. Study the detailed example provided in the section titled, "Adding and Dropping Product Lines."

1. Notice that costs are classified as being either "avoidable" or "not avoidable" according to the guidelines given earlier.

2. In deciding whether a product line should be retained or dropped:

a. If the contribution margin which will be lost by dropping a product line is *greater* than the costs which will be avoided, then the product line should be retained.

b. If the contribution margin which will be lost by dropping a product line is *less* than the costs which will be avoided, then the line should be dropped.

3. An alternate approach to deciding whether to retain or drop a product line or other segment of a company is found in Exhibit 13-3. In this approach two income statements are prepared: one showing present operations, and another showing what costs and revenues would be if the product line was dropped. Study Exhibit 13-3 to see how this analysis is organized.

4. The decision to keep or drop a product line or other segment of a company is often clouded by the allocation of common fixed costs.

    a. Such allocations can make a product line or other segment *appear* to be unprofitable, when in fact the product line may be contributing substantially to the overall profits of the company.

    b. Common fixed costs should never be allocated to segments of a company; segments should be charged only with those costs which are directly traceable to them, as shown in Exhibit 13-4.

E. A decision to produce a particular part internally, rather than to buy the part externally from a supplier, is often called a "make or buy" decision. "Make or buy" really relates to vertical integration in a company. When a company is involved in more than one of the steps from the extracting of raw material to the fabrication of a finished product, it is said to be vertically integrated.

    1. There are several advantages to vertical integration. These include (a) less dependence on suppliers, (b) assurance of quality control of products, and (c) cost savings made possible by "making" rather than "buying."

    2. The disadvantages of integration include: (a) severance of existing suppliers may disrupt long-run relationships, (b) if the firm needs goods from former suppliers, the former suppliers may be uncooperative, (c) changing technology may make continued production of one's own parts more costly than purchasing from the outside.

    3. An example of make or buy is contained in the text, in Exhibit 13-5. Notice from the exhibit that the costs which are relevant in a make or buy decision are those costs which are *differential* between the make or buy alternatives.

    4. Opportunity cost is a key factor in a make or buy decision.

    a. If there are no alternative uses of facilities currently being used to make a part or a product, then opportunity cost is zero and it does not need to be considered in make or buy computations.

    b. On the other hand, if buying from outside the company would free up facilities or time which could be used to produce some new product, then an opportunity cost is present. This opportunity cost is the segment margin which could be obtained from the new product; it becomes part of the cost of the "make" alternative in a make or buy decision.

F. There are scarce resources in every firm. The scarce resource might be floor space, labor time available, machine time available, or advertising space available.

    1. To maximize total contribution margin, firms may not necessarily want to promote those products that have the highest individual contribution margins. Rather, total contribution margin will be maximized by promoting those products that promise the greatest contribution margin in relation to the scarce resources of the firm.

    2. The manager should compute contribution margin for products in terms of the amount generated per unit of scarce resource, and use this as a guide to which products should be produced and sold.

G. The manufacturing processes of some firms are such that several end products are produced from a single raw material input. Such products are known as *joint products,* with the common input from which they are derived known as the *joint product cost.* The *split-off point* is that point in the manufacturing process at which the joint products can be recognized as individual units of output.

    1. Decisions as to whether a joint product should be sold at the split-off point or processed further and then sold are known as "sell or process further" decisions.

    2. Joint product costs incurred up to the split-off point are irrelevant in decisions regarding whether or not a product should be processed further, since they are sunk costs.

    3. It will always be profitable to continue processing joint products after the split-off point *so long as the incremental revenue from such processing exceeds the incremental processing costs.* An example of a "sell or process further" analysis is provided in Exhibit 13-7.

H. When activity-based costing is being used, managers must exercise caution against reading more into the "traceability" of costs than really exists.

    1. Some managers assume that if a cost is traceable to a segment, then the cost is automatically an avoidable cost in decision making. This is an incorrect assumption.

    2. Even if a cost is traceable to a segment on an activity basis, managers must still apply the principles

discussed in this chapter to see if the cost can be avoided in special decision situations.

Appendix G: Linear Programming

A. Linear programming is a mathematical tool designed to assist management in making decisions in those situations where constraining or limiting factors are present. Linear programming seeks to identify the "right" mix of products that will maximize profits, given the limiting factors (scarce resources) faced by a firm.

1. A graphic approach can be used to solve a linear programming problem in those situations where only two products are involved.

2. The four basic steps in a linear programming graphic analysis are:

a. Determine the objective function and express it in algebraic terms.

b. Determine the constraints under which the firm must operate and express them in algebraic terms.

c. Determine the feasible production area on a graph. This area will be bounded by the constraint equations derived in "b" above, after the constraint equations have been expressed on the graph in linear form.

d. Determine from the feasible production area that mix of products which will maximize (or minimize) the objective function.

3. The objective function represents the goal which is to be achieved, expressed in terms of the variables involved. The goal might be to maximize total contribution margin or it might be to minimize total cost.

4. Constraint equations are algebraic representations of the constraints under which the firm must operate. These constraints may be raw material, machine hours, labor hours, product demand, etc.

5. The feasible production area is formed by the constraint equations on the graph. The firm can operate *anywhere* within the feasible production area.

6. The optimal product mix will always fall on a corner of the feasible production area.

7. In the graphic representation of constraints, the following should be remembered:

a. If the constraint equation is stated in terms of less than or equal to ($\leq$), the direction of the constraint will be *inward* toward the origin of the graph.

b. If the constraint equation is stated in terms of greater than or equal to ($\geq$), the direction of the constraint will be *outward* away from the origin of the graph.

8. The *simplex* method is a more complex approach to solving linear programming problems than is the graphic method. The simplex method is used in those situations where *more than* two products are involved.

9. Linear programming has been successfully used in many areas of our economy where multiple constraints exist.

REVIEW AND SELF TEST
Questions and Exercises

True or False

For each of the following statements, enter a T or an F in the blank to indicate whether the statement is true or false.

_____ 1. All costs are relevant in decision making, except those costs which are not avoidable.

_____ 2. Variable costs are relevant costs in decision making, whereas fixed costs are not relevant.

_____ 3. A sunk cost is an avoidable cost.

_____ 4. Depreciation is a relevant cost if it relates to equipment which has not yet been purchased.

_____ 5. Future costs are always relevant in decision making.

_____ 6. Costs which are relevant in one decision situation are not necessarily relevant in another decision situation.

_____ 7. One way to define relevant costs is to say that they are costs which are avoidable.

_____ 8. If by dropping a product line a company is able to avoid more in fixed costs than it loses in contribution margin, then it will be better off if the line is eliminated.

_____ 9. Allocation of common fixed costs to product lines and to other segments of a company helps the manager to see if the product line or segment is profitable.

_____ 10. If a product line has a negative segment margin, it is conclusive evidence that the product line should be discontinued.

_____ 11. Opportunity cost is a key factor in a make or buy decision.

_____ 12. A company should always promote that product which has the highest contribution margin per unit sold.

_____ 13. A joint product should continue to be processed after the split-off point so long as the incremental revenue from such processing exceeds the incremental processing costs.

_____ 14. Joint product costs are irrelevant in decisions regarding what to do with joint products after the split-off point.

_____ 15. (Appendix G) The purpose of linear programming is to help management make decisions in those situations where constraining or limiting factors are present.

_____ 16. (Appendix G) The objective function equation expresses the constraints under which the firm must operate.

_____ 17. (Appendix G) The feasible production area is bounded by the lines of the constraint equations.

_____ 18. (Appendix G) The corners of the feasible production area are the points where the optimal product mix can be found that will maximize profits.

Multiple Choice

Choose the best answer or response by placing the identifying letter in the space provided.

_____ 1. All of the following costs are relevant in a make or buy decision except: a) the opportunity cost of space; b) costs that are avoidable by "buying" rather than "making"; c) variable costs of producing the item; d) costs that are differential between the "make" and "buy" alternatives; e) all of the above costs are relevant.

_____ 2. One of Simplex Company's product lines has a contribution margin of $50,000 and fixed costs totaling $60,000. If the product line is dropped, $40,000 of the fixed costs will continue unchanged. As a result of dropping the product line, the company's net income should: a) decrease by $50,000 per period; b) increase by $30,000 each period; c) decrease by $30,000 each period; d) increase by $10,000 each period; e) none of these.

_____ 3. Allocated common costs: a) are necessary in order to determine the profitability of a product line; b) are always relevant in decision making; c) are sometimes relevant in decision making; d) are never relevant in decision making; e) none of these.

_____ 4. Halley Company produces 2,000 parts per year, which are used in the assembly of one of its products. The unit cost of producing this part is (based on 2,000 units per year):

Variable cost	$ 7.50
Fixed cost	6.00
Total cost	$13.50

The part can be purchased from an outside supplier at $10 per unit. If the part is purchased from the outside supplier, two-thirds of the fixed costs incurred in producing the part can be eliminated. The annual gain or loss realized from purchasing the part would be: a) $3,000 gain; b) $1,000 loss; c) $7,000 gain; d) $5,000 loss; e) none of these.

_____ 5. Product A has a contribution margin of $8 per unit, a contribution margin ratio of 50 percent, and requires 4 machine-hours to produce. Product B has a contribution margin of $12 per unit, a contribution margin ratio of 40 percent, and requires 5 machine-hours to produce. If the company has limited machine-hours available, then it should produce and sell: a) Product A since it has the highest contribution margin ratio; b) Product B since it has the highest contribution margin per machine-hour; c) Product A since it requires fewer machine-hours per unit than does Product B; d) Product B since it has the highest contribution margin per unit; e) none of these.

_____ 6. Products A and B are joint products. Product A can be sold for $1,200 at the split-off point, or be processed further at a cost of $600 and then sold for $1,700. Product B can be sold for $3,000 at the split-off point, or be processed further at a cost of $800 and then sold for $4,000. The company should process further: a) Product A; b) Product B; c) both products; d) none of these.

_____ 7. (Appendix G) A company produces two products, X and Y. The contribution margin per unit of X is $15, and the contribution margin per unit of Y is $12. The company has 60 hours of production time available each period, and it takes 4 hours to produce one unit of X and 7 hours to produce one unit of Y. The company's objective function equation would be: a) $15X + $12Y = $60; b) $15X + $12Y ≤ 60; c) Z = $15X + $12Y; d) none of these.

_____ 8. (Appendix G) Refer to the data in question 7 above. The company's constraint equation for production time would be: a) 4X + 7Y ≤ 60; b) 4X + 7Y = 60; c) Z = 4X + 7Y; d) none of these.

Complete the Statements

Fill in the necessary words to complete the following statements.

1. All costs are relevant in decision making except those costs which are not _____.

2. Depreciation on equipment which has already been purchased is a _____ cost.

3. If by dropping a product line a company is not able to avoid as much in _____ as

it loses in contribution margin, then the product line should be retained.

4. One of the great dangers in allocating _____ fixed costs is that such allocations can make a product line look less profitable than it really is.

5. A decision to produce a fabricated part internally, rather than to buy the part externally from a supplier, is often called a _____ _____ _____ decision.

6. If a company is involved in more than one of the steps from the extraction of raw materials to the completion of a final product, it is said to be _____ _____.

7. One of the key considerations in a make or buy decision is the _____ cost of the space being used to make a part rather than to buy it.

8. Total contribution margin will be maximized by promoting those products or accepting those orders that promise the highest contribution margin in relation to the _____ resources of the firm.

9. Two or more products that are produced from a common input are known as _____ products.

10. The _____-_____ point is that point in the manufacturing process at which the joint products can be recognized as individual units of output.

11. (Appendix G) In linear programming, the _____ represents the goal that is to be achieved. This goal could be either to maximize total contribution margin or to minimize total cost.

12. (Appendix G) A key step in a linear programming solution is to recognize the _____ under which a firm must operate, and express them in equation form.

13. (Appendix G) The solution to a linear programming problem is found in the _____ _____ _____, which is bounded by the lines formed by the constraint equations.

Exercises

13-1. The most recent income statement for Department C of Merrill's Department Store is given below:

Sales		$500,000
Less variable expenses		200,000
Contribution margin		300,000
Less fixed expenses:		
Salaries and wages	$150,000	
Insurance on inventories	10,000	
Depreciation of equipment	65,000*	
Advertising	100,000	325,000
Net income (loss)		$(25,000)

*Six year remaining useful life, with little or no current resale value.

Management is thinking about dropping the department, due to its poor showing. If the department is dropped, one employee will be retained. Her salary is $30,000. The equipment has no resale value. Prepare an analysis to determine whether or not the department should be dropped.

Contribution margin lost if the
  department is dropped $
Less fixed costs that can
  be avoided if the department is
  dropped:

_____ $

_____

_____   _____   _____

Increase (decrease) in overall
  company net income $_____

Based on the analysis above, Department C (should/should not) _____ be dropped.

Redo the analysis, using the alternate format shown below:

	Keep Department C	Drop Department C	Difference: Net income increase or (decrease)
Sales	$500,000	$	$
Less variable expenses	200,000		
Contribution margin	300,000		
Less fixed expenses:			
Salaries and wages	150,000		
Insurance on inventories	10,000		
Depreciation of equipment	65,000		
Advertising	100,000		
Total fixed expenses	325,000		
Net income (loss)	$(25,000)	$	$

13-2. Watson Company produces two products from a common input. Data relating to the two products are given below:

	Product A	Product B
Sales value at the split-off point	$60,000	$120,000
Allocated joint product costs	45,000	90,000
Sales value after further processing	90,000	200,000
Cost of further processing	20,000	85,000

Determine which of the products should be sold at the split-off point, and which should be processed further before sale.

Sales value after further processing	$	$
Sales value at the split-off point	————	————
Incremental revenue from further processing		
Less cost of further processing	————	————
Profit (loss) from further processing	$	$

13-3. Petre Company is now producing a small part that is used in the production of one of its product lines. The company's accounting department reports the following costs of producing the part internally:

	Per Part
Direct materials	$15
Direct labor	10
Variable overhead	2
Fixed overhead, direct	4
Fixed overhead, common, but allocated	5
Total cost	$36

The direct fixed overhead costs consist of 75 percent depreciation of special equipment, and 25 percent supervisory salaries. The special equipment has no resale value.

An outside supplier has offered to sell the parts to Petre Company for $30 each, based on an order of 5,000 parts per year. Determine whether Petre Company should accept this offer, or continue to make the parts internally:

	Per Unit Differential Costs		5,000 Parts	
	Make	Buy	Make	Buy
Outside purchase price				
Cost of making internally:				
Total cost	$	$	$	$
Difference in favor of (making/buying) ————		$		$

13-4.   (Appendix G) Monson Company manufactures two products, A and B. The company operates under three constraints: the weight of the products, the amount of raw materials available, and the amount of available production capacity. A graphic analysis of these three constraints is given below:

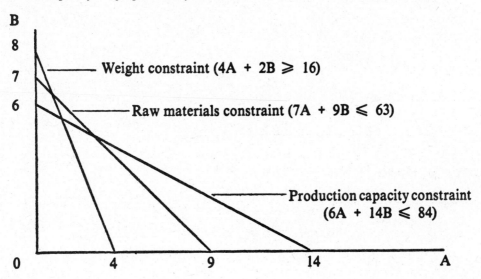

Shade the feasible production area on the above graph. Be careful to watch the direction of the constraint!

13-5.   (Appendix G) H-P Company manufactures two products, H and P. It takes four hours to manufacture H and two hours to manufacture P. The company operates three eight-hour shifts. H requires one pound of raw material per unit and P requires three pounds per unit. The supplier of raw material will provide only 30 pounds of raw material per day. Upon completion, H weighs 16 ounces, and P weighs 2½ pounds. The combination of products shipped to customers should weigh at least 10 pounds. H has a contribution margin of $4.50 per unit, and P has a contribution margin of $8 per unit.

   a.   What is the objective function equation?

   b.   Determine the constraint equations for:

       (1)   Time constraint:

       (2)   Raw material constraint:

       (3)   Shipping constraint:

13-6. **Critical thought writing exercise:** "The easiest way to distinguish between relevant and irrelevant costs is by cost behavior; variable costs are relevant costs and fixed costs are irrelevant costs." Explain why you do or do not agree with this statement.

_____

_____

_____

_____

_____

_____

_____

_____

Chapter 13
Answers to Questions and Exercises

True or False

1. T This statement is true by definition; as stated in the text, costs which are not avoidable fall into two categories: (1) sunk costs, and (2) future costs that do not differ between alternatives.

2. F Fixed costs can be relevant in decision making, so long as they are not sunk costs or future costs that will not differ between alternatives.

3. F Sunk costs are never avoidable costs, since by definition they have already been incurred and thus can't be avoided.

4. T Depreciation is an irrelevant cost only if it relates to equipment which has already been purchased.

5. F Future costs are relevant only if they differ between alternatives; future costs that do not differ between alternatives are not relevant costs.

6. T For example, costs which are relevant in setting a selling price for a product may not be relevant in a decision about whether to drop or retain the product.

7. T This statement is true by definition.

8. T This statement represents one way in which a manager can determine whether a product should be dropped or retained.

9. F Allocation of common fixed costs to product lines and to other segments of a company can result in misleading data and can make a product line appear to be unprofitable when in fact it may be one of a company's best products.

10. F Even if a product line has a negative segment margin, the product's costs still must be analyzed to determine if the product should be dropped.

11. T The opportunity cost represents the segment margin that could be obtained by best alternative use of the space currently being utilized to make an item rather than to buy it.

12. F A company should promote that product which has the highest contribution margin *per unit of limiting factor*. A product might have a high contribution margin per unit, for example, but it may require a large amount of machine time as compared to other products. If machine time is a limiting factor, then the other products may be more desirable.

13. T This statement is true by definition; the principles involved are illustrated in Exhibit 13-7.

14. T At the split-off point, joint product costs have already been incurred and thus they are sunk costs and not relevant in decision making.

15. T This statement is true by definition.

16. F The objective function equation expresses the goal that management is trying to achieve. This goal might be to maximize total contribution margin or it might be to minimize total cost.

17. T This statement is true by definition, and it is illustrated in Exhibit G-1.

18. T This statement is true by definition, and it is illustrated in Exhibit G-1.

Multiple Choice

1. e   These costs are all relevant because they all represent costs which are avoidable (differential) in choosing one alternative over another.

2. c   The computations are:

Contribution margin lost	$(50,000)
Less fixed costs that can be avoided	20,000*
Net decrease in net income	$(30,000)

*$60,000 − $40,000 = $20,000

3. d   Common costs are either sunk costs or future costs that will not differ; thus, they are not relevant in decision making.

4. a   The computations are:

	Differential Cost	
	Make	*Buy*
Variable costs	$ 7.50	—
Fixed cost avoidable	4.00	—
Outside purchase price	—	$10.00
Total relevant cost	$11.50	$10.00

2,000 units × $1.50 = $3,000

5. b   The computations are:

	A	B
Contribution margin per unit (a)	$8	$12
Machine-hours to produce (b)	4	5
CM per machine-hour (a) ÷ (b)	$2	$ 2.40

6. b   The computations are:

	A	B
Sale value after further processing	$1,700	$4,000
Sale value at split-off	1,200	3,000
Incremental sale value	500	1,000
Incremental processing cost	600	800
Advantage (disadvantage) of further processing	$ (100)	$ 200

7. c   The objective function equation expresses the goal that management is trying to achieve. Since the central issue of this question is contribution margin, we can assume that the maximization of contribution margin represents management's overall goal. Thus, the total contribution margin, Z, will equal the contribution margin per unit times the number of units produced and sold, as expressed in response (c).

8. a   The constraint equation for production time would be expressed by multiplying the time needed to produce each unit times the number of units, with the total time utilized equal to or less than the 60 hours of production time available, as expressed in response (a).

Complete the Statements

1. avoidable
2. sunk
3. fixed cost
4. common
5. make or buy
6. vertically integrated
7. opportunity
8. scarce
9. joint
10. split-off
11. objective function
12. constraints
13. feasible production area

Exercises

13-1.

Contribution margin lost if the department is dropped		$(300,000)
Less fixed costs that can be avoided if the department is dropped:		
Salaries and wages ($150,000 − $30,000)	$120,000	
Insurance on inventories	10,000	
Advertising	100,000	230,000
Decrease in overall company net income		$ (70,000)

Based on the analysis above, Department C should not be dropped. Solution using the alternate format:

	Keep Department C	Drop Department C	Difference: Net income increase or (decrease)
Sales	$500,000	$ -0-	$(500,000)
Less variable expenses	200,000	-0-	200,000
Contribution margin	300,000	-0-	$(300,000)
Less fixed expenses:			
Salaries and wages	150,000	30,000	120,000
Insurance on inventories	10,000	-0-	10,000
Depreciation of equipment	65,000	65,000	-0-
Advertising	100,000	-0-	100,000
Total fixed expenses	325,000	95,000	230,000
Net income (loss)	$(25,000)	$(95,000)	$ (70,000)

13-2.

	Product A	Product B
Sales value after further processing	$ 90,000	$200,000
Sales value at the split-off point	60,000	120,000
Incremental revenue from further processing	30,000	80,000
Less cost of further processing	20,000	85,000
Profit (loss) from further processing	$ 10,000	$ (5,000)

13-3.

	Per Unit Differential Costs		5,000 Parts	
	Make	Buy	Make	Buy
Outside purchase price		$30		$150,000
Cost of making internally:				
Direct materials	$15		$ 75,000	
Direct labor	10		50,000	
Variable overhead	2		10,000	
Fixed overhead, direct	1*		5,000	
Fixed overhead, common, but allocated	--		--	
Total cost	$28	$30	$140,000	$150,000
Difference in favor of making		$2		$10,000

*$4 × 25% = $1. The depreciation on the equipment and the common fixed overhead would not be avoidable costs.

13-4.

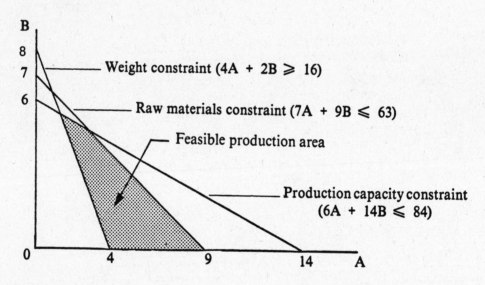

Remember that the direction of a constraint is *inward* if the equation is expressed in terms of less than or equal to (≤), whereas the direction of the constraint is *outward* if the equation is expressed in terms of greater than or equal to (≥).

13-5. a. $Z = 4.50H + 8P$

b. (1) Time constraint: $4H + 2P \leq 24$
    (2) Raw material constraint: $H + 3P \leq 30$
    (3) Shipping constraint: $H + 2.5P \geq 10$

13-6. This statement is not true. Variable costs are not automatically relevant costs, and fixed costs are not automatically irrelevant costs. Whether or not a cost is relevant depends on whether or not the cost is avoidable. A fixed cost can be avoidable, the same as a variable cost can be avoidable. On the other hand, a variable cost may not be avoidable in a particular decision situation and therefore not relevant to the decision. For example, the variable costs in obsolete goods that are already manufactured and in a warehouse would not be relevant to a decision as to whether the goods should be sold at a discount price or simply junked.

Chapter 14

Capital Budgeting Decisions

Chapter Study Suggestions

To understand the material in this chapter, you must have a solid understanding of the concept of present value. If you have not worked with present value before, study Appendix H title, "The Concept of Present Value" until you thoroughly understand what present value is and how it is computed. Then turn to Review Problem 1 and follow its solution through step by step.

Once you understand present value, you will be ready to tackle the capital budgeting methods illustrated in the chapter. The first of these methods is called the net present value method. This method is illustrated in Exhibits 14-1 and 14-4. Follow through each number in the exhibits, and trace the factors back into the tables given at the end of the chapter. Unless you do this, you won't really understand what is going on. Also note the format in which the data are presented. You should use a similar format in your own homework problems.

The second method presented for capital budgeting is called the time-adjusted rate of return method. It is illustrated in Example D and Exhibit 14-5. This method is very different from the net present value method, so spend an equal amount of time studying how it is computed.

At the end of the chapter, two methods of making capital budgeting decisions are illustrated that do not utilize discounted cash flows. These are: 1) the payback method, and 2) the simple rate of return method. Formulas are provided for both methods that should be committed to memory. Pay particular attention to the formula for the simple rate of return. It is somewhat complex and can be tricky to apply in a problem situation.

CHAPTER HIGHLIGHTS AND STUDY GUIDE

A. The term capital budgeting is used to describe those actions relating to the planning and financing of capital outlays, such as for the purchase of new equipment, for the introduction of new product lines, and for the modernization of plant facilities. Capital budgeting is an investment concept, since it involves a commitment of funds now in order to receive some desired return in the future.

1. Typical capital budgeting decisions encountered by the business executive are:

    a. Cost reduction decisions.
    b. Plant expansion decisions.
    c. Equipment selection decisions.
    d. Equipment replacement decisions.

2. Capital budgeting decisions fall into two broad categories:

    a. Screening decisions: Those decisions relating to whether or not a proposed project meets some preset standard of acceptance.

    b. Preference decisions: Those decisions relating to the selection of a proposed project from among several *competing* courses of action.

3. Business investments have two key characteristics that must be recognized in a study of capital budgeting methods.

    a. The first characteristic is that most business investments involve depreciable assets. The return provided by such investments must be sufficient to do two things: (1) provide a return *on* the original investment; and (2) return the total amount of the original investment itself.

    b. The second characteristic is that the returns on most business investments extend over long periods of time.

B. Because business investments tend to be long-term in nature, a business should pay particular attention to the time value of money in investment decisions. The discounted cash flow methods give full recognition to the time value of money, and at the same time provide for full recovery of original capital. There are two discounted cash flow methods available—net present value and time-adjusted rate of return.

C. The net present value method is illustrated in Example A (Exhibit 14-1) and in Example C (Exhibit 14-4). The basic steps in this method are:

1. Determine the required investment.

2. Determine the future cash inflows or outflows associated with the investment.

3. Use the appropriate present value tables to determine the present value of the future cash flows.

4. Subtract the initial investment from the present value of the future cash flows. This difference is called the *net present value*.

5. If the net present value determined from step (4) is zero or positive, the investment should be accepted. If the net present value is negative, the investment should be rejected. To summarize, note the following example:

	Case 1	Case 2	Case 3
Initial investment (outflow)	$(5,000)	$(4,500)	$(5,200)
Present value of future cash inflows	5,000	5,000	5,000
Net Present Value	$ -0-	$ 500	$ (200)
Decision	Accept	Accept	Reject

D. The emphasis of discounted cash flow analysis is on *cash flows*—not on accounting net income. Accounting net income must be ignored in cash flow analysis, since accounting net income does not take into account the timing of cash flows into and out of an organization.

1. Typical cash flows associated with an investment are:

    a. Cash Outflows: Initial investment (including installation costs).
    Increased working capital needs.
    Repairs and maintenance.
    Incremental operating costs.

    b. Cash Inflows: Incremental revenues.
    Reductions in costs.
    Salvage value.
    Release of working capital.

2. Depreciation is not considered in capital budgeting analysis. There are two reasons why it is not considered:

a. Depreciation is an accounting concept not involving a current cash outflow. As indicated above, in capital budgeting the emphasis is on cash flows.

b. Discounted cash flow methods automatically provide for return of the original investment, thereby making a depreciation deduction unnecessary. This is illustrated in Exhibits 14-2 and 14-3.

3. There are two limiting assumptions in discounted cash flow analysis. These are:

a. All cash flows occur at the *end* of a period.

b. All cash flows generated by an investment project are immediately reinvested in another project which yields a rate of return at least as large as the first project.

E. The time-adjusted rate of return (or internal rate of return) is another discounted cash flow method used in capital budgeting decisions.

1. The time-adjusted rate of return can be defined as the true interest yield promised by an investment project over its useful life.

2. The time-adjusted rate of return can be computed by finding that discount rate which will equate the present value of the investments (cash outflows) required by a project with the present value of the returns (cash inflows) that the project promises.

3. The formula for computing the time-adjusted rate of return is:

$$\frac{\text{Investment}}{\text{Annual cash inflows}} = \frac{\text{Factor of the time-}}{\text{adjusted rate of return.}}$$

For example, assume an investment of $3,791 is made in a project which will last five years and has no salvage value. Also assume that the annual cash inflow from the project will be $1,000.

$$\frac{\$3,791}{\$1,000} = \frac{\text{Factor of the time-adjusted rate of}}{\text{return for a 5-year annuity.}}$$

$$3.791 = \frac{\text{Factor of the time-adjusted rate of}}{\text{return for a 5-year annuity.}}$$

From Table J-4 in Appendix J, scanning along the 5-year row, it can be seen that this factor represents a 10 percent rate of return.

4. If the cash flows are uneven, *a trial and error approach* must be used to find the time-adjusted rate of return.

5. Interpolation is a process used if the factor for the time-adjusted rate of return falls between two factors from the present value tables. The interpolation process is illustrated in the chapter.

6. The time-adjusted rate of return can be compared against the required rate of return (usually the cost of capital) a company has selected for investment projects. If the time-adjusted rate of return is less than the cost of capital, the project is rejected. If it is greater than or equal to the cost of capital, the project is accepted.

F. The cost of capital is a screening tool to help managers screen out undesirable investment projects. The cost of capital is a broad concept involving a blending of the cost of *all* sources of capital funds, both debt and equity.

1. Under the time-adjusted rate of return method, the cost of capital is the *hurdle* rate which the project must clear for acceptance.

2. Under the net present value method, the cost of capital becomes the *actual discount rate* used to compute the net present value of a proposed project.

G. The net present value method has a number of advantages over the time-adjusted rate of return method.

1. The net present value method is easier to use.

2. The net present value method makes it easier to adjust for risk.

3. The net present value method provides more usable information.

H. Investments in automated equipment differ in three ways from investments in other types of equipment.

1. The cost of automating a process tends to be very large, even when only a few items are purchased. Moreover, costs for engineering, software development, and implementation of the system can exceed the cost of the equipment itself.

2. Purchases of automated equipment must be carefully evaluated in terms of a company's long-term goals and objectives, since automation is sometimes

viewed as being a "cure all" for competitive deficiencies.

3. The benefits from automation are both tangible and intangible in nature, with the intangible benefits often being the most significant of the two. However, the intangible benefits are hard to quantify and therefore are frequently overlooked in capital budgeting analyses.

a. Lists of tangible benefits are provided in the text. Tangible benefits represent potential *cost savings,* whereas intangible benefits represent potential *revenue enhancements.*

b. One of the most significant intangible benefits from automation is the avoidance of capital decay. Capital decay is defined as a loss in market share from technologically obsolete products and operations.

I. A decision framework is available that can be used for purchases of automated equipment. This framework consists of five steps, which are listed in the chapter.

1. Study the five steps from the chapter with care, paying particular attention to step 5 and the illustration that accompanies step 5.

2. Note from step 5 that you are working backwards in that you have a negative net present value and you are trying to find the amount of cash flow that will eliminate that negative net present.

J. Two common approaches used in the net present value method are the *total-cost* approach and the *incremental* cost approach.

1. The total-cost approach is the most flexible and the most widely used method.

a. Follow through Exhibit 14-7 to see how this approach is used.

b. Note in Exhibit 14-7 that *all* cash inflows and *all* cash outflows are included in the solution under each alternative.

2. The incremental cost approach is a simpler and more direct route to a decision. This approach focuses on differential costs. Follow through Exhibit 14-8 which shows this approach.

3. The final net present value figure that serves as a criterion for the decision is the *same* under the total-cost approach or incremental approach.

K. Sometimes no revenue or cash inflow is directly involved in a decision. In this situation, the company will select the *least-cost* project. The least cost can be determined by either the total-cost approach or the incremental approach. Least-cost decisions are illustrated in Exhibits 14-9 and 14-10.

L. There are other methods to aid in capital budgeting decisions that do not involve discounted cash flow. One of these is the payback method.

1. The payback method computes the time period that is required for an investment project to recoup its own initial cost out of the cash receipts which it generates. The payback period is expressed in years. The formula is:

$$\frac{\text{Payback}}{\text{Period}} = \frac{\text{Investment Required}}{\text{Net Annual Cash Inflow}}$$

a. In computing the "Investment Required," if new equipment is replacing old equipment, then the cost of the new equipment should be reduced by any salvage value obtained from the old equipment.

b. In computing the "Net Annual Cash Inflow," if new equipment is replacing old equipment, then only the *incremental* cash inflow provided by the new equipment over the old equipment should be used.

2. The payback method is not a measure of profitability. Rather it is a measure of how long it takes for a project to recoup its own investment cost.

3. Major defects in the payback method are that it ignores the time value of money, and that it does not discriminate between projects of different useful lives.

M. Another capital budgeting method that does not involve discounted cash flow is the simple rate of return method.

1. The simple rate of return method focuses on accounting net income, rather than on cash flows. The formula for its computation is:

$$\frac{\text{Simple}}{\text{rate of}} = \frac{[\text{Incremental revenue}] - \text{Incremental expenses (including depreciation)}}{\text{Initial investment}}$$

or

$$\text{Simple rate of return} = \frac{\text{Incremental net income}}{\text{Initial investment}}$$

2. If the project is a cost reduction project, the formula becomes:

$$\text{Simple rate of return} = \frac{\text{Cost savings} - \text{Depreciation on new equipment}}{\text{Initial investment}}$$

If new equipment is replacing old equipment, then the "Initial Investment" in the new equipment is the cost of the new equipment reduced by any salvage value obtained from the old equipment.

3. A major defect of the simple rate of return method is that it does not consider the time value of money. Therefore, the rate of return computed by this method will not be an accurate guide as to the profitability of an investment project.

Appendix H: The Concept of Present Value

A.   Since most business investments extend over long periods of time, it is important to recognize the time value of money in capital budgeting analysis. Essentially, the time value of money says that a dollar received today is more valuable than a dollar received in the future. There are two reasons why a dollar received today is more valuable:

1. The first reason is that the dollar received today can be invested and earn an immediate return.

2. The second reason is that there is uncertainty about the future, and therefore a dollar in the future may never be received.

B.   Present value analysis makes it possible for the manager to recognize the time value of money in capital budgeting decisions.

1.   Present value analysis involves the expressing of a future cash flow in terms of present dollars. When a future cash flow is expressed in terms of its present value, the process is called *discounting*.

2. To determine the present value of a single sum to be received in the future, Table J-3 in Appendix J to the chapter should be used. This table contains factors for various rates of interest for various periods, which when multiplied by the future sum, will give the sum's present value.

3. To determine the present value of an *annuity*, or stream, of cash flows, Table J-4 in Appendix J to the chapter should be used. This table contains factors which, when multiplied by the stream of cash flows, will give the stream's present value.

Appendix I: Inflation and Capital Budgeting

A.   Inflation has an impact on the numbers which are used in a capital budgeting analysis, but it does not have an impact on the *results* which are obtained.

B.   Refer to the data in Exhibit I-1. In "Solution B," inflation is given full consideration. Note the following points about Solution B:

1. Annual cash inflows are adjusted for the effects of inflation by multiplying each year's cash inflow by a price-index number which reflects the current inflation rate. (Note from the exhibit how the index number is computed.)

2. The cost of capital is adjusted for the effects of inflation by adding together three cost elements.

a. These elements are (1) the cost of capital, (2) the inflation rate, and (3) a combined factor which allows for the reinvestment of inflation-generated earnings.

b. For example, if the cost of capital is 15 percent and the inflation rate is 8 percent, then the inflation-adjusted cost of capital would be:

Cost of capital	15.0%
Inflation rate	8.0
Combined effect (15% × 8%)	1.2
Inflation-adjusted cost of capital	24.2%

c. A frequent error in adjusting data for inflation is to omit part or all of the computations in "b" above.

3. If the computations in "2" are properly made, then the same net present value will be obtained in a capital budgeting analysis as if no adjustments had been made.

a. The reason the same net present value is obtained is that in adjusting the data for the effects of inflation we adjust *both* the cash flows and the discount rate, and thus the inflationary effects cancel themselves out.

C. In actual practice, not all companies make adjustments for inflation when doing a capital budgeting analysis.

1. The reasons no adjustments are made are: 1) the computations are very complex, and 2) the same net present value can be obtained using unadjusted data.

2. If no adjustments are made for inflation when the original capital budgeting analysis is made, then some adjustments should be made in the post-audit to ensure that both estimated and actual data are comparable. This can be accomplished by either adjusting the estimated data for the *actual* inflation which has taken place, or by adjusting the actual data downward to remove any inflationary element.

REVIEW AND SELF TEST
Questions and Exercises

True or False

For each of the following statements, enter a T or an F in the blank to indicate whether the statement is true or false.

_____ 1. The commitment of funds by a business into inventory, equipment, and like assets is an investment, the same as a purchase of stocks or bonds by an individual.

_____ 2. Under the net present value method, the present value of all cash inflows associated with an investment project are compared against the present value of all cash outflows, with the difference, or net present value, determining whether or not the project is an acceptable investment.

_____ 3. If the net present value of an investment project is zero, then the project should be rejected since it is not providing any return on the investment involved.

_____ 4. One key shortcoming of discounted cash flow methods is that they ignore the recovery of original investment.

_____ 5. Although depreciation is an important element in the computation of accounting net income, it is not used in capital budgeting computations, since it does not involve a cash flow.

_____ 6. Although a cash outlay for a noncurrent asset such as a machine would be considered in a capital budgeting analysis, a cash outlay for a working capital item such as inventory would not be considered.

_____ 7. Cost of capital is a broad concept, involving a blending of the costs of all sources of capital, both debt and equity.

_____ 8. In discounted cash flow analysis, cash flows are assumed to occur uniformly throughout a period.

_____ 9. The time-adjusted rate of return is that discount rate which will cause a project's net present value to be zero.

_____ 10. If the cash flows of a project are uneven, then the project's time-adjusted rate of return can't be computed

_____ 11. Depreciation is an example of an out-of-pocket cost.

_____ 12. To be acceptable, a project's time-adjusted rate of return can't be less than the company's cost of capital.

____ 13. The time-adjusted rate of return method is simpler to use, makes it easier for the manager to adjust for risk, and provides more usable information than the net present value method.

____ 14. In present value analysis, the higher the discount rate, the higher is the present value of a given sum.

____ 15. In comparing two investment alternatives, the net present value obtained using the total-cost approach would be the same as that obtained using the incremental-cost approach.

____ 16. Capital decay is a term used to describe the physical deterioration of buildings and equipment.

____ 17. If an investment in automated equipment can't be justified by a reduction in direct labor cost, then the investment probably shouldn't be made.

____ 18. The simple rate of return method explicitly considers depreciation in deriving a rate of return figure.

____ 19. A very useful guide for making investment decisions is: Projects with short payback periods are more profitable than projects with long payback periods.

____ 20. The payback method can be used even if cash flows are uneven from year to year.

____ 21. Although it deals with cash flows, the payback method gives no consideration to the time value of money.

____ 22. (Appendix H) The present value of a sum discounted over 5 years would be greater than the present value of the same sum discounted over 10 years.

Multiple Choice

Choose the best answer or response by placing the identifying letter in the space provided.

____ 1. Returns provided by depreciable assets must be sufficient to: a) provide an adequate return on the original investment; b) provide a return at least as great as the cost of the investment multiplied by the cost of capital; c) provide a return on the original investment, plus return the total amount of the original investment itself; d) provide a return equal to the charge for depreciation.

____ 2. All of the following are limiting assumptions when dealing with discounted cash flows, *except*: a) cash flows are assumed to occur at the end of a period; b) cash flows are assumed to be reinvested immediately in another investment project; c) cash flows are assumed to occur evenly during a period; d) reinvested cash flows are assumed to earn a rate of return at least as great as the current discount rate; e) all of these responses are limiting assumptions.

The following data relate to questions 3 and 4.

Peters Company is considering the purchase of a machine to further automate its production line. The machine would cost $30,000, and have a ten-year life with no salvage value. It would save $8,000 per year in labor costs, but would increase power costs by $1,000 annually. The cost of capital is 12 percent.

____ 3. The present value of the net annual cost savings would be: a) $39,550; b) $45,200; c) $5,650; d) none of these.

____ 4. The net present value of the proposed machine would be: a) $(15,200); b) $5,650; c) $9,550; d) none of these.

____ 5. Acme Company is considering investing in a new machine which costs $84,900, and which has a useful life of 12 years with no salvage value. The machine will generate $15,000 annually in net cash inflows. The time-adjusted rate of return on the machine is: a) 8 percent; b) 10 percent; c) 12 percent; d) 14 percent; e) none of these.

____ 6. White Company's cost of capital is 12%. The company is considering an investment opportunity that would yield a return of $10,000 in five years. What is the most that the company would be willing to invest in this project? a) $36,050; b) $5,670; c) $17,637; d) $2,774; e) none of these.

____ 7. If a company uses its cost of capital to discount the cash flows associated with an investment project, and if the resulting net present value is positive, then it can be concluded that: a) the company will earn a profit on the project equal to the net present value; b) the return on the investment exceeds the company's cost of capital; c) the discount rate used is *not* the company's true cost of capital; d) this project is clearly more desirable than other possible uses of the investment funds; e) none of these.

____ 8. Dover Company is considering an investment project in which a working capital investment of $30,000 would be required. The investment would provide cash inflows of $10,000 per year for six years. If the company's cost of capital is 18 percent, and if the working capital is released at the end of the project, then the project's net present value is: a) $4,980; b) $(4,980); c) $16,080; d) $(12,360); e) none of these.

____ 9. Whiting Company has completed a net present value analysis for a project that shows a $113,000 *negative* net present value. This project involves a purchase of automated equipment that would have a 10-year useful life. The company's cost of capital is 12%. What amount of cash inflow each year would have to be provided by the intangible benefits associated with the project in order for the project to be acceptable? a) $11,300; b) $13,560; c) $18,000; d) $20,000.

____ 10. Frumer Company has purchased a machine that cost $30,000, that will save $6,000 per year in cash operating costs, and that has an expected life of 15 years. The payback period on the machine will be: a) 2 years; b) 7.5 years; c) 5 years; d) none of these.

____ 11. Refer to the data in question (10) above. The simple rate of return on the machine will be approximately: a) 20%; b) 13.3%; c) 18%; d) 10%; e) none of these.

Complete the Statements

Fill in the necessary words to complete the following statements.

1. Capital budgeting decisions tend to fall into two broad categories—_____ decisions and _____ decisions.

2. The _____ _____ _____ of an investment project is determined by deducting the present value of its cash inflows from the present value of its cash outflows.

3. The _____–_____ rate of return can be defined as the true interest yield of an investment project over its useful life.

4. In computing the net present value of a project, a company generally will use its _____ _____ _____ as the discount rate.

5. In addition to the cost of new equipment, when a firm undertakes a new project it often will have to make an investment in _____ _____, which includes amounts expended for added inventory, accounts receivable, and like assets.

6. The cost of capital acts as a _____ tool, helping the manager to cull out undesirable investment projects.

7. Decisions in which revenues are not directly involved are called _____–_____ decisions.

8. The loss in market share resulting from technologically obsolete products and operations is called _____ _____.

9. The _____ period can be defined as the length of time that it takes for an investment project to recoup its own initial cost out of the cash receipts which it generates.

10. If new equipment is replacing old equipment, then any salvage received on disposal of the old equipment should be deducted from the cost of the new equipment, and only the _____ investment used in a payback computation.

11. The payback period is computed by dividing a project's initial investment by its net annual _____ _____.

12. The simple rate of return is computed by dividing a project's _____ _____, as shown on the income statement, by the project's initial investment.

13. The most damaging criticism of the simple rate of return method is that it does not consider the _____ _____ of money.

14. (Appendix H) A series, or stream, of cash flow is known as an _____.

15. (Appendix H) When interest is paid on interest the process is called _____ of interest.

Exercises

14-1. You have recently won $100,000 in a contest. You have been given the option of receiving $100,000 today or receiving $12,000 at the end of each year for the next 20 years.

Which of these two options would you select if you can invest money at:

a.   8 percent.

Item	Year(s)	Amount of Cash Flows	8 Percent Factor	Present Value of Cash Flows
Receive the annuity		$		$
Receive the lump sum				
Net present value in favor of the _____				$

b.   12 percent.

Item	Year(s)	Amount of Cash Flows	12 Percent Factor	Present Value of Cash Flows
Receive the annuity		$		$
Receive the lump sum				
Net present value in favor of the _____				$

14-2. Lynde Company has been offered a contract to provide a key part for the U.S. Army. The contract would expire in eight years. The projected cash flows that would be associated with the contract are given below:

Cost of new equipment	$300,000
Working capital needed	100,000
Net annual cash receipts from the Army	85,000
Salvage value of the equipment in eight years	50,000

The company's cost of capital is 16 percent. Complete the analysis below to determine whether or not the contract should be accepted.

Item	Year(s)	Amount of Cash Flows	16 Percent Factor	Present Value of Cash Flows
Cost of new equipment		$		$
Working capital needed				
Net annual cash receipts				
Salvage value of equipment				
Working capital released				
Net present value				$

Should the contract be accepted? Explain.

_____

_____

_____

_____

14-3. Swift Company wants to purchase a new machine which will cost $20,000. The machine will provide revenues of $9,000 per year. Out-of-pocket operating costs will be $6,000 per year. The new machine will have a useful life of 10 years. The company's cost of capital is 12 percent.

a. What is the time-adjusted rate of return? (Interpolate if necessary.)

Annual revenue .... $ _____

Annual operating costs .... _____

   Net annual cash inflow .... _____

$$\frac{\text{Initial investment}}{\text{Net annual cash inflow}} = \text{Factor of the time-adjusted rate of return}$$

_____ =

                                                                 Present Value Factor

_____ percent factor ....

True factor ....

_____ percent factor .... _____ _____

   Difference ....

TAROR = _____ percent + (_____ × 2%) =

b. Should the company buy the new machine? Why or why not?

_____

_____

_____

_____

_____

_____

_____

14-4. Hardee Company would like to purchase a new machine which dispenses yogurt. The machine costs $450,000. Annual revenues and expenses which would be associated with the new yogurt machine follow:

Sales revenue		$300,000
Less operating expenses:		
Advertising	$100,000	
Salaries of operators	70,000	
Maintenance	30,000	
Depreciation	40,000	
Total expenses		240,000
Net income		$ 60,000

a. Hardee Company will not invest in new equipment unless it promises a payback period of 4 years or less. Compute the payback period on the yogurt machine. Ignore income taxes.

Computation of the net annual cash inflow:

Net income	$ _____
Add: Noncash deduction for depreciation	_____
Net annual cash inflow	$ _____

Computation of the payback period:

$$\frac{\text{Investment required}}{\text{Net annual cash inflow}} = \text{Payback period}$$

$$\underline{\hspace{4cm}} = \qquad \text{years}$$

Should the machine be purchased? Explain. _____

_____

_____

b. Assume that Hardee requires a 16 percent return on all equipment purchases. Compute the simple rate of return promised by the new machine. Ignore income taxes.

$$\frac{\overset{\text{Incremental}}{\text{revenue}} - \overset{\text{Operating}}{\text{expenses}} = \overset{\text{Net}}{\text{income}}}{\text{Initial investment}} = \text{Simple rate of return}$$

$$\underline{\hspace{4cm}} = \qquad \%$$

Should the machine be purchased? Explain. _____

_____

_____

14-5. **Critical thought writing exercise:** As the discount rate increases, the present value of a given future sum also increases. Do you agree? Why or why not?

_____

_____

_____

_____

_____

_____

_____

_____

Chapter 14
Answers to Questions and Exercises

True or False

1. T   A commitment of funds for the purposes indicated represents an investment, since a return is expected from the funds committed.

2. T   This point is illustrated in Exhibit 14-4.

3. F   If the present value of an investment project is zero, then it is providing a return equal to the discount rate.

4. F   Discounted cash flow methods automatically provide for recovery of original investment, as illustrated in Exhibit 14-3.

5. T   The cash flow occurs when equipment is purchased; depreciation is a bookkeeping adjustment and involves no cash flow.

6. F   A cash outlay for a working capital item represents an investment, the same as a cash outlay for a machine; thus, it would be considered in a capital budgeting analysis.

7. T   This statement is true by definition.

8. F   Cash flows are assumed to occur at the end of a period.

9. T   This statement is true by definition; the principle involved is illustrated in Exhibit 14-5.

10. F   The project's time-adjusted rate of return can still be computed, but it must be done by a trial and error process.

11. F   Depreciation is not an out-of-pocket cost, since an out-of-pocket cost involves a cash outflow such as for salaries or rent.

12. T   This statement is true by definition; the cost of capital represents the "cutoff" or "hurdle" rate.

13. F   The opposite is true—the net present value method is the method that is simpler to use, and so forth.

14. F   The opposite is true—the higher the discount rate, the *lower* is the present value of a given sum.

15. T   The total-cost approach and the incremental-cost approach are just different ways of obtaining the same result.

16. F   Capital decay means a loss of market share due to technologically obsolete products and operations.

17. F   Only rarely will a reduction in direct labor cost justify an investment in automated equipment. Typically, the justification for such an investment will come from intangible benefit such as greater throughput or greater flexibility in operations.

18. T   This point is illustrated in formulas (3) and (4) in the text.

19. F   The payback method does not measure profitability; thus, a project with a short payback is not necessarily more profitable than a project with a long payback period.

20. T   This point is illustrated in Exhibit 14-12 in the text.

21. T   This is a major defect of the payback method—dollars are given the same weight regardless of the year in which they are received.

22. T   When discounting a single sum, the shorter the time period, the greater the present value.

Multiple Choice

1. c   To be acceptable, *all* projects must provide a return on the original investment. In the case of depreciable assets, the asset will be used up at the end of its life; therefore, the returns provided must be great enough to provide a return of the original investment in the asset as well as a return *on* this investment.

2. c   As stated in response (a), cash flows are assumed to occur at the end of a period.

3. a   The computations are:

Savings in labor costs	$ 8,000
Less increased power costs	1,000
Net cost savings	$ 7,000
Present value factor for 12% for 10 years (Table J-4)	× 5.650
Present value of cost savings	$39,550

4. c   The computations are:

Investment in the machine	$(30,000)
Present value of cost savings	39,550
Net present value	$ 9,550

5. d   The computations are:

$$\frac{\text{Investment in the Project}}{\text{Annual Cash Inflow}} = \frac{\text{Factor of}}{\text{the TAROR}}$$

$$\frac{\$84,900}{\$15,000} = 5.660$$

A factor of 5.660 equals a return of 14% from the 12-year row in Table J-4.

6. b   The computations are:

Return in 5 years	$10,000
Factor for 12% for 5 years (Table J-3)	× 0.567
Present value and the maximum amount that the company would be willing to invest	$ 5,670

7. b   If the net present value of a project is positive, then the return promised by that project is greater than the discount rate that has been used in the present value computations. Since in the case at hand the discount rate was the company's cost of capital, the return promised by the project exceeds the cost of capital.

8. c   The computations are:

	Year(s)	Amount	18% Factor	Present Value
Working capital investment	Now	$(30,000)	1.000	$(30,000)
Cash inflow	1-6	10,000	3.498	34,980
Working capital released	6	30,000	0.370	11,100
Net present value				$ 16,080

9. d   The computations are:

$$\frac{\text{Net Present value} \quad (\$113,000)}{\text{Factor for 12\% } 5.650 \text{ over 10 years}} = \$20,000$$

10. c   The computation is:

$30,000 \div \$6,000 = 5$ years

11. b   The computation is:

$$\frac{\$6,000 - \$2,000*}{\$30,000} = 13.3\%$$

*$30,000 \div 15$ years = $2,000/year

Complete the Statements

1. preference, screening	6. screening	11. cash flow
2. net present value	7. least-cost	12. net income
3. time-adjusted	8. capital decay	13. time value
4. cost of capital	9. payback	14. annuity
5. working capital	10. incremental	15. compounding

Exercises

14-1. a. You would prefer to receive the annuity:

Item	Year(s)	Amount of Cash Flows	8 Percent Factor	Present Value of Cash Flows
Receive the annuity	1-20	$ 12,000	9.818	$117,816
Receive the lump sum	Now	100,000	1.000	100,000
Net Present Value in Favor of the Annuity				$ 17,816

b. You would prefer to receive the lump sum:

Item	Year(s)	Amount of Cash Flows	12 Percent Factor	Present Value of Cash Flows
Receive the annuity	1-20	$ 12,000	7.469	$ 89,628
Receive the lump sum	Now	100,000	1.000	100,000
Net Present Value in Favor of the Lump Sum				$ 10,372

14-2.

Item	Year(s)	Amount of Cash Flows	16 Percent Factor	Present Value of Cash Flows
Cost of new equipment	Now	($300,000)	1.000	($300,000)
Working capital needed	Now	(100,000)	1.000	(100,000)
Net annual cash receipts	1-8	85,000	4.344	369,240
Salvage value of equipment	8	50,000	0.305	15,250
Working capital released	8	100,000	0.305	30,500
Net present value				$ 14,990

Yes, the contract should be accepted. The net present value is positive, which means that the contract will provide more than the company's 16 percent required rate of return.

14-3. a.

Annual revenue	$9,000
Annual operating costs	6,000
Incremental Cash Inflow	$3,000

$$\frac{\text{Initial Investment}}{\text{Annual Cash Inflow}} = \text{Factor of the time-adjusted rate of return}$$

$$\frac{\$20,000}{\$\ 3,000} = 6.667.$$

Since the 6.667 factor falls between the 8 percent and 10 percent rates of return in Table J-4, it will be necessary to interpolate to find the exact rate of return:

Present Value Factor

8 percent factor	6.710	6.710
True rate	6.667	
10 percent factor		6.145
Difference	.043	.565

$$\text{Time-adjusted rate of return} = 8 \text{ percent} + \left(\frac{.043}{.565} \times 2 \text{ percent}\right)$$

Time-adjusted rate of return = 8.15 percent.

b. No, reject the machine since the 8.15 percent time-adjusted rate of return is less than the 12 percent cost of capital.

14-4. a. The net annual cash inflow would be:

Net income	$ 60,000
Add: Noncash deduction for depreciation	40,000
Net annual cash inflow	$100,000

The payback period would be:

$$\frac{\$450,000}{\$100,000} = 4.5 \text{ years.}$$

The machine should not be purchased since it will not provide the 4 year payback period required by the company.

b. The simple rate of return would be:

$$\frac{\$60,000}{\$450,000} = 13.3\%.$$

The machine should not be purchased since the simple rate of return which it promises (13.3%) is less than the 16 percent return required by the company.

14-5. No. As the discount rate increases, the present value of a given future sum *decreases*. The reason is that as the discount rate increases, more interest is taken out of a future sum, thus leaving a smaller present value. For example, the factor for a discount rate of 12 percent for a single sum to be received ten years from now is 0.322, whereas the factor for a discount rate of 14 percent over the same period is 0.270. If the sum to be received in ten years is $10,000, the present value in the first case is $3,220, but only $2,700 in the second case. Thus, as the discount rate increases, the present value of a given sum decreases.

Chapter 15

Further Aspects of Investment Decisions

Chapter Study Suggestions

This chapter builds on the discounted cash flow methods introduced in Chapter 14 and discusses the impact of income taxes on capital budgeting decisions. The formulas showing the computation of after-tax cost and after-tax benefit should be committed to memory. In addition, the formula for the tax shield associated with depreciation should be memorized. Exhibit 15-7 provides a comprehensive illustration of the computation of net present value when income tax factors are considered. Study this exhibit and the related text material with special care; the computations on the exhibit are complex and will take some time to digest.

Two methods are illustrated in the chapter for ranking investment projects according to preference. These are: 1) the time-adjusted rate of return method, and 2) the profitability index. Notice that the profitability index is based on the net present value concepts discussed in the preceding chapter. It is tricky to compute, so follow the text example through step-by-step.

CHAPTER HIGHLIGHTS AND STUDY GUIDE

A.   Income taxes have an effect on the cash flows of profit-making entities and therefore must be considered in discounted cash flow methods of capital budgeting. Nonprofit entities such as hospitals, schools, or governmental units are not subject to income taxes and will always use the approaches illustrated in Chapter 14.

B.   Since expenses are tax deductible in most companies, managers generally look at their expenses on an after-tax basis, rather than on a before-tax basis.

1. The true cost of a tax-deductible item is not the dollars paid out, but the amount of the payment that will remain after taking into account any reduction in income taxes that the payment will bring about.

2. An expenditure net of its tax effects is known as *after-tax cost*. For example, assume that a company needs to overhaul a machine at a cost of $6,000. The overhaul is tax-deductible. If the income tax rate is 30 percent, the after-tax cost is:

Cost of overhaul	$6,000
Reduction in taxes due to the overhaul	
(30 percent × $6,000)	(1,800)
After-Tax Cost	$4,200

3. The concept of after-tax cost is very useful to the manager, since it measures the *actual* amount of cash that will be leaving a company as a result of a particular expenditure decision.

4. The formula that will give the after-tax cost of *any* tax-deductible expenditure is:

$(1 - \text{Tax rate}) \times \text{Cash expense} = \text{After-tax cost}$

C.   In capital budgeting decisions, taxable cash receipts must also be placed on an after-tax basis.

1. The cash inflow from a taxable cash receipt should not be measured by the dollars received. Rather, it should be measured by the amount that will remain after deducting related income taxes.

2. A receipt net of its tax effect is known as *after-tax benefit*. For example, assume that a company receives $100,000 from a sublessee. If the tax rate is 30 percent, the after-tax benefit is:

Revenue	$100,000
Income tax payment required	
(30 percent × $100,000)	(30,000)
After-Tax Benefit	$ 70,000

3. If a company has a savings in cost by using machine A instead of machine B, the savings are treated the same as a revenue item in determining the net after-tax cash inflow.

4. Not all cash receipts are taxable. For example, the release of working capital at the termination of an investment project is not a taxable cash inflow.

5. The formula that will give the after-tax cash inflow from revenue or other *taxable* cash receipts is:

$$(1 - \text{Tax rate}) \times \frac{\text{Cash}}{\text{receipt}} = \frac{\text{After-tax benefit}}{\text{(net cash inflow)}}$$

D.   Depreciation deductions in and of themselves do not involve cash flows. However, because the depreciation deduction does have an effect on the amount of taxes that a firm will pay, it does have an effect on the cash outflow paid for taxes.

1. The depreciation deduction acts as a *shield* against tax payments. In effect, depreciation deductions *shield* revenues from taxation and thereby *lower* the amount of income taxes that a company has to pay.

2. The formula used to compute the depreciation tax shield is:

$$\frac{\text{Depreciation}}{\text{deduction}} \times \frac{\text{Tax}}{\text{rate}} = \frac{\text{Tax savings from the}}{\text{depreciation tax shield}}$$

E.   For tax purposes, companies must use the Modified Accelerated Cost Recovery System (MACRS) to depreciate assets. MACRS should also be used to compute depreciation for capital budgeting purposes.

1. Under MACRS, assets are placed into one of eight property classes. Assets are placed in these classes according to their useful life.

2. Each property class has a preset depreciation period and method. In all classes, the *half-year convention* must be observed, which means that only one half year's depreciation can be taken in the first and last year of the asset's life. In effect, this adds a full year onto the recovery period, as shown in Exhibit 15-5.

3. Under MACRS, salvage value is not considered in computing depreciation deductions.

4. In lieu of the MACRS tables, taxpayers can elect to use the optional straight-line method.

a. Under the optional straight-line method, taxpayers can depreciate an asset somewhat evenly over its property class life rather than use the MACRS tables.

b. The half-year convention must also be observed when using the optional straight-line method.

F. A comprehensive example of income taxes and capital budgeting is given in Exhibit 15-7. The reader should turn to this example and follow it through step by step.

1. Notice that all cash flows involving tax deductible expenses and taxable receipts have been placed on an after-tax basis by multiplying the cash flow in each case by one minus the tax rate.

2. Also notice that the depreciation deductions have to be multiplied *by the tax rate itself* to determine the tax savings (cash inflow) resulting from the tax shield. *These two points should be studied with great care until both are thoroughly understood.*

G. Preference decisions involve the ranking of investment projects.

1. Because investment funds are usually limited, a company needs some means of selecting among investment projects that compete for those funds.

2. Preference decisions are sometimes called *ranking* decisions or *rationing* decisions because they attempt to ration limited investment funds among competing investment opportunities.

3. When using the time-adjusted rate of return to rank competing investment projects, the preference rule is: *The higher the time-adjusted rate of return, the more desirable the project.*

4. If the net present value method is being used to rank competing investment projects, the net present value of one project can't be compared directly to the net present value of another project, unless the investments in the projects are of equal size.

a. To make a valid comparison between projects, a *profitability index* must be computed. The formula for the profitability index is:

$$\frac{\text{Present value of cash inflows}}{\text{Investment required}} = \frac{\text{Profitability}}{\text{index}}$$

b. The preference rule using the profitability index is: *The higher the profitability index, the more desirable the project.*

5. The profitability index is conceptually superior to the time-adjusted rate of return as a method of making preference decisions because the profitability index will always give the correct signal as to the relative desirability of alternatives, even if alternatives have different lives and different patterns of earnings.

REVIEW AND SELF TEST
Questions and Exercises

True or False

For each of the following statements, enter a T or an F in the blank to indicate whether the statement is true or false.

_____ 1. The after-tax cost of a tax-deductible item is computed by the formula: Tax rate × Cash expense = After-tax cost.

_____ 2. The "cash flow" in a company is computed by adding noncash deductions (such as depreciation) to net income.

_____ 3. Taxpayers must observe the half-year convention when using the optional straight-line method, but they do not observe it when using the MACRS tables.

_____ 4. Since salvage value is not considered when computing depreciation under MACRS, any salvage value received on sale of an asset is fully taxable as income.

_____ 5. The MACRS tables allow a greater total amount of depreciation to be taken over the life of an asset than is allowed under the optional straight-line method.

_____ 6. The release of working capital at the termination of an investment project would be a taxable cash inflow.

_____ 7. Although companies are not allowed to use sum-of-the-years'-digits depreciation for tax purposes, they can still use this method in preparing financial statements.

_____ 8. In general, a larger present value of tax savings from the depreciation tax shield will result from using the MACRS tables than from using the optional straight-line method.

_____ 9. In ranking investment projects, a project with a high net present value should always be ranked above a project with a lower net present value.

_____ 10. In preference decision situations, the net present value and time-adjusted rate of return methods may give conflicting rankings of projects.

_____ 11. The profitability index is computed by dividing an asset's net present value by the investment required in the project.

_____ 12. In the MACRS tables, all assets are depreciated using 200% declining balance depreciation.

_____ 13. Under the optional straight-line method, a taxpayer is required to depreciate an asset over its useful life rather than over its MACRS property class life.

_____ 14. For capital budgeting purposes, taxpayers should use the same depreciation method as is being used for financial statement purposes.

Multiple Choice

Choose the best answer or response by placing the identifying letter in the space provided.

_____ 1. For 19X1, Kinnard Company's depreciation deduction was $50,000 and its tax rate was 30 percent. The company's tax savings from the depreciation tax shield for the year was: a) $15,000; b) $35,000; c) $50,000; d) none of these.

_____ 2. Vidmar Company has purchases an asset that cost $100,000 and has a $5,000 salvage value. The asset has a useful life of 12 years and is in the MACRS 7-year property class. If the MACRS tables are used for depreciation purposes, the asset: a) can be depreciated using either the 7-year property class life or the 12-year useful life; b) must be depreciated using the 7-year property class life; c) must be depreciated using the 7-year property class life, but only $95,000 in depreciation can be taken; d) none of these.

_____ 3. Project A requires an investment of $40,000, has a present value of cash inflows of $50,000, and has a net present value of $10,000. The project's profitability index would be: a) 0.80; b) 1.25; c) 4.0; d) none of these.

_____ 4. Leeds Company has purchased a machine that cost $90,000, has an $8,000 salvage value, and is in the MACRS 5-year property class. The machine was purchased on December 1 of the current year. If the optional straight-line method is used, the depreciation in the first year will be: a) $1,200; b) $7,200; c) $1,500; d) $9,000; e) none of these.

_____ 5. Information on three investment projects is given below:

Project	Investment Required	Net Present Value
1	$ 80,000	$20,000
2	150,000	30,000
3	60,000	18,000

Rank the projects in terms of preference: a) 2, 1, 3; b) 1, 3, 2; c) 3, 1, 2; d) none of these.

_____ 6. Polar Company is studying a project that would require a $200,000 working capital investment. If the company's tax rate is 30 percent, then the working capital should be shown in the capital budgeting analysis as a cash outflow of: a) $200,000; b) $140,000; c) $60,000; d) none of these.

Complete the Statements

Fill in the necessary words to complete the following statements.

1. An expenditure net of its tax effect is known as _____-_____ cost.

2. A decision as to which of two otherwise acceptable projects should be selected is called a _____ decision.

3. When using the time-adjusted rate of return method to rank competing investment projects, the preference rule is: The _____ the time-adjusted rate of return, the more desirable the project.

4. Preference decisions are sometimes called _____ decisions, since they attempt to ration limited investment funds among many competing investment opportunities.

5. The _____ index is used to make preference decisions between investment projects, when the net present value method has been used for screening purposes.

6. Under the optional straight-line method, depreciation in the first and last years of an asset's life is limited to _____ _____ of the depreciation allowable in other years. This is known as the _____ – _____ _____.

Exercises

15-1. Martin Company is acquiring a new copier for use in its office. The following data relate to the new copier:

Cost of the new copier	$150,000
Annual savings in cash operating costs	40,000
Salvage value of the new copier	6,000
Overhaul of the new copier required in the third year	5,000
Life of the new copier	8 years

The new copier is replacing an old machine that is fully depreciated, but which has a remaining book value of $18,000. The old machine can be sold now for $10,000.

Assume that the company's tax rate is 30 percent.

a. Compute the after-tax savings in annual cash operating costs. $_____

b. Compute the after-tax cost of the overhaul required in the third year. $_____

c. Compute the tax savings from the depreciation tax shield. You may assume that the company uses the MACRS tables and that the copier is in the 5-year property class. The company does not consider salvage value in computing depreciation deductions.

Year	Cost	MACRS Percentage	Depreciation Deduction	Tax Rate	Tax Shield: Income Tax Savings
1	$150,000			30%	
2					
3					
4					
5					
6					

d. Compute the after-tax benefit from the salvage value of the new copier. $_____

e. Compute the after-tax cash inflow from sale of the old machine. (This is a tough one, and you may have to refer to the computations in Exhibit 15-8 in the text.)

Cash received from the sale $ _____

Tax savings from loss on sale:
    Current book value $ _____
    Sale price now
    Loss on disposal   _____
    Multiply by the tax rate   _____ × 30%
Tax savings from loss $ _____

15-2. Marvel Company has $50,000 to invest and is considering two alternatives:

	Investment X	Investment Y
Cost of equipment	$60,000	—
Working capital needed	—	$60,000
Annual cash inflows	20,000	20,000
Salvage value	3,000	—
Life of the project	5 years	5 years

The company's cost of capital is 12 percent, and the tax rate is 30 percent.

a. Compute the net present value of each investment. The company uses straight-line depreciation on all equipment. The equipment is in the MACRS 3-year proper class. [Place your solution to Part (a) on the following page.]

b. Compute the profitability index for each investment, and explain which investment should be chosen.

$$\frac{\text{Present Value of Cash Inflows}}{\text{Investment Required}} = \text{Profitability Index}$$

Investment X: Investment Y:

_____ =   _____ =

_____

_____

_____

15-2. Part (a), *(continued)*

Items and computations	Year(s)	(1) Amount	(2) Tax effect	(1) × (2) After-tax cash flows	12 percent factor	Present value of cash flows

Investment X:

Cost of equipment..................

Annual cash inflows ....

Depreciation deductions:

Year	Cost	Dep'n deduction
1		
2		
3		
4		

Salvage value ....

Net present value ....

Investment Y:

Working capital needed ....

Annual cash inflows ....

Working capital released ....

Net present value ....

15-3. **Critical thought writing exercise:** On an income statement, cash expenses (such as salaries) and depreciation expenses are added together and deducted from revenues to determine net income. Assume that a company has cash operating expenses of $50,000 and depreciation expenses of $20,000. Can these amounts be added together and treated as one in a capital budgeting analysis, or should they be kept separate? Explain your answer.

_____

_____

_____

_____

_____

_____

_____

_____

Chapter 15
Answers to Questions and Exercises

True or False

1. F   The formula is: $(1 - \text{Tax rate}) \times \text{Cash expense} = \text{After-tax cost}$.

2. T   This statement is true by definition; the computation involved is illustrated in Exhibit 15-2.

3. F   The half-year convention must be observed with either the MACRS tables or the optional straight-line method.

4. T   The salvage value is fully taxable as income since the taxpayer will already have recovered the original investment in the asset by deducting its entire cost through the depreciation process.

5. F   The same total amount of depreciation (equal to the original cost of the asset) is taken regardless of the depreciation method used. This point is illustrated in Exhibit 15-6 (where a total of $300,000 depreciation is taken under both methods).

6. F   The release of working capital would simply be a return of the taxpayer's original investment and thus would not be taxable as income.

7. T   MACRS only governs the depreciation method to be used for tax purposes; it says nothing about the method(s) that can be used in preparing financial statements.

8. T   This point is illustrated in Exhibit 15-6.

9. F   Net present value can't be used in ranking projects, since one project may have a higher net present value than another simply because it is larger and requires a greater investment. When the net present value method is used, a profitability index must be considered in order to compare projects.

10. T   This is because the time-adjusted rate of return method tends to favor short-term, high-yield projects, whereas the net present value method tends to favor longer-term projects.

11. F   The profitability index is computed by dividing the present value of an asset's *total cash inflows* by the investment required.

12. F   Various depreciation methods and rates are used, as shown in Exhibit 15-4.

13. F   Under the optional straight-line method, a taxpayer depreciates assets over their MACRS property class life.

14. F   For capital budgeting purposes, taxpayers should use the same depreciation method as is being used for tax purposes.

Multiple Choice

1. a   The computation is:

$$30\% \times \$50,000 = \$15,000.$$

2. b   When the MACRS tables are used, assets must be depreciated over their property-class life.

3. b   The computation is:

$$\frac{\text{Present Value of Cash Inflows}}{\text{Investment Required}} = \frac{\$50,000}{\$40,000} = 1.25$$

4. d   The computations are:

$90,000 \div 5 \text{ years} = \$18,000$;
$18,000 \times 1/2 = \$9,000$.

5. c   The computations are:

Project

1   $(\$\ 80,000 + \$20,000) \div \$\ 80,000 = 1.25$
2   $(\$150,000 + \$30,000) \div \$150,000 = 1.20$
3   $(\$\ 60,000 + \$18,000) \div \$\ 60,000 = 1.30$

6. a   Working capital represents an investment, not an expense, so no tax adjustment is needed. This point is discussed in connection with Exhibit 15-7.

Complete the Statements

1. after-tax
2. preference
3. higher
4. rationing or ranking
5. profitability

6. one half; half-year convention

Exercises

15-1. a. (1 − Tax Rate) × Total Amount Received = After-Tax Benefit
        (1 − 0.30) × $40,000 = $28,000

   b. (1 − Tax Rate) × Total Amount Paid = After-Tax Cost
        (1 − 0.30) × $5,000 = $3,500

   c. The tax shield from depreciation is:

   Depreciation Deduction × Tax Rate = Tax Savings from Depreciation Tax Shield

Year	Cost	MACRS Percentage	Depreciation Deduction	Tax Rate	Tax Shield: Income Tax Savings
	(1)	(2)	(1) × (2) = (3)	(4)	(3) × (4)
1	$150,000	20.0	$30,000	30%	$ 9,000
2	$150,000	32.0	48,000	30%	14,400
3	$150,000	19.2	28,800	30%	8,640
4	$150,000	11.5	17,250	30%	5,175
5	$150,000	11.5	17,250	30%	5,175
6	$150,000	5.8	8,700	30%	2,610

   d. (1 − Tax Rate) × Total Amount Received = After-Tax Benefit
        (1 − 0.30) × $6,000 = $4,200

   e. Cash flow from disposal of the old machine:

   Cash received from sale $10,000

   Tax savings from loss on sale:
Current book value	$18,000
Sale price now	10,000
Loss on disposal	8,000
Multiply by the tax rate	× 30%
Tax savings from loss	$ 2,400

15-2.

a.

Investment X:

Items and computations	Year(s)	(1) Amount	(2) Tax effect	(1) × (2) After-tax cash flows	12 percent factor	Present value of cash flows
Cost of equipment	Now	$(60,000)	—	$(60,000)	1.000	$(60,000)
Annual cash inflows	1-5	20,000	1 - 30%	14,000	3.605	50,470

Depreciation deductions:

Year	Cost	Dep'n deduction						
1	$60,000	$10,000	1	10,000	30%	3,000	0.893	2,679
2	60,000	20,000	2	20,000	30%	6,000	0.797	4,782
3	60,000	20,000	3	20,000	30%	6,000	0.712	4,272
4	60,000	10,000	4	10,000	30%	3,000	0.636	1,908
Salvage value			5	3,000	1 - 30%	2,100	0.567	1,191

Net present value .... $ 5,302

Investment Y:

Items and computations	Year(s)	(1) Amount	(2) Tax effect	(1) × (2) After-tax cash flows	12 percent factor	Present value of cash flows
Working capital needed	Now	$(60,000)	—	$(60,000)	1.000	$(60,000)
Annual cash inflows	1-5	20,000	1 - 30%	14,000	3.605	50,470
Working capital released	5	60,000	—	60,000	0.567	34,020

Net present value .... $ 24,490

b. Investment X:

$$\frac{\$65,302}{\$60,000} = 1.09 \text{ (rounded)}$$

Investment Y:

$$\frac{\$84,490}{\$60,000} = 1.41 \text{ (rounded)}$$

Investment Y should be chosen, since its profitability index is higher than Investment X's profitability index.

15-3. The two amounts should be kept separate. The reason is that cash operating expenses represent cash outflows; these outflows on an after-tax basis are measured by multiplying the expenses by (1 - Tax Rate). By contrast, depreciation expenses will trigger a cash inflow through the depreciation tax shield. The amount of the inflow will be measured by multiplying the depreciation expenses by the tax rate itself.

Chapter 16

Service Department Costing:
An Activity Approach

Chapter Study Suggestions

There are three key exhibits in this chapter—Exhibits 16-2, 16-4, and 16-7. Exhibits 16-2 and 16-4 illustrate the direct method and the step method of allocating service department costs to operating departments. Follow the computations in the exhibits through step-by-step, and note the difference in the way the two exhibits handle the cost data.

Exhibit 16-7 expands on Exhibits 16-2 and 16-4 by showing how costs can be broken down into their variable and fixed components, and thus can be allocated by behavior. Spend the bulk of your study time on the sections titled, "Allocating costs by behavior," and "A summary of cost allocation guidelines." Then note from Exhibit 16-7 how the ideas in these two sections are implemented in an actual allocation problem. This is a very important exhibit, since it is the basis for many of the longer, more difficult homework problems.

CHAPTER HIGHLIGHTS AND STUDY GUIDE

A. The two broad classes of departments within a firm are: 1) operating departments, and 2) service departments.

1. Operating departments include those departments or units where the central purposes of the organization are carried out. Examples of such departments or units include the surgery department in a hospital, the various programs in a university, and producing departments in a manufacturing firm.

2. Service departments do not engage directly in operating activities. Rather, they provide service or assistance that facilitates the activities of the operating departments. Examples of such departments include the cafeteria, personnel, and purchasing.

3. The costs of service departments must be allocated to operating departments. These allocated costs are then added to the overhead costs of the operating departments, and included in billing rates and predetermined overhead rates.

4. There are four broad areas that must be considered in deciding how to make an equitable allocation of service department costs to operating departments. These four areas are discussed in sections B, C, D, and E below.

B. Care must be taken to select an allocation base which reflects as accurately as possible the benefits to be received by the various operating departments from the services involved.

1. Examples of allocation bases that are frequently used are provided in Exhibit 16-1. Criteria for selecting a particular allocation base include:

   a. Direct, traceable benefits from the service involved.
   b. The extent to which space or equipment is made available.
   c. The ease of making an allocation.

2. Selection of an allocation base represents *a major policy decision* that is reviewed only at very infrequent intervals, or when it appears that some major inequity exists.

C. Service departments not only provide service to operating departments, but also to each other. Services provided by one service department to another are called *inter-departmental services*. A cafeteria for all

company employees, including service department employees, is an example of an inter-departmental service.

1. There are three approaches to handling the allocation of inter-departmental service costs: 1) the direct method, 2) the step method, and 3) the reciprocal method.

2. The *direct method* ignores the costs of services between service departments, and allocates all service department costs directly to operating departments. The direct method is illustrated in Exhibit 16-2.

   a. Because the direct method ignores inter-departmental services, it is less accurate than the step method.

   b. When a cost allocation is not accurate, it distorts the predetermined overhead rates which, in turn, can lead to ineffective pricing.

3. The *step method* provides for the allocation of a department's costs to other service departments, as well as to operating departments, in a sequential manner.

   a. The sequence of allocation typically begins with the department which provides the greatest amount of service to other departments.

   b. Exhibits 16-3 and 16-4 provide graphical and numerical examples of the step method.

   c. Once a service department's costs have been allocated out, no costs are subsequently reallocated back to it.

4. The reciprocal method allocates costs both forward and backward. This is done through the use of simultaneous linear equations. Although the reciprocal method is very accurate, it is too complex for most firms.

D. Whenever possible, service department costs should be separated into fixed and variable classifications and allocated separately. By allocating fixed and variable costs separately, a company can avoid possible inequities in allocation as well as provide data which are useful for planning and controlling operations.

1. Variable costs represent direct costs of providing services, and will generally vary in total proportionately with fluctuations in the level of service consumed.

    a. As a general rule, variable costs should be charged to consuming departments according to whatever activity base controls the incurrence of the cost involved.

    b. The assigning of variable service costs to consuming departments can more accurately be termed "charges" than allocations.

2. The fixed costs of service departments represent the cost of having long-run service capacity available. These costs are most equitably allocated to consuming departments on the basis of *predetermined, lump-sum amounts.*

    a. The lump-sum amount may be based either on long-run average servicing needs, or on peak-period servicing needs of other departments.

    b. Once set, lump-sum allocations of fixed costs will not vary from period to period.

E. Some pitfalls to avoid in allocating service department costs are:

1. A company should not allocate fixed costs by the use of a *variable* allocation base. An inequity will arise since fixed costs allocated to one department will be influenced heavily by what happens in other departments.

2. A company should not allocate actual service department costs to operating departments, but instead should allocate *budgeted* costs. The allocation of actual costs passes on the inefficiencies in operations by service department managers to operating department managers.

3. Any variance over budgeted costs should be retained in the service department and closed out against cost of goods sold, along with operating department variances.

F. The amounts allocated to operating departments are included in the performance evaluations of these departments, and also included in determining their individual profitability. In addition, these allocated costs are used in developing overhead rates.

1. The overhead rate development process is illustrated in Exhibit 16-5.

2. Typically, the flexible budget serves as the means for combining allocated service department costs with operating department costs and for computing overhead rates. A flexible budget containing allocated costs is provided in Exhibit 16-6.

G. Five guidelines for allocating service department costs are:

1. If possible, the distinction between variable and fixed costs should be maintained.

2. Variable costs should be allocated at the budgeted rate, according to whatever activity measure controls the incurrence of the cost involved.

3. Fixed costs should be allocated in predetermined, lump-sum amounts.

4. If it is not feasible to maintain a distinction between variable and fixed costs in a service department, the costs of the department should be allocated to consuming departments according to that base which appears to provide the best measure of benefits received.

5. Where feasible, reciprocal services between departments should be recognized.

H. As a general rule, any service department costs that are incurred as a result of specific service provided to operating departments should be allocated back to these departments and used to compute overhead rates and to measure profitability. This rule is not followed, however, if it is felt by management that doing so would produce an undesirable response from operating departments.

1. Sometimes a service (such as for internal auditing or systems design) is provided free in order to facilitate its acceptance by operating departments.

2. Rather than provide a service free, a retainer fee is sometimes charged to operating departments. This is done to encourage the operating departments to use the service involved up to the specified level for which the retainer fee has been paid.

I. Sales dollars are sometimes used as an allocation base.

1. One reason for using sales dollars is that the sales dollar figure is simple and easy to work with. Another reason is that managers tend to view sales dollars as a measure of well-being, or "ability to pay."

2. However, since sales dollars represent a variable allocation base, inequities can result if fixed costs are being allocated.

3. Sales dollars should be used as an allocation base only in those cases where there is a direct causal relationship between sales dollars and the service department costs being allocated.

REVIEW AND SELF TEST
Questions and Exercises

True or False

For each of the following statements, enter a T or an F in the blank to indicate whether the statement is true or false.

_____ 1. The major difference between service departments and operating departments is that service departments are quite small whereas operating departments are quite large.

_____ 2. Service department costs should be included as part of the cost of a company's products and services, the same as costs for materials, labor, and overhead.

_____ 3. For purposes of equity, the bases used to allocate service department costs should be changed at least once each year.

_____ 4. The overhead rates used in operating departments should include allocated costs from service departments.

_____ 5. As costs are allocated from service departments to operating departments, these costs should be included on the operating departments' flexible budgets.

_____ 6. If a service department (such as a cafeteria) generates revenues, these revenues should not be considered in allocating the service department's costs to operating departments.

_____ 7. In allocating costs by the step method, the allocation sequence typically begins with the service department which provides the greatest amount of service to other departments.

_____ 8. Under the step method of cost allocation, costs are allocated backward as well as forward.

_____ 9. The step method and the direct method generally will result in the same total amount of service department cost being allocated to a given operating department.

_____ 10. Variable costs of service departments should be allocated to operating departments in predetermined, lump-sum amounts.

_____ 11. If a variable allocation base (such as direct labor hours) is used to allocate fixed service department costs, inequities may result in the amount of cost allocated to the various operating departments.

_____ 12. Budgeted costs, rather than actual costs, should always be allocated from service departments to operating departments.

_____ 13. The direct method of cost allocation is much simpler than the step method, in that services provided between service departments are ignored.

_____ 14. Sales dollars represent a good allocation base, because sales dollars are easy to work with and show a department's "ability to pay."

_____ 15. Under the retainer fee approach, operating departments are charged only for the amount of services which they actually consume.

Multiple Choice

Choose the best answer or response by placing the identifying letter in the space provided.

_____ 1. Allocation bases used to allocate service department costs to operating departments: a) should be simple and easy to understand; b) remain unchanged for long periods of time, once they are chosen; c) have a heavy influence on the amount of cost ultimately charged to a unit of product; d) responses a, b, and c are all correct; e) responses b and c are both correct.

The following information applies to multiple choice questions 2-6.

The budgeted and peak-period machine hours of Wasatch Company's two operating departments follow

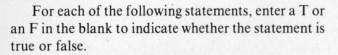

	Machine Hours	
	Budgeted	Peak-Period
Operating Department #1	15,000	20,000
Operating Department #2	25,000	30,000
Total Machine Hours	40,000	50,000

The Wasatch Company has a repair department which services these two operating departments. The variable servicing costs are budgeted at $.20 per machine hour. Fixed costs are budgeted at $12,000 per year. Fixed service costs are allocated to operating departments on the basis of peak-period machine hours.

At the end of the year, the actual machine hours worked by the operating departments were 16,000 hours for Department #1 and 24,000 hours for Department #2. The actual repair department costs were: variable costs—$8,600, and fixed costs—$13,000.

_____ 2. The amount of variable cost allocated to Department #1 at the beginning of the year will be: a) $3,000; b) $5,000; c) $4,800; d) $7,200; e) none of the above.

_____ 3. The amount of fixed cost allocated to Department #2 at the beginning of the year will be: a) $3,000; b) $5,000; c) $4,800; d) $7,200; e) none of the above.

_____ 4. The amount of variable cost allocated to Department #1 at the end of the year will be: a) $4,800; b) $5,200; c) $3,200; d) $7,200; e) none of the above.

_____ 5. The amount of fixed cost allocated to Department #2 at the end of the year will be: a) $4,800; b) $7,800; c) $3,200; d) $7,200; e) none of the above.

_____ 6. The total spending variance for fixed and variable costs of the repair department at the end of the year will be: a) $600; b) $1,600; c) $1,000; d) $1,400; e) none of the above.

Complete the Statements

Fill in the necessary words to complete the following statements.

1. One allocation method, known as the _____ method, provides for allocation of a service department's costs to other service departments, as well as to operating departments, in a sequential manner.

2. Another allocation method, known as the _____ method, ignores the cost of services between departments, and allocates all service department costs directly to operating departments.

3. Technically, the assigning of variable service department costs to consuming departments can be more accurately termed "_____" than allocations, since the service department is charging the consuming department at some fixed rate per unit of service provided.

4. Fixed costs of service departments should be allocated to consuming departments in predetermined _____-_____ amounts.

5. A _____ allocation base should never be used to allocate fixed costs from service departments to operating departments.

6. A service department should always allocate _____ costs, rather than actual costs, to other departments.

7. Under the _____ fee approach for assigning service department costs to operating departments, each department is charged a flat amount each year, regardless of how much or how little of the service it utilizes.

8. Under the step method, allocation always begins with the department that provides the _____ amount of service to other departments

Exercises

16-1. Piney Company has three service departments and two operating departments. Following are costs and other data relating to these departments:

	Service Departments			Operating Departments	
	Janitorial	Cafeteria	Engineering	Assembly	Finishing
Overhead costs before allocation	$60,000	$42,600	$75,000	$230,000	$300,000
Square feet	1,500 sq. ft.	2,000 sq. ft.	1,000 sq. ft.	4,000 sq. ft.	3,000 sq. ft.
Number of employees	15	12	50	200	400

The Janitorial department performs the greatest amount of service to the other departments, followed by the Cafeteria, with the Engineering department last. Allocate Janitorial costs on the basis of square feet. The Cafeteria and Engineering costs should be allocated on the basis of the number of employees. The company makes no distinction between variable and fixed service department costs.

Allocate service department costs to the operating departments using the step method.

	Service Departments			Operating Departments	
	Janitorial	Cafeteria	Engineering	Assembly	Finishing
Overhead costs before allocation					
Allocation:					
Janitorial					
Cafeteria					
Engineering					
Total overhead costs after allocation					

16-2. Refer to the data in Exercise 16-1. Allocate service department costs to the operating departments using the direct method.

	Service Departments			Operating Departments	
	Janitorial	Cafeteria	Engineering	Assembly	Finishing
Overhead costs before allocation					
Allocation:					
Janitorial					
Cafeteria					
Engineering					
Total overhead costs after allocation					

16-3. **Critical though writing exercise:** "Since sales dollars is a measure of ability to pay, it is probably the most equitable base for allocating service department costs to operating departments." Explain why you do or do not agree with this statement.

_____

_____

_____

_____

_____

_____

_____

_____

Chapter 16
Answers to Questions and Exercises

True or False

1. F   The major difference is in the type of work each department performs. Operating departments are those where the central purposes of the organization are carried out. Service departments provide assistance or support to the operating departments.

2. T   Since the work of service departments assists or supports the operating departments, the costs of service departments should be included in the cost of products and services.

3. F   Once selected, allocation bases should remain unchanged unless it becomes obvious that a major inequity exists in the allocation of costs.

4. T   The way in which service department costs are charged to products and services is through the overhead rates of operating departments.

5. T   The inclusion of allocated costs on the flexible budget of an operating department is illustrated in Exhibit 16-6.

6. F   The revenues are deducted from the service department's costs, and only the net amount is allocated to other departments.

7. T   This statement is true by definition.

8. F   Service department costs are always allocated forward—never backward.

9. F   The total amount of cost allocated to a given operating department can differ greatly between the two methods.

10. F   Fixed costs—not variable costs—should be allocated in predetermined, lump-sum amounts.

11. T   The inequities that can result are discussed in the section of the chapter titled, "Pitfalls in allocating fixed costs."

12. T   Budgeted costs should be allocated in order to avoid passing inefficiencies on from one department to another.

13. T   The accuracy of this statement is illustrated in Exhibit 16-2, which provides an example of the direct method.

14. F   Sales dollars represents a poor allocation base, as discussed in the chapter.

15. F   Under the retainer fee approach, departments are charged a flat fee regardless of how much a service is used.

Multiple Choice

1. d   These points are all discussed in the section of the chapter titled, "Selecting allocation bases."

2. a   The computations are:

    15,000 hours × $0.20 = $3,000.

3. d   Department 2 had 60% (30,000 hours ÷ 50,000 hours) of the peak-period hours realized in the company each year. Therefore, the amount of fixed cost allocated to Department 2 would be: 60% × $12,000 = $7,200.

4. c   The computations are:

    16,000 hours × $0.20 = $3,200.

5. d   Fixed costs are always allocated in predetermined, lump-sum amounts. Therefore, the allocation at the end of the year will be the same as at the beginning of the year.

6. b   The computations are:

Actual costs		
($8,600 + $13,000)		$21,600
Allocated costs:		
Variable		
(16,000 hours + 24,000		
hours) × $0.20	8,000	
Fixed (budgeted amount)	12,000	20,000
Spending variance		$ 1,600

Complete the Statements

1. step
2. direct
3. charges
4. lump-sum

5. variable
6. budgeted
7. retainer
8. greatest

Exercises

16-1.

	Service Departments			Operating Departments	
	Janitorial	*Cafeteria*	*Engineering*	*Assembly*	*Finishing*
Overhead costs before allocation	$60,000	$42,600	$75,000	$230,000	$300,000
Allocation:					
Janitorial[1]	(60,000)	12,000	6,000	24,000	18,000
Cafeteria[2]..........		(54,600)	4,200	16,800	33,600
Engineering[3]			(85,200)	28,400	56,800
Total overhead costs after allocation	-0-	-0-	-0-	$299,200	$408,400

$$1. \quad \frac{\text{Janitorial cost}}{\text{Total square feet}} = \frac{\$60,000}{10,000 \text{ sq. ft.}} = \$6/\text{sq. ft.}$$

$$2. \quad \frac{\text{Cafeteria cost}}{\text{Number of employees}} = \frac{\$54,600}{650} = \$84/\text{employee}$$

$$3. \quad \frac{\text{Engineering cost}}{\text{Number of employees}} = \frac{\$85,200}{600} = \$142/\text{employee}$$

16-2.

	Service Departments			Operating Departments	
	Janitorial	*Cafeteria*	*Engineering*	*Assembly*	*Finishing*
Overhead costs before allocation	$60,000	$42,600	$75,000	$230,000	$300,000
Allocation:					
Janitorial[1]	(60,000)			34,286	25,714
Cafeteria[2]..........		(42,600)		14,200	28,400
Engineering[3]			(75,000)	25,000	50,000
Total overhead costs after allocation	-0-	-0-	-0-	$303,486	$404,114

$$1. \quad \frac{\text{Janitorial cost}}{\text{Total square feet}} = \frac{\$60,000}{7,000 \text{ sq. ft.}} = \$8.57/\text{sq. ft. (rounded)}$$

$$2. \quad \frac{\text{Cafeteria cost}}{\text{Number of employees}} = \frac{\$42,600}{600} = \$71/\text{employee}$$

$$3. \quad \frac{\text{Engineering cost}}{\text{Number of employees}} = \frac{\$75,000}{600} = \$125/\text{employee}$$

16-3. Sales dollars is not a good base for allocating service department costs to other departments. This is because there generally is no cause-and-effect relationship between sales in operating departments and the incurrence of costs in the service departments. Thus, if sales dollars is used to allocate service department costs to other departments, inequities can result in the allocations. The amount of cost allocated to a given department will depend in large part on what is happending in other departments. A drop in sales in one department will result in it being relieved of allocated costs, and these costs will be shifted to other departments. As a consequence, the better departments will be penalized for lack of effectiveness elsewhere that is beyond their control.

"How Well Am I Doing?"—Statement of Cash Flows

Chapter Study Suggestions

This chapter shows how the statement of cash flows is prepared and how it is used by managers, investors, and creditors in assessing the well being of a company. The chapter is divided into three major sections. The first section discusses general concepts relating to the statement of cash flows. Much of the material in this section is summarized in Exhibit 17-1 where general rules are given for cash flows relating to *operating, investing,* and *financing* activities in an organization.

The other two sections deal with actual preparation of a statement of cash flows. One of these sections shows preparation without the use of working papers. Exhibits 17-2 and 17-3 are the key exhibits in this section; you should spend considerable time studying the material they contain. The other section shows preparation of a statement of cash flows with the use of working papers. Exhibits 17-10 and 17-11 are the key exhibits in this section of the chapter.

Finally, you should note that two methods of preparing the Operating Activities portion of the statement of cash flows are presented in the chapter. These are the *indirect method* and the *direct method.* The indirect method is used as the basis for much of the discussion in the chapter. The direct method is illustrated near the end of the chapter in Exhibit 17-13.

CHAPTER HIGHLIGHTS AND STUDY GUIDE

A. The purpose of the statement of cash flows is to highlight the major activities that have provided cash and that have used cash during a period, and to show the resulting effect on the overall cash balance.

1. The term *cash* is broadly defined to include both cash and cash equivalents. Cash equivalents consist of short-term, highly liquid investments such as treasury bills, commercial paper, and money market funds.

2. Investments such as those described in (1) are considerd to be "equivalent" to cash in that they are made solely for the purpose of generating a return on cash that is temporarily idle.

B. To provide comparability of data, the FASB requires that the statement of cash flows be divided into three sections. These sections relate to *operating activities, investing activities,* and *financing activities.*

1. As a general rule, any transactions that enter into the determination of net income are classified as operating activities. These transactions are summarized in Exhibit 17-1.

2. Any transactions that are involved in the acquisition or disposition of non-current assets are classified as investing activities. These transactions include gains and losses on disposition of non-current assets, as shown in Exhibit 17-1.

3. As a general rule, any transactions involving borrowing from creditors (other than the payment of interest), and any transactions involving the owners of a company (except stock dividends and stock splits), are classified as financing activities. Again, these transactions are summarized in Exhibit 17-1.

C. Companies sometimes acquire assets or dispose of liabilities through *direct exchange transactions*. Examples include the issue of capital stock in exchange for property and equipment and the conversion of long-term debt into common stock.

1. Such exchanges have a common identifying characteristic in that they affect only non-current balance sheet accounts and have no effect on cash.

2. Although direct exchanges have no effect on cash they must still be reported, since they involve significant financing and investing activities. This reporting is done in a separate, accompanying schedule to the statement of cash flows.

D. For both financing and investing activities, items on the statement of cash flows must be presented in gross amounts rather than in net amounts. For example, if a company issues $100,000 of common stock and retires $80,000 of other common stock, the two amounts must be shown separately.

E. The net result of the cash inflows and outflows arising from operating activities is referred to as the *cash provided by operations*. This figure can be computed by using the *direct method* or the *indirect method.*

1. Under the direct method, the income statement is reconstructed on a cash basis from top to bottom. The model used in making the necessary adjustments to the income statement is illustrated in Exhibit 17-13.

2. Under the indirect method, the amount of cash provided by operations is computed by starting with net income and adjusting it to a cash basis. The steps to follow in this adjustment process are illustrated in Exhibit 17-2.

a. Since depreciation is a noncash item, i must be added back to net income in computing the cash provided by operations under the indirect method. By adding depreciation back to net income, its effects are cancelled out, thus leaving as part of net income only those items of revenue and expense that *do* affect cash.

b. Adjustments needed under the indirect method for current asset and current liability accounts are explained in Exhibit 17-3.

c. Deferred income taxes represent amounts deducted currently on the income statement as income tax expense but not paid until a later time. In adjusting the net income figure to a cash basis, changes in the Deferred Income Taxes account follow the same rules as for current liabilities.

F. There are four basic steps to follow in preparing a statement of cash flows. These steps are:

1. Find the change that has taken place in the cash account during the year.

2. Determine the *net cash provided by operating activities* by analyzing the changes in the appropriate balance sheet accounts and by following the model given in Exhibit 17-2 for the indirect method or by following the model given in Exhibit 17-13 for the direct method.

3. Analyze each additional balance sheet account and determine whether the change in the account was the result of an investing activity or a financing activity.

4. Summarize the cash flows obtained in steps 2 and 3 into operating, investing, and financing activities. The net result of the cash flows for these three activities will equal the change in cash obtained in step 1.

G. The section titled, "An Example of the Statement of Cash Flows" provides a step-by-step example of the preparation of a statement of cash flows. The reader should carefully study this example before going on.

H. The section titled, "A Working Paper Approach to the Statement of Cash Flows" provides an example of how working papers can assist in statement preparation.

1. Exhibit 17-11 contains a set of completed working papers. Notice that a T-account is provided for each balance sheet account, including an account for Cash into which entries are made for cash "provided" and "used."

2. Each account is analyzed, and the entry(s) explaining the change in the account are entered into it, with offsetting entries being made in the Cash T-account.

3. The use of T-accounts greatly simplifies the computation of the net cash provided by operating activities. This is because the T-accounts automatically show the correct adjustment to make for changes in current asset and current liability accounts in adjusting the net income figure to a cash basis.

I. The similarities and differences between the direct and indirect methods of computing the cash provided by operating activities are as follows:

1. Both methods will yield the same cash provided by operating activities figure; this is because the two methods are just different roads to the same destination.

2. The adjustments for accounts that affect revenue are the same under the two methods. In either case, we deduct increases in the accounts and we add decreases in the accounts in adjusting figures to a cash basis.

3. The adjustments for accounts that affect expenses are handled in opposite ways under the two methods.

a. This is because under the indirect method we are making our adjustments to *net income,* whereas under the direct method we are making our adjustments to the *expense accounts* themselves.

b. These differences can be seen by comparing the model for the indirect method (Exhibit 17-2) with the model for the direct method (Exhibit 17-13).

REVIEW AND SELF TEST
Questions and Exercises

True or False

For each of the following statements, enter a T or an F in the blank to indicate whether the statement is true or false.

_____ 1. Cash equivalents consists of any investments in stocks, bonds, treasury bills, or money market funds.

_____ 2. The term *funds* should not be used in a statement of cash flows.

_____ 3. Dividends received on stock held as an investment would be included in the operating activities section of the statement of cash flows.

_____ 4. Interest paid on amounts borrowed would be included in the investing activities section of the statement of cash flows.

_____ 5. Payments made for items that appear as expenses on the income statement would be classified as part of a company's operating activities on the statement of cash flows.

_____ 6. The lending of money to another entity (such as to a subsidiary) would be classified as a financing activity.

_____ 7. Gains and losses on the sale of noncurrent assets would be included in the operating activities section of the statement of cash flows.

_____ 8. Neither stock dividends nor stock splits are included in the statement of cash flows.

_____ 9. The payment of cash dividends to the owners of a company would be classified as a financing activity.

_____ 10. All forms of debt, including accounts payable, short-term borrowing, and long-term borrowing, are classified as financing activities on the statement of cash flows.

_____ 11. For both financing and investing activities, items on the statement of cash flows should be presented in gross amounts rather than in net amounts.

_____ 12. Under the direct method of computing the net cash provided by operating activities, the income statement is reconstructed on a cash basis from top to bottom.

_____ 13. As shown by the indirect method of computing the net cash provided by operating activities, depreciation is a significant source of cash in most organizations.

_____ 14. All changes in current assets are added to net income in computing the net cash provided by operating activities under the direct method.

_____ 15. Generally, the direct and indirect methods will yield different figures for the net cash provided by operating activities.

_____ 16. In computing the net cash provided by operating activities, depreciation is added to net income under the indirect method, but it is deducted from operating expenses under the direct method.

_____ 17. Only changes in noncurrent accounts (assets, liabilities, and owners' equity) are analyzed in preparing a statement of cash flows.

_____ 18. The cash account will always increase during the year if a company is profitable.

Multiple Choice

Choose the best answer or response by placing the identifying letter in the space provided.

_____ 1. Given the following accounts: 1) Prepaid Expenses; 2) Inventory; 3) Accounts Receivable; 4) Accounts Payable; and 5) Accrued Liabilities. Which of these accounts would be involved in adjusting cost of goods sold to a cash basis under the direct method? a) 1 and 2; b) only 2; c) 2 and 4; d) 2, 3, and 4; e) all of these accounts except 3 would be involved.

For questions 2 through 10 below, indicate whether the transaction involved would be treated as: a) an operating activity; b) an investing activity; c) a financing activity; or d) not appear at all on a statement of cash flows.

_____ 2. Deferred income taxes increased by $40,000 during a year.

_____ 3. By use of a 90-day note, $100,000 was borrowed from a bank.

_____ 4. Interest was paid on the note in (3).

_____ 5. A $25,000 stock dividend was declared and issued.

_____ 6. Fully depreciated equipment was retired.

_____ 7. An $80,000 loan was made to a subsidiary.

_____ 8. Common stock was sold for cash.

_____ 9. Equipment was purchased for $60,000 cash.

_____ 10. Treasury bills were purchased for $25,000 cash.

3. Interest received from bonds held for long-term investment would be included as part of _____ activities on a statement of cash flows.

4. All forms of debt except _____ _____ are included as part of financing activities on a statement of cash flows.

5. The issue of capital stock for property and equipment would be called a _____ _____ _____ .

6. The indirect method of computing the net cash provided by operating activities is also known as the _____ method.

7. In preparing a statement of cash flows, the manager must analyze both the _____ and _____ balance sheet accounts.

8. Depreciation is added to net income in computing the net cash provided by operating activities under the _____ method.

9. Under the indirect method, an increase in Accounts Receivable must be _____ _____ net income to show that cash-basis sales are (greater/less) _____ than reported sales.

10. Both _____ activities and _____ activities must be shown in gross amounts rather than in net amounts on the statement of cash flows.

Complete the Statements

Fill in the necessary words to complete the following statements.

1. The FASB has stated that the term *Cash* must be broadly defined to include both _____ and _____ _____ .

2. A gain on the sale of equipment would be included as part of _____ activities on a statement of cash flows.

Exercises

17-1. Balance sheet account data for Ingalls Company follow:

	19x5	19x4
Cash	$ 6	$ 10
Accounts receivable, net	20	14
Inventory	67	48
Prepaid expenses	3	6
Buildings and equipment	175	140
Accumulated depreciation	(52)	(40)
Investments in other companies	8	12
Total Assets	$227	$190
Accounts payable	$ 49	$ 35
Accrued liabilities	8	15
Bonds payable	40	20
Common stock	100	106
Retained earnings	30	14
Total Liabilities and Equity	$227	$190

Income statement data for 19x5 follow:

Sales	$350
Cost of goods sold	225
Gross margin	125
Less operating expenses	100
Net Income	$ 25

During 19x5 the company declared and paid $9 in cash dividends. Depreciation expense of $12 is included in the 19x5 operating expenses above.

Using the indirect method, compute the net cash provided by operating activities for the year:

Net income $25
    Adjustments needed to convert net income to a cash basis:
      Depreciation expense for the year
      Add (deduct) changes in current asset accounts:

    Add (deduct) changes in current liability accounts:

Net cash provided by operating activities .... $

17-2. Refer to the data for Ingalls Company in Exercise 17-1. Using the direct method, adjust the company's income statement to a cash basis.

Sales	$350	
Adjustments to a cash basis:		
	———	
Sales adjusted to a cash basis		$
Cost of goods sold	$225	
Adjustments to a cash basis:		
	———	
Cost of goods sold adjusted to a cash basis		$
Operating expenses	$100	
Adjustments to a cash basis:		
Operating expenses adjusted to a cash basis	———	$___
Net cash provided by operating activities		═══

17-3. Refer to the data for Ingalls Company in Exercises 17-1 and 17-2. Prepare a statement of cash flows for the year (it is not necessary to show the details for the "Net cash provided by operating activities" figure).

INGALLS COMPANY
Statement of Cash Flows

Operating activities
    Net cash provided by operating activities . . . .

Investing activities
    Cash was provided by:

    Cash was used to:

    Net cash _____ investing activities . . . .

Financing activities
    Cash was provided by:

    Cash was used to:

    Net cash _____ financing activities . . . .

Net decrease in cash . . . . (4)

Cash balance, January 1, 19x5 10

Cash balance, December 31, 19x5 . . . . $ 6

17-4. Critical thought writing exercise: A recent article in *Forbes* magazine stated, "During the last year, depreciation has been one of X Company's biggest sources of cash." Do you agree that depreciation is a source of cash? Explain your answer

_____

_____

_____

_____

_____

_____

_____

Chapter 17
Answers to Questions and Exercises

True or False

1. **F** Cash equivalents consist of investments in short-term, highly liquid investments. Stocks and bonds do not fall in this category, since they represent long-term investments.

2. **T** The term *funds* is subject to misinterpretation and therefore is no longer used in a statement of cash flows.

3. **T** The reason it is not included in the "investing activities" section is that the dividends enter into the determination of net income and investing activities are narrowly defined to include only the principal amount invested in stocks and bonds.

4. **F** Interest paid on amounts borrowed would be included in the operating activities section since the interest enters into the determination of net income.

5. **T** This statement is true by definition.

6. **F** The lending of money to another entity would be classified as an investing activity.

7. **F** Gains and losses on the sale of noncurrent assets are included in the investing activities section of the statement of cash flows, along with the assets to which they relate.

8. **T** This statement is true by definition, because neither transaction involves a cash flow.

9. **T** The dividends represent payments to owners for providing capital to the organization.

10. **F** Transactions involving accounts payable are included among operating activities—not financing activities.

11. **T** This statement is true by definition; only transactions involving operating activities are presented in net amounts.

12. **T** This statement is true by definition.

13. **F** Depreciation is not a source of cash; it is added back to net income under the indirect method in order to cancel out its effect (since it was previously deducted in obtaining the net income figure).

14. **F** Changes in current assets may be either added or deducted, depending on the nature of the change (increases are deducted and decreases are added).

15. **F** The two methods will yield the same figure for cash provided by operating activities, since they are simply different roads to the same destination.

16. **T** Depreciation is added to net income under the indirect method in order to cancel out its effect (as explained in question 13 above), but it is deducted from the operating expenses under the direct method to cancel out its effect.

17. **F** Changes in all accounts, current as well as noncurrent, are analyzed in preparing a statement of cash flows.

18. **F** The cash account could decrease during the year even if a company is profitable, and the opposite could also be true (it could increase even if the company is unprofitable). Changes in the cash account hinge on cash management—not on whether a company is profitable or unprofitable.

Multiple Choice

1. c   Only inventory and accounts payable would be involved, as shown in the model in Exhibit 17-13.

2. a   Income taxes enter into the determination of net income and therefore would be classified as an operating activity.

3. c   All borrowing of cash (short term or long term) is included as a financing activity.

4. a   Since interest payments enter into the determination of net income, they are included as operating activities.

5. d   Neither stock dividends nor stock splits appear on a statement of cash flows.

6. d   No cash flow would be associated with the retirement of equipment.

7. b   Loans to other entities are investing activities, by definition.

8. c   Sales of capital stock are financing activities, by definition.

9. b   All purchases of noncurrent assets are investing activities, by definition.

10. d   A treasury bill would be a cash equivalent and therefore would be included as part of cash on the statement of cash flows. Thus, there would be no change in the amount of cash available if treasury bills were purchased.

Complete the Statements

1. cash, cash equivalents
2. investing
3. operating
4. accounts payable
5. direct exchange transaction
6. reconciliation
7. current, noncurrent
8. indirect
9. deducted from, less
10. investing, financing

Exercises

17-1. Net income .... $ 25
    Adjustments needed to convert net income to a cash basis:
        Depreciation expense for the year 12
        Add (deduct) changes in current asset accounts:
            Increase in accounts receivable .... (6)
            Increase in inventory.. (19)
            Decrease in prepaid expenses 3
        Add (deduct) changes in current liability accounts:
            Increase in accounts payable 14
            Decrease in accrued liabilities .... (7)
    Net cash provided by operating activities .... $ 22

17-2. Sales $350
    Adjustments to a cash basis:
        Increase in accounts receivable .... − 6
    Sales adjusted to a cash basis $344

    Cost of goods sold.. 225
    Adjustments to a cash basis:
        Increase in inventory .... +19
        Increase in accounts payable .... −14
    Cost of goods sold adjusted to a cash basis 230

    Operating expenses 100
    Adjustments to a cash basis:
        Decrease in prepaid expenses.................................. − 3
        Decrease in accrued liabilities .... + 7
        Depreciation expense for the year .... −12
    Operating expenses adjusted to a cash basis 92
    Net cash provided by operating activities .... $ 22

17-3.
INGALLS COMPANY
Statement of Cash Flows

Operating activities

Net cash provided by operating activities . . . . $ 22

Investing activities

Cash was provided by:

Sale of investments in other companies . . . . $ 4

Cash was used to:

Purchase buildings and equipment . . . . (35)

Net cash used for investing activities . . . . (31)

Financing activities

Cash was provided by:

Sale of bonds 20

Cash was used to:

Acquire common stock . . . . (6)

Pay cash dividends to owners . . . . (9)

Net cash provided by financing activities 5

Net decrease in cash . . . . (4)

Cash balance, January 1, 19x5 10

Cash balance, December 31, 19x5 . . . . $ 6

17-4. Depreciation is not a source of cash. The adding back of depreciation charges to net income in order to compute the amount of cash provided by operations only creates the illusion that depreciation is a source of cash. Actually, any cash provided by operations comes as a result of sales revenues, not as result of depreciation charges. Depreciation is added back to net income for the reason that it requires no cash outlay during a period, yet it is deducted as an expense in arriving at net income. Thus, by adding it back, we are able to cancel out its effect and leave as part of net income only those items of revenue and expense that do affect the amount of cash provided during a period. A company could double or triple it's depreciation charges, and there would be no effect on the amount of cash provided by operations.

Chapter 18

"How Well Am I Doing?"—
Financial Statement Analysis

Chapter Study Suggestions

The chapter is divided into two parts. The first part discusses the preparation and use of statements in comparative and common-size form. Your study time in this part should be focused on Exhibits 18-1 through 18-4. These exhibits show how statements in comparative and common-size form are prepared and used by the manager to assess the well-being of the firm.

The second part of the chapter deals with ratio analysis. Altogether, some seventeen ratios are presented in this part of the chapter. In your study, you should memorize the formula for each ratio since you will be expected to know these formulas on quizzes and examinations. You should also learn how to interpret each ratio. A summary of the ratios is given in Exhibit 18-7 to aid you in your study.

CHAPTER HIGHLIGHTS AND STUDY GUIDE

A. The purpose of financial statement analysis is to assist statement users in predicting the future course of events in an organization.

1. All users of financial data—stockholders, creditors, and management—have concerns that can be resolved to some degree by the predictive ability of statement analysis.

2. To be most useful for predictive purposes, the results of any financial statement analysis should be in comparative form.

a. This comparison should be against other periods, as well as against other firms within the industry.

b. Unfortunately, comparisons between firms are often made difficult by differences in accounting methods in use.

3. The analyst must be careful not to rely just on ratios and other analytical tools in making a judgment about a firm.

a. Rather than an end, ratios should be viewed as being a starting point, and as being indicators of what to pursue in greater depth.

b. The analyst must also look at industry trends, technological changes, changes in consumer tastes, and so forth, in judging the probable future of a firm.

B. Three common analytical techniques for financial statement analysis are: 1) dollar and percentage changes on statements; 2) common-size statements; and 3) ratios.

1. Dollar and percentage changes on statements are determined through a technique known as *horizontal analysis*. Horizontal analysis involves the placing of two or more statements side by side and analyzing the changes between years.

a. Showing changes in dollar form identifies key factors affecting profitability or financial position.

b. Showing changes in percentage form helps the analyst to gain perspective, and to gain a feel for the significance of the changes that have taken place.

c. Horizontal analysis can also be done by computing *trend percentages*. Trend percentages state several years' financial statements in terms of a base year.

2. A common-size statement is one that shows the separate items on it in percentage form, rather than in dollar form. Preparation of common-size statements is known as *vertical analysis*.

a. Showing the balance sheet and the income statement in common-size form helps the manager to see the relative importance of the various assets, and also to see the relative importance of the various expense items in relation to sales.

b. Common-size statements are also very helpful in pointing out efficiencies and inefficiencies that otherwise might go unnoticed.

3. In addition to the above analytical techniques, ratios can be prepared to assist stockholders, short-term creditors, and long-term creditors in assessing the well-being of a firm. Ratios which are designed to meet the needs of these three different groups are discussed in sections C, D, and E following.

C. The common stockholder wants to measure his or her well-being. There are several ratios which act as indicators of shareholder well-being.

1. *Earnings per share* is an important measure of the annual earnings remaining for common shareholders. The formula is:

$$\frac{\text{Net income} - \text{Preferred dividends}}{\text{Common shares outstanding}} = \frac{\text{Earnings per}}{\text{share}}$$

a. If a company has extraordinary gains or losses appearing as part of net income, the company must show two earnings per share figures. First, earnings per share must be shown for *normal* operations; and second, the effect on earnings per share must be shown for *extraordinary items*.

b. By showing the effect of extraordinary items on earnings per share, the distorting influence of the extraordinary items on net income is highlighted. In addition, the trend of normal earnings can be evaluated by the analyst.

c. When reporting extraordinary items separately, they must be shown "net of their tax effect."

d. If a company has convertible securities, the earnings per share figure must again be computed in two ways. First, it must be computed assuming no conversion of the convertible securities into common stock; and second, it must be computed assuming full conversion of the convertible securities into common stock. The latter computation is referred to as earnings per share computed on a *fully diluted* basis.

2. The *price-earnings ratio* is a measure used to gauge stock values. It shows the relationship between the market price of a share of stock and the stock's current earnings per share. The price-earnings ratio is computed by the following formula:

$$\frac{\text{Market price}}{\text{Earnings per share}} = \text{Price/earnings ratio}$$

3. The *dividend payout ratio* gauges the portion of current earnings being paid out as dividends. The formula is:

$$\frac{\text{Dividends per share}}{\text{Earnings per share}} = \text{Dividend payout ratio}$$

4. The *dividend yield ratio* provides the investor with a measure of the opportunity cost of his or her investment in terms of yield. The ratio is computed by the following formula:

$$\frac{\text{Dividends per share}}{\text{Market price per share}} = \text{Dividend yield ratio}$$

5. The *return on total assets* ratio is a measure of how well assets have been employed by a firm. It is a measure of *operating performance*. The formula is:

$$\frac{\text{Net Income} + \left[\begin{array}{c} \text{Interest expense} \times \\ (1 - \text{tax rate}) \end{array} \right]}{\text{Average total assets}} = \begin{array}{c} \text{Return on} \\ \text{total assets} \end{array}$$

a. Notice that the interest expense is placed on an after-tax basis before being added back to net income.

b. The reason for adding the interest expense back to net income is to derive a net income figure that shows earnings *before* any distributions have been made to either creditors or stockholders. Thus we eliminate the matter of how the assets were financed from influencing the measurement of how well the assets have been employed.

6. The *return on common stockholders' equity* is a measure of a company's ability to generate income for the benefit of common stockholders. The formula is:

$$\frac{\text{Net income} - \text{Preferred dividends}}{\begin{array}{c} \text{Average common stockholders' equity} \\ \text{(Average total stockholders' equity less} \\ \text{Preferred stock)} \end{array}} = \begin{array}{c} \text{Return on} \\ \text{common} \\ \text{stockhold-} \\ \text{ers' equity} \end{array}$$

a. The return on common stockholders' equity is usually higher than the return on total assets because of financial leverage (sometimes called "trading on the equity").

b. Financial leverage involves the financing of assets in a company with funds that have been acquired from creditors or from preferred stockholders at a fixed rate of return. If the assets in which the funds are invested earn a greater return than the fixed rate of return required by the suppliers of the funds, then financial leverage is *positive*. Leverage is *negative* if the assets earn a return which is less than the fixed rate required by the suppliers of the funds.

c. Leverage sources include long-term debt, preferred stock, and current liabilities.

d. Since interest on long-term debt is tax-deductible, it is a more effective source of positive leverage than is preferred stock.

e. The leverage principle amply illustrates that prudent use of debt in the capital structure can substantially benefit the common stockholder.

7. The *book value per share* measures the net assets per share of common stock. The formula is:

$$\frac{\begin{array}{c} \text{Common stockholders' equity (Total} \\ \text{stockholders' equity} - \text{Preferred stock)} \end{array}}{\text{Number of common shares outstanding}} = \begin{array}{c} \text{Book} \\ \text{value} \\ \text{per share} \end{array}$$

a. A book value per share that is less than the market value per share is not an indication that the stock is overpriced. Market value is geared toward future earnings and dividends; by contrast, book value is geared toward the past, in that it reflects the results of already completed transactions.

b. Book value is of limited usefulness to the manager, since it is geared to the past rather than to the future.

D.   The short-term creditor is concerned with the near-term prospects of having obligations paid on time. As such, he or she is more interested in cash flows and in working capital management than in how much accounting net income is being reported by a company.

1.   *Working capital* is a measure of the assets financed from long-term capital sources that do not require near-term payment. Working capital is computed by the following formula:

Current assets − Current liabilities = Working capital

2.   The *current ratio* is a widely used measure of short-term debt-paying ability. The formula is:

$$\frac{\text{Current assets}}{\text{Current liabilities}} = \text{Current ratio}$$

a.   Although widely regarded as a measure of debt-paying ability, the current ratio must be interpreted with a great deal of care. The manager must look at the *composition* of the assets and liabilities that go into the computation of the ratio, rather than just looking at their total amount.

b.   The general rule of thumb calls for a current ratio of 2 to 1. However, this general rule is subject to many exceptions, depending on the industry and firm involved.

3.   The *acid-test or quick ratio* is designed to measure how well a company can meet its short-term obligations using only its *most liquid* current assets. The formula is:

$$\frac{\text{Cash + Marketable securities + Current receivables}}{\text{Current liabilities}} = \text{Acid-test ratio}$$

4.   The *accounts receivable turnover* provides a rough gauge of how well accounts receivable are turning into cash. The formula is:

$$\frac{\text{Sales on account}}{\text{Average accounts receivable balance}} = \frac{\text{Accounts receivable}}{\text{turnover}}$$

By dividing the turnover rate into 365 (the number of days in a year), the *average collection period* for accounts receivable can be computed.

5.   The *inventory turnover* measures how many times a company's inventory has been sold during the year. The formula is:

$$\frac{\text{Cost of goods sold}}{\text{Average inventory balance}} = \text{Inventory turnover}$$

The number of days being taken to sell the entire inventory one time (called the *average sale period*) can be computed by dividing 365 by the inventory turnover figure.

E.   The long-term creditor's position differs from that of the short-term creditor, since the long-term creditor is concerned with both the near-term and the long-term ability of a firm to meet its commitments.

1.   The long-term creditor uses the *times interest earned ratio* to gauge the ability of a firm to meet its near-term commitments. The formula is:

$$\frac{\text{Earnings before interest expense and income taxes}}{\text{Interest expense}} = \frac{\text{Times interest}}{\text{earned}}$$

Interest expense has a claim on earnings *before* any income taxes are paid. Therefore, earnings before income taxes is used in the computation above, rather than earnings after taxes.

2.   The *debt-to-equity ratio* indicates the amount of assets being provided by creditors for each dollar of assets being provided by the owners of a company. The formula is:

$$\frac{\text{Total liabilities}}{\text{Stockholders' equity}} = \text{Debt-to-equity ratio}$$

Creditors would like the debt-to-equity ratio to be low, since that would mean that stockholders were providing most of the long-term financing for the company, thereby giving creditors a large cushion of protection.

REVIEW AND SELF TEST
Questions and Exercises

True or False

For each of the following statements, enter a T or an F in the blank to indicate whether the statement is true or false.

_____ 1. In trend analysis, percentage figures are usually computed by using the most recent year as a base.

_____ 2. Common-size statements are statements of companies of similar size and operations.

_____ 3. An extremely high current ratio may be an indication that receivables and inventories are excessive.

_____ 4. Trend percentages in financial statements would be an example of vertical analysis.

_____ 5. A common-size statement is one that shows the separate items appearing on it in percentage form, with each item stated as a percentage of some total of which that item is a part.

_____ 6. The earnings per share figure is computed *after* deducting preferred dividends from the net income of a company.

_____ 7. In computing the earnings per share figure, extraordinary gains and losses should be included with ordinary income and expense items.

_____ 8. If a company has convertible securities, then it should adjust its earnings per share figure to a fully diluted basis.

_____ 9. If earnings remain unchanged and the price/earnings ratio goes up, then one would expect the market price of a stock to go down.

_____ 10. Investors seeking capital gains would like the dividend payout ratio to be high.

_____ 11. Dividing the market price of a share of stock by the dividends per share gives the price/earnings ratio.

_____ 12. Book value per share is not a good predictor of either earnings potential or debt paying ability.

_____ 13. In computing the dividend yield ratio, the investor should use the current market price for the stock, rather than the price which he or she paid for it.

_____ 14. In placing a before-tax item on an after-tax basis, the item should be multiplied by $1 -$ tax rate.

_____ 15. If the return on total assets is greater than the after-tax cost of long-term debt, then leverage is positive, and the common stockholders will benefit.

_____ 16. The inventory turnover is computed by dividing sales by average inventory.

_____ 17. Companies that experience high earnings on some occasions and suffer losses on other occasions should rely heavily on the use of financial leverage.

_____ 18. If a company's return on total assets is substantially higher than its cost of borrowing, then the common stockholders would normally want the company to have a high debt/equity ratio.

Multiple Choice

Choose the best answer or response by placing the identifying letter in the space provided.

_____ 1. Common stockholders would be *least* concerned with which of the following ratios? a) earnings per share; b) dividend yield ratio; c) price/earnings ratio; d) acid-test ratio; e) dividend payout ratio.

_____ 2. Black Company has an acid-test ratio of 1.4 to 1. Which of the following events will cause this ratio to decrease? a) the sale of merchandise on account; b) the payment of a cash dividend already declared; c) borrowing on a short-term note; d) the sale of equipment at a loss; e) none of these.

_____ 3. If the return on total assets is 10 percent, and if the return on common stockholders' equity is 12 percent, then: a) financial leverage is negative; b) the after-tax cost of long-term debt is probably greater than 10 percent; c) the after-tax cost of long-term debt is probably less than 10 percent; d) none of these.

_____ 4. The acid-test ratio: a) can be expected to be less than the current ratio; b) can be expected to be greater than the current ratio; c) could be either greater or less than the current ratio; d) none of these.

_____ 5. The payment of a current liability would cause the current ratio to: a) increase; b) decrease; c) remain unchanged; d) none of these.

_____ 6. An increase in the average collection period for accounts receivable would be explained by: a) an increase in the accounts receivable turnover ratio; b) a decrease in the average accounts receivable balance, with sales remaining unchanged; c) a tightening of credit policy in the company; d) none of these.

_____ 7. Which of the following transactions would result in a decrease in a company's working capital? a) the collection of an account receivable; b) a payment to a short-term creditor; c) the purchase of inventory on account; d) the sale of equipment at a loss; e) none of these.

_____ 8. Hall Company reported net income of $80,000 for 19x5. The company has 20,000 shares of common stock outstanding, and 5,000 shares of $100 par value, 7 percent preferred stock outstanding. The earnings per share of common stock for the year is: a) $4.00; b) $3.20; c) $2.25; d) $3.72; e) none of these.

_____ 9. Given the following data:

Assets	$1,000,000
Liabilities	400,000
Stockholders' equity	600,000
Common stock	300,000
Preferred stock	100,000

If the company has 40,000 shares of common stock and 10,000 shares of preferred stock outstanding, then the book value per share of common stock is: a) $22.50; b) $12.50; c) $20.00; d) $12.00; e) $7.50; f) none of these.

_____ 10. Given the following data:

Number of common shares outstanding	30,000
Number of preferred shares outstanding	10,000
Net income	$180,000
Dividend rate per share of preferred stock	6

The preferred stock is convertible into common stock on a basis of two shares of common for each share of preferred. The fully diluted earnings per share would be: a) $3.60; b) $4.00; c) $2.40; d) $3.00; e) none of these.

Complete the Statements

Fill in the necessary words to complete the following statements.

1. Preparation of common-size statements is known as _____ analysis.

2. The excess of current assets over current liabilities is known as _____ _____.

3. If a firm has convertible securities in its capital structure, then it should report its earnings per share on a fully _____ basis.

4. The dividend yield ratio is computed by dividing the dividends per share by the (market/original purchase) _____ price per share.

5. In order to place a before-tax item on an after-tax basis, the before-tax item should be multiplied by _____.

6. _____ _____ involves the securing of funds for investment at a fixed rate of return to the suppliers of the funds, normally with the thought in mind of enhancing the well-being of the common stockholders.

7. If the return to the common stockholders is greater than the return on total assets, then financial leverage is (positive/negative) _____.

8. The _____ _____ ratio measures how many times a company's inventory has been sold during the year.

9. The relationship between the market price of a share of stock and the stock's current earnings per share is often quoted in terms of a _____/ _____ ratio.

10. Trend percentages would be an example of (vertical/horizontal) _____ analysis of financial statements.

Exercises

18-1. The financial statements of Amfac, Inc., are given below:

AMFAC, INC.
Balance Sheet
December 31, 19x0

Assets

Cash	$ 8,000
Accounts receivable, net...	36,000
Merchandise inventory...	40,000
Prepaid expenses...	2,000
Plant and equipment, net..	214,000
Total Assets	$300,000

Equities

Current liabilities	$ 40,000
Long-term liabilities (10%)	60,000
Preferred stock (8%)..	50,000
Common stock, $10 par..	30,000
Retained earnings	120,000
Total Equities	$300,000

AMFAC, INC.
Income Statement
For the Year Ended December 31, 19x0

Sales	$450,000
Cost of goods sold	270,000
Gross margin	$180,000
Operating expenses...	129,000
Net operating income	$ 51,000
Interest expense...	6,000
Net income before taxes...	$ 45,000
Income taxes (30%)...	13,500
Net Income	$ 31,500

Accounts receivable and inventory remained relatively constant during the year. There are no convertible securities. Assets at the beginning of the year totaled $250,000, and the stockholders' equity at the beginning of the year totaled $180,000. Preferred stock did not change during the year.

Compute the following:

a.   Current ratio.

b.   Acid-test ratio.

c.   Debt-to-equity ratio.

d.   Accounts receivable turnover in days.

e.   Inventory turnover.

f.   Times interest earned.

g.   Return on total assets.

h.   Return on common stockholders' equity.

i.   Is financial leverage positive or negative? Explain.

_____

_____

_____

18-2. Cartwright Company has reported the following data relating to sales and accounts receivable in its most recent annual report:

	19x5	19x4	19x3	19x2	19x1
Sales	$700,000	$675,000	$650,000	$575,000	$500,000
Accounts Receivable	$ 72,000	$ 60,000	$ 52,000	$ 46,000	$ 40,000

Express the data above in trend percentages. Use 19x1 as the base year.

	19x5	19x4	19x3	19x2	19x1
Sales	_____	_____	_____	_____	_____
Accounts Receivable	_____	_____	_____	_____	_____

Comment on the significant information revealed by your trend percentages:

_____

_____

_____

_____

18-3. Consider the following 19x1 and 19x2 income statements of Eldredge Company:

ELDREDGE COMPANY
Income Statements
For the Years Ended December 31, 19x1 and 19x2

	19x2	19x1
Sales	$600,000	$500,000
Cost of goods sold	420,000	331,000
Gross margin	180,000	169,000
Operating expenses:		
Selling expenses	87,000	72,500
Administrative expenses	46,800	51,000
Total operating expenses	133,800	123,500
Net operating income	46,200	45,500
Interest expense	1,200	1,500
Net income before taxes	45,000	44,000
Income taxes (30%)	13,500	13,200
Net Income	$ 31,500	$ 30,800

a. Express the income statements for both years in common-size percentages. Round percentages to one decimal point.

	19x2	19x1
Sales		
Cost of goods sold	———	———
Gross margin	———	———
Operating expenses:		
Selling expenses		
Administrative expenses	———	———
Total operating expenses	———	———
Net operating income		
Interest expense		
Net income before taxes		
Income taxes (30%)	———	———
Net Income	═══	═══

b. Comment briefly on the changes between the two years.

_____

_____

_____

_____

_____

_____

_____

_____

_____

18-4. **Critical though writing exercise:** Company X and Company Y are in the same industry, are about the same size, and have equal earnings. Why might these two companies have different price-earnings ratios?

_____

_____

_____

_____

_____

_____

_____

Chapter 18
Answers to Questions and Exercises

True or False

1. F   Percentage figures are computed using some prior year as the base.

2. F   A common-size statement is one that shows the separate items appearing on it in percentage form rather than in dollar form. Each item is stated as a percentage of some total of which that item is a part.

3. T   Excessive receivables and inventories cause the current assets to be high, which in turn causes the current ratio to be high.

4. F   Trend percentages would be an example of horizontal analysis.

5. T   This point is discussed in connection with question 2 above.

6. T   The earnings per share figure is computed for common stock, and the portion of net income belonging to the common stockholders is that amount which remains after paying preferred dividends.

7. F   Extraordinary gains and losses should not be included in earnings per share computations; however, the per share effect of extraordinary gains and losses should be computed and reported to stockholders.

8. T   This adjustment is needed to avoid misleading statement users.

9. F   The opposite is true—one would expect the market price of the stock to go up. If the price/earnings ratio goes up, then the stock is selling for a higher market price per dollar of earnings.

10. F   The opposite is true—they would like the dividend payout ratio to be low. This is because they prefer to get their return in the form of capital gains rather than in the form of dividends.

11. F   Dividing the market price of a share of stock by the *earnings per share* gives the price/earnings ratio.

12. T   Book value per share is just the balance sheet carrying value of already completed transactions—it tells nothing about the future.

13. T   Using the current market price tells the investor the opportunity cost of the investment in terms of its current yield.

14. T   This statement is true by definition.

15. T   Any time the return on total assets is greater than the after-tax cost of long-term debt, leverage is positive.

16. F   The inventory turnover is computed by dividing *cost of goods sold* by average inventory.

17. F   Companies that experience stability in earnings should rely more heavily on the use of financial leverage. Companies with unstable earnings should be wary of financial leverage since it can increase the volitility of the earnings figure.

18. T   If a company's return on total assets is higher than its cost of borrowing, then financial leverage is positive. Therefore, the common stockholders would want the company to use this positive financial leverage to their advantage by having a high amount of debt in the company.

Multiple Choice

1. d   The acid-test ratio is of more interest to creditors than it is to stockholders.

2. c   Borrowing on a short-term note will cause both the "quick" assets and the current liabilities to increase by the same amount; this will cause the acid-test ratio to decrease. As proof, assume that the company borrows $60,000 on a short-term note:

Before: $\dfrac{\$140,000}{\$100,000} = 1.4$ to 1   After: $\dfrac{\$200,000}{\$160,000} = 1.25$ to 1

3. c   Note that the return on common stockholders' equity is greater than the return on total assets; therefore, financial leverage is positive. In order to have positive financial leverage, the after-tax cost of long-term debt is probably less than the return on total assets (we say "probably" because the positive financial leverage could be caused by preferred stock or by current liabilities).

4. a   The acid-test ratio will always be less than the current ratio because it contains less assets in its computation but the same amount of liabilities.

5. a   As proof, assume current assets of $300,000, current liabilities of $150,000, and the payment of a $50,000 debt:

Before: $\dfrac{\$300,000}{\$150,000} = 2.0$ to 1   After: $\dfrac{\$250,000}{\$100,000} = 2.5$ to 1

6. d   An increase in the average collection period would mean that it is taking longer to collect an account. Therefore, a) the accounts receivable turnover ratio is *decreasing;* b) there is an *increase* in the average accounts receivable balance (with sales remaining unchanged); c) credit policy must be getting looser, since it is taking longer to collect an account.

7. e   Item a would leave current assets unchanged; items b and c would change current assets and current liabilities by the same amount in each case; item d would not affect working capital; so item e is correct.

8. c   The computations are:

Net income	$80,000
Less preferred dividends:	
5,000 shares × ($100 × 7%)	35,000
Net income for common	$45,000

$45,000 ÷ 20,000 shares = $2.25 per share.

9. b   The computations are:

Stockholders' equity	$600,000
Less preferred stock	100,000
Remainder to common	$500,000

$500,000 ÷ 40,000 shares = $12.50 per share.

10. a   The computations are:

$$\frac{\text{Net income} \quad \$180,000}{\text{Total shares} \quad 30,000 + (10,000 \times 2)} = \$3.60 \text{ per share}$$
after conversion

Complete the Statements

1. vertical
2. working capital
3. diluted
4. market
5. 1 − tax rate
6. Financial leverage
7. positive
8. inventory turnover
9. price/earnings
10. horizontal

Exercises

18-1.

a. $\dfrac{\$86,000}{\$40,000} = 2.15 \text{ to } 1$

b. $\dfrac{\$44,000}{\$40,000} = 1.10 \text{ to } 1$

c. $\dfrac{\$100,000}{\$200,000} = 0.5 \text{ to } 1$

d. $\dfrac{\$450,000}{\$36,000} = 12.5 \text{ times (Accounts Receivable Turnover)}$

$$\dfrac{365}{\text{Accounts Receivable Turnover}} = \dfrac{365}{12.5} = 29.2 \text{ days}$$

e. $\dfrac{\$270,000}{\$40,000} = 6.75 \text{ times}$

f. $\dfrac{\$51,000}{\$6,000} = 8.5 \text{ times}$

g. $\dfrac{\$31,500 + [\$6,000 \times (1 - 0.30)]}{\left(\dfrac{\$250,000 + \$300,000}{2}\right)} = 13.0\% \text{ (rounded)}$

h.

	Beginning of Year	End of Year
Total stockholders' equity	$180,000	$200,000
Less preferred stock	50,000	50,000
Common stockholders' equity	$130,000	$150,000

$$\dfrac{\$31,500 - (8\% \times \$50,000) = \$27,500}{\left(\dfrac{\$130,000 + \$150,000}{2}\right)} = 19.6\% \text{ (rounded)}$$

i. Financial leverage is positive, since the return on the common stockholders' equity is greater than the return on total assets.

18-2.

	19x5	19x4	19x3	19x2	19x1
Sales	140%	135%	130%	115%	100%
Accounts Receivable	180%	150%	130%	115%	100%

Sales grew by 15 percent per year through 19x3, and then dropped off to a 5 percent growth rate for the next two years. The accounts receivable grew at a 15 percent rate through 19x3, but then rather than dropping off to a 5 percent rate the accounts receivable grew at an even faster rate through 19x5. This suggests that the company is granting credit too liberally, and that large bad debts may soon be encountered.

18-3.

a.

ELDREDGE COMPANY
Common-Size Comparative Income Statements
For the Years Ended December 31, 19x1 and 19x2

	19x2	19x1
Sales	100.0	100.0
Cost of goods sold	70.0	66.2
Gross margin	30.0	33.8
Operating expenses:		
Selling expenses	14.5	14.5
Administrative expenses	7.8	10.2
Total operating expenses	22.3	24.7
Net operating income	7.7	9.1
Interest expense	0.2	0.3
Net income before taxes	7.5	8.8
Income taxes	2.2	2.6
Net Income	5.3	6.2

b.   The two primary areas affecting the percentage decrease in net income were cost of goods sold and administrative expenses. Cost of goods sold increased from 66.2 percent of sales in 19x1 to 70.0 percent of sales in 19x2—an increase of 3.8 percentage points. On the other hand, administrative expenses dropped from 10.2 percent of sales in 19x1 to only 7.8 percent of sales in 19x2—a decrease of 2.4 percentage points. The net effect was a decrease in net income as a percentage of sales, which fell from 6.2 percent of sales in 19x1 to only 5.3 percent of sales in 19x2.

18-4.   Price-earnings ratios are determined by how investors see a firm's *future* earnings prospects. Current reported earnings are generally considered to be useful only so far as they can assist investors in judging what will happen in the future. For this reason, two firms might have the same current earnings, but one might have a much higher price-earnings ratio if investors view it to have superior *future* prospects. In some cases, firms with very small current earnings enjoy very high price-earnings ratios. This is simply because investors view these firms as having very favorable prospects for earnings in future years.

Appendix K

Quality Costs and Reports

In the first few pages of the appendix a distinction is made between *grade, quality of design,* and *quality of conformance.* Be sure you understand the difference between these three concepts.

The remainder of the appendix is spent discussing quality of conformance. Four types of costs are associated with quality of conformance, as listed in Exhibit K-2. These four types of costs are the heart of the appendix and you should spend most of your time studying them. You must learn the proper distribution of these costs, and learn how to structure them into a quality cost report such as is illustrated in Exhibit K-4.

APPENDIX HIGHLIGHTS AND STUDY GUIDE

A. Quality means conformance to customer expectations in terms of features and performance of the product or service involved.   Three factors underlie quality: grade, quality design, and quality of conformance.

1. Grade relates to differences in degree, worth, or ranking between products that have the same functional use. Companies provide products and services that differ in grade because of differences in purchasing power between consumers.

2. Quality of design is the degree to which a company's design specifications for a product or service meet customers' expectations *for the grade level chosen.* A product or service has a high quality of design if it contains all the features and operates in the way that customers would expect it to operate.

3. Quality of conformance is the degree to which the actual product that is manufactured meets its design specifications and is free of defects or other problems that might affect appearance or performance.

B. The bulk of all quality costs incurred by a company are associated with quality of conformance. These costs can be broken down into four broad groups as shown in exhibit K-2.

1. Two of these groups—known as *prevention costs* and *appraisal costs*—are incurred in an effort to keep poor quality of conformance from occurring.

2. The other two groups—known as *internal failure costs* and *external failure costs*—are incurred because poor quality of conformance has occurred.

C. See Exhibit K-2 for examples of the four types of quality costs.

1. Prevention costs relate to any activity that will reduce or eliminate the manufacture of defective products or the providing of substandard service in a company.

   a. Quality circles, which are part of prevention costs, consist of small groups of employees that meet on a regular basis to discuss ways to improve the quality of output.

   b. Statistical process control is a technique whereby workers use charts to monitor the quality of parts or components that pass through their workstations.

2. Appraisal costs, which are sometimes called inspection costs, are incurred to identify defective products *before* the products are shipped to customers.

3. Internal failure costs result from identification of defects during the appraisal process. Such costs include scrap, reworking of defective units, and downtime. If failure costs are going to occur, then it is better to identify them internally rather than ship defective units to customers.

4. External failure costs result when a defective product is delivered to a customer. These are the least desirable of all quality costs. Even if a problem is corrected under a warranty, customer ill-will can still occur.

D. Quality costs should be distributed more toward prevention and appraisal, and less toward internal and external failure. This will result in less total quality cost, as shown in Exhibit K-3.

E. Quality costs are summarized for management on a quality cost report such as is illustrated in Exhibit K-4. Several benefits accrue from such a report. Quality cost information:

1. Helps managers to see the financial significance of quality.

2. Helps managers identify the relative importance of the quality problems faced by the firm.

3. Helps managers to see whether their quality costs are poorly distributed and, when needed, it helps them to work toward a better distribution of costs.

4. Provides a basis for establishing budgets for quality costs as management seeks to reduce the total cost involved. The budgets, in turn, provide a basis for performance evaluation from year to year.

F. Three limitations exist to quality cost information.

1. Simply measuring and reporting quality costs does not solve quality problems. Problems can be solved only by action on the part of management.

2. A lag will usually exist between when quality improvement programs are put into effect and when the results are seen. Initially, total quality costs may even increase as quality control systems are designed and installed.

3. Some important quality costs are typically omitted from the quality cost report. These costs include the opportunity cost of lost sales arising from poor product design or customer ill will, and the cost of top management time in designing and administering the quality cost program.

G. Quality has become a matter of international importance.

1. The emphasis on quality programs started in other countries—particularly Japan—and has slowly filtered to the United States.

2. The level of quality in products sold in Europe is now monitored by a set of quality control guidelines known as the *ISO 9000 Standards*.

a. These standards have become an international measure of quality and are being adopted by many companies in the United States.

b. The key to receiving certification under ISO 9000 is documentation. A company must document every aspect of its quality control program.

REVIEW AND SELF TEST
Questions

True or False

For each of the following statements, enter a T or an F in the blank to indicate whether the statement is true or false.

_____ 1.   A product that is high in grade is not necessarily high in quality.

_____ 2.   If features are lacking in a product that customers expect, the product has a poor quality of design.

_____ 3.   To have a high quality of design, all grades of product should have the same features and perform in the same way.

_____ 4.   A product containing defects has a poor quality of conformance.

_____ 5.   The best quality systems are those that put their emphasis on appraisal costs, which are incurred to catch defects during the manufacturing process.

_____ 6.   It is better to incur internal failure costs than to incur external failure costs.

_____ 7.   Initially, increases in appraisal costs typically lead to increases in internal failure costs.

_____ 8.   Increased emphasis on prevention and appraisal costs will cause total quality costs to rise.

_____ 9.   Quality cost reports focus on quality costs associated with the manufacturing process.

_____ 10. Even if a company doesn't sell products in Europe, it still must be concerned about the ISO 900 standards.

Appendix K
Answers to Questions

True or False

1. T   A product that is high in grade could be poorly designed, thereby making it low in quality in the eyes of customers.

2. T   Quality of design is the degree to which a product's design features meet customers' expectations.

3. F   Products of different grades will have different design features. Customers expect more features and better performance out of higher grade products.

4. T   Quality of conformance indicates how well a product meets its design specifications and is free of defects and other problems.

5. F   The best quality systems are those that put their emphasis on *prevention* costs.

6. T   Internal failure costs keep defective products from being shipped to customers, which reduces customer ill will and other opportunity costs.

7. T   As a company increases its appraisal activities, defective products are identified, which results in greater internal failure costs. As a company identifies defective products, it incurs more cost for rework, scrap, and so forth.

8. F   The opposite is true, as depicted in Exhibit K-3.

9. F   Quality cost reports focus on all quality costs in an organization from R&D through customer servicing.

10. T   The ISO standards have become an international measure of quality and these standards are being adopted by organizations in the United States and elsewhere. Companies such as IBM require their suppliers to adhere to ISO 9000 standards even if the suppliers are not selling directly in Europe.

Appendix L

Pricing Products and Services

Appendix Study Suggestions

This appendix contains two major topics, both of which relate to pricing issues. The first major topic deals with cost-plus pricing. Exhibits L-1 through L-5 contain the essential computations involved in cost-plus pricing under both the absorption and contribution approaches. Also study the section titled *Determining the Markup Percentage* with care, and commit the two formulas in this section to memory.

The second major topic deals with time and material pricing. Carefully study Exhibit L-7 and the accompying text, which illustrates how the time component and material component are computed.

APPENDIX HIGHLIGHTS AND STUDY GUIDE

A. The most common approach to product pricing is to employ some type of cost-plus pricing formula. Under this method a cost base is computed, to which a markup is added in order to arrive at a target selling price.

1. Cost-plus pricing can be used to compute a target selling price under either the absorption approach or the contribution approach.

    a. The absorption approach defines the cost base as the cost to manufacture one unit of product. Selling the administrative expenses are not included in this cost base, but rather are provided for through the markup which is added on to arrive at the target selling price. The format is:

Unit cost to manufacture	$50
Markup to cover selling and administrative expenses, and desired profit—40% of cost to manufacture	20
Target selling Price	$70

    b. The contribution approach defines the cost base as consisting of variable production, selling, and administrative expenses. A markup designed to cover fixed costs and to provide the desired profit element is added to this variable cost base. The format is:

Variable manufacturing costs	$35
Variable selling and administrative expenses	5
Total variable expenses	40
Markup to cover fixed expenses and desired profit—75% of variable expenses	30
Target selling price	$70

    c. In both cases above, the term "cost plus" is a misnomer, since part of the costs are buried in the "plus" or markup part of the formula. For the absorption approach, the selling and administrative expenses are included as part of the markup; for the contribution approach, the fixed costs are included as part of the markup.

B. By far the most crucial element in the cost-plus pricing formulas is the percentage markup added to the cost base. This is because the markup must be large enough to cover a portion of the costs of the firm, and to provide for the desired profit element.

1. One approach to determining the markup percentage is to base it on some desired return on investment (ROI). A formula exists which can be used to determine the appropriate markup percentage, given the ROI figure which management wishes to achieve.

2. If absorption costing is being used, the formula is:

$$\text{Markup Percentage} = \frac{\begin{array}{c}\text{Desired Return} \\ \text{on Assets} \\ \text{Employed}\end{array} + \begin{array}{c}\text{Selling and} \\ \text{Administrative} \\ \text{Expenses}\end{array}}{\begin{array}{c}\text{Volume in} \\ \text{Units}\end{array} \times \begin{array}{c}\text{Unit Cost to} \\ \text{Manufacture}\end{array}}$$

3. If the contribution approach is being used, the formula is:

$$\text{Markup Percentage} = \frac{\begin{array}{c}\text{Desired Return} \\ \text{on Assets} \\ \text{Employed}\end{array} + \text{Fixed Costs}}{\begin{array}{c}\text{Volume in} \\ \text{Units}\end{array} \times \begin{array}{c}\text{Unit Variable} \\ \text{Expenses}\end{array}}$$

4. In the case of both formulas, the target ROI will be attained only if the budgeted sales volume is attained.

C. Target costing is used in those situations where a company already knows what price should be charged, and the problem is to develop a product that can be marketed profitably at the desired price. The formula for target costing is:

Anticipated selling price - Desired Profit
= Target Cost

D. Rather than compute prices by means of a cost-plus formula, some companies use an alternative approach called time and material pricing. Under this method two pricing rates are established—one based on direct labor time and a second based on direct material used.

1. The time component is typically expressed as a labor rate per hour. The rate is computed by adding together three elements: (1) the direct costs of the employee, including salary and fringe benefits; (2) an allowance for selling, general and administrative expenses of the company; and (3) an allowance for a desired profit.

2. The material component is determined by adding a material loading charge to the invoice cost of the materials used on the job. This charge is designed to cover the costs of ordering, handling, and carrying materials in stock, plus a profit margin on the materials.

3. Time and material pricing is typically used by service organizations, ranging from doctors' offices to TV repair shops.

REVIEW AND SELF-TEST
Questions and Exercises

True or False

For each of the following statements, enter a T or an F in the blank to indicate whether the statement is true of false.

_____ 1. In cost-plus pricing, the cost base is generally the same under either the absorption or the contribution approaches.

_____ 2. The contribution approach to cost-plus pricing defines the cost base as consisting of a product's variable costs, including variable selling and administrative expenses.

_____ 3. If a company has a 20% desired ROI, then it should add a 20% markup to its products.

_____ 4. Time and material pricing is more appropriate for service-type organizations than for manufacturing firms.

_____ 5. In time and material pricing, the material loading charge includes a profit element.

_____ 6. The markup in cost-plus pricing consists of the desired profit of a firm.

_____ 7. When basing markup percentages on ROI, the markup percentage computed under the absorption approach will be different from the markup percentage computed under the contribution approach.

_____ 8. Under target costing, a firm knows how much a product will cost and efforts are directed toward determining an appropriate selling price.

Multiple Choice

Choose the best answer or response by placing the identifying letter in the space provided.

_____ 1. Given the following data (based on 15,000 units produced and sold each year):

Direct materials	$8
Direct labor	7
Variable overhead	2
Variable selling	3

Fixed overhead cost totals $15,000 per year and fixed selling and administrative expenses total $30,000 per year. If the company uses the absorption approach to pricing and desires a 50 percent markup, the target selling price per unit would be: a) $34.50; b) $31.50; c) $27.00; d) $23.00; e) none of these.

_____ 2. Refer to the data in question 1 above. If the company uses the contribution approach to pricing and desires a 35 percent markup, the target selling price per unit would be: a) $29.70; b) $22.95; c) $20.00; d) $27.00.

_____ 3. The material loading charge: a) includes the invoice cost of materials plus a desired profit margin on the materials; b) includes the invoice cost of materials plus costs of ordering, handling, and carrying the materials; c) includes only a profit margin on the materials; d) includes costs of ordering, handling and carrying materials plus a profit margin on the materials; e) none of these.

Complete the Statements

Fill in the necessary words to complete the following statements.

1. Under the _____ approach to cost-plus pricing, the cost base is defined as the cost to manufacture one unit of product.

2. One of the most common ways to determine the percentage markup that should be added to products is to base the markup on the company's desired _____ _____ _____.

3. The material component in time and material pricing is computed by adding a _____ _____ _____ to the invoice cost of any materials used on the job.

4. Under the contribution approach to cost plus pricing, the _____ costs are included as part of the markup which is added to the cost base.

5. Under _____ _____, a company already knows what price should be charged for a product; the problem is to develop a product that can be profitablity sold at that price.

Exercises

L-1. Manufacturing costs and other costs relating to a product produced by Mackey Company are given below:

Direct materials	$10
Direct labor	12
Variable overhead	1
Fixed overhead ($210,000 total)	7
Variable selling and administrative	2
Fixed selling and administrative ($90,000 total)	3

a.   Assume that the company uses the absorption approach to cost-plus pricing, and adds a 50% markup to obtain target selling prices. Compute the target selling price for the product above.

_____ $

_____

_____

_____ ___

    Total cost to manufacture

Markup—50% × $_____ ___

Target selling price $___

b.   Assume that the company uses the contribution approach to cost-plus pricing, and adds an 80% markup to obtain target selling prices. Compute the target selling price for the product above.

_____ $

_____

_____

_____ ___

    Total variable expenses

Markup—80% × $_____ ___

Target selling price $___

L-2. a. Speckart Company has determined that an investment of $800,000 is needed in order to produce and market 30,000 units of Product A each year. The company's cost accountant estimates that it will cost $50 to manufacture a unit of Product A at a 30,000-unit level of activity, and that selling and administrative expenses will total $400,000 per year. Compute the required markup percentage for Product A, assuming that the company uses the absorption approach to costing, and has a 25% desired ROI.

$$\text{Markup Percentage} = \frac{\text{Desired Return on Assets Employed} + \text{Selling and Administrative Expenses}}{\text{Volume in Units} \times \text{Unit cost to Manufacture}}$$

$$\text{Markup Percentage} =$$

b. Hansen Company has determined that an investment of $750,000 is needed in order to produce and market 25,000 units of Product B each year. The company estimates that variable costs associated with Product B will total $24 per unit, and that fixed costs will total $300,000 per year. Compute the required markup percentage for Product B, assuming that the company uses the contribution approach to costing, and has a 20% desired ROI.

$$\text{Markup Percentage} = \frac{\text{Desired Return on Assets Employed} + \text{Fixed Costs}}{\text{Volume in Units} \times \text{Unit variable Expenses}}$$

$$\text{Markup Percentage} =$$

Appendix L
Answers to Questions and Exercises

True or False

1. F   The cost base is different under the two approaches, as shown in Exhibits L-2 and L-7.

2. T   This point is shown in Exhibit L-7.

3. F   The markup also includes some element of cost under both the absorption and contribution approaches.

4. T   Time and material pricing is designed specifically for service-type organizations.

5. T   The material loading charge consists of two elements: (1) the cost of ordering, handling, and carrying materials in stock, and (2) a profit margin on the materials themselves.

6. F   The markup consists of the desired profit plus some element of cost. Under the absorption approach, this element is the selling and administrative expenses; under the contribution approach it is the fixed costs.

7. T   The markup percentages will be different because of differences in the cost bases used by the two costing methods. This point is discussed in the section of the chapter titled *Determining the Markup Percentage*.

8. F   The opposite is true; a firm knows what price to charge, but it does not know what the product will cost to manufacture and sell.

Multiple Choice

1. c   The computations are:

Direct materials	$ 8
Direct labor	7
Variable overhead	2
Fixed overhead ($15,000 ÷ 15,000 units)	1
Cost to manufacture	18
Markup-50%	9
Target selling price	$27

2. d   The computations are:

Direct materials	$ 8
Direct labor	7
Variable overhead	2
Variable selling	3
Total variable expenses	20
Markup—35%	7
Target selling price	$27

3. d   Response (d) is correct by definition.

Complete the statements

1. absorption
2. return on investment
3. material loading charge
4. fixed
5. target costing

Exercises

L-1. a.

Direct materials	$10
Direct labor	12
Variable overhead	1
Fixed overhead	7
Total cost to manufacture	$30
Markup—50% x $30	15
Target selling price	$45

   b.

Direct materials	$10
Direct labor	12
Variable overhead	1
Variable selling and administrative	2
Total variable costs	$25
Markup—80% x $25	20
Target selling price	$45

L-2. a.

$$\text{Markup Percentage} = \frac{(25\% \times \$800,000) + \$400,000}{30,000 \text{ units} \times \$50}$$

$$= \frac{\$600,000}{\$1,500,000}$$

$$= 40\%$$

   b.

$$\text{Markup Percentage} = \frac{(20\% \times \$750,000) + \$300,000}{25,000 \text{ units} \times \$24}$$

$$= \frac{\$450,000}{\$600,000}$$

$$= 75\%$$